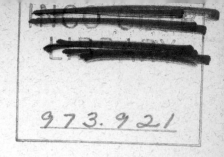
KHRUSHCHEV
IN
AMERICA

Full texts of the speeches made by
N. S. KHRUSHCHEV
Chairman of the Council of Ministers of the USSR
on his tour of the United States
September 15-27, 1959

Translated from the book published in the USSR
entitled
"LIVE IN PEACE AND FRIENDSHIP!"

CROSSCURRENTS PRESS

NEW YORK 1960

CONTENTS

NIKITA S. KHRUSHCHEV
Chairman of the Council of Ministers of the USSR

Cheers along the road for Chairman of the USSR Council of Ministers Khrushchev.

PREFACE

KHRUSHCHEV IN AMERICA contains the full texts of the speeches made by N. S. Khrushchev, Chairman of the Council of Ministers of the Union of Soviet Socialist Republics, on his tour of the United States, September 15-27, 1959. These speeches are translated from the authoritative collection entitled LIVE IN PEACE AND FRIENDSHIP! published and widely circulated in the Soviet Union.

The translation includes a condensation of explanatory material from the Soviet book describing the place and circumstances of each speech or discussion. The translation also contains several instances of pointed editorial commentary on remarks made to Khrushchev in question periods and discussions. These were written by and express the opinions of the Soviet editors of LIVE IN PEACE AND FRIENDSHIP! They are retained in order to convey accurately to the reader the Soviet point of view on various aspects of the Khrushchev trip.

Khrushchev's American speeches constitute an historical document of first-rate importance. They place before the reader Khrushchev the man, the political leader, the master of repartee and wit. They reflect the position of his government on a wide range of issues. But most important of all, these speeches are the principal record of a trip that has already exercised a profound influence on the course of world affairs and perhaps opened a new and more hopeful chapter in relations between the two powers on which the future depends—the United States and the Soviet Union.

The publisher takes pleasure in making available, in permanent form, the record of this eventful trip.

New York, N. Y.
January 2, 1960

ON THE EXCHANGE OF VISITS BETWEEN N. S. KHRUSHCHEV, CHAIRMAN OF THE COUNCIL OF MINISTERS OF THE USSR, AND PRESIDENT DWIGHT D. EISENHOWER OF THE USA

(Official Announcement Published on August 4, 1959)

The President of the United States has invited N. S. Khrushchev, Chairman of the Council of Ministers of the USSR, to make an official visit to the United States in September 1959. N. S. Khrushchev has accepted the invitation with pleasure.

The President has also accepted with pleasure the invitation of N. S. Khrushchev to make an official visit to the USSR later in the autumn of this year.

N. S. Khrushchev will spend two or three days in Washington and will tour the United States for approximately ten days. He will have unofficial talks with the President, which will present an opportunity for an exchange of opinions on problems of mutual interest.

During his tour of the United States, N. S. Khrushchev will have an opportunity of personally seeing the country and its people and getting acquainted with their life.

President Eisenhower will visit Moscow and will also spend several days touring the Soviet Union. This will provide another opportunity for unofficial talks and an exchange of opinions with the Chairman of the Council of Ministers of the USSR on problems of mutual interest.

During his tour of the Soviet Union President Eisenhower will also have an opportunity of personally seeing the country and its people and getting acquainted with their life.

Both governments express the hope that the forthcoming visits will contribute to better understanding between the USA and the USSR, and promote the cause of peace.

N. S. KHRUSHCHEV'S REPLY TO LETTERS AND TELEGRAMS RECEIVED ON THE EVE OF U.S. TOUR

In connection with my visit to the United States of America I have received many letters and telegrams from Soviet people and from citizens of other countries, including Americans. These letters and telegrams express the hope that my visit will serve to improve relations between the USSR and the USA, and that the exchange of views with Mr. Eisenhower, the President of the United States, will be a good start in improving the international situation.

Mankind is now living in a wonderful time. It is a time when science and technology, economy and culture are flourishing, when, indeed, the fantastic is becoming reality. Our visit to the United States coincides with two immensely important events: The world's first space rocket has been successfully sent to the moon from the earth by Soviet people, and the world's first atomic icebreaker, the *Lenin,* has set out on her maiden voyage.

How many fantastic novels, tales and poems have been written about flights to the moon! For ages people have dreamed of inter-planetary flight, and at last we are about to see this daring dream come true. For decades scientists have striven to build a ship which could break her way to the North Pole, and at last such a ship has been launched.

How can we, Soviet people—and not only we, but all people of good will—help rejoicing and admiring the great feat of Soviet scientists, engineers, technicians and workers, who calculated to the minute and second and accomplished the marvelous flight of a rocket from the earth to the moon. How can we help congratulating the Soviet scientists, engineers, technicians and workers who built the world's first atomic icebreaker, which will stay at sea for months, crushing the ice of many centuries.

The exploit of the Soviet conquerors of outer space has ushered in a new era, when man, possessing a most profound knowledge of the laws of physics, chemistry, mathematics, astronomy and other sciences, has created a force capable of sending a powerful spaceship from the earth to another heavenly body, and of directing it exactly to a predetermined point.

Why were the Soviet people the first in the world to successfully solve such a difficult and truly grandiose problem as sending a rocket to the moon—a problem with many unknowns? This triumph became possible because these same Soviet people had with their own hands, their heroic labor, in a historically short period, succeeded in solving the supreme social problem. They have built a socialist society and are confidently building communism.

The unparalleled flight of the Soviet rocket to the moon and the launching of the atomic icebreaker *Lenin* convincingly show that, acting upon the historic decisions of the Twenty-first Party Congress, our people are successfully developing the material and technical basis of communist society. Only people who deliberately close their eyes and refuse to look reality in the face can doubt the boundless possibilities for human progress offered by communism.

Soviet people are pleasantly stirred and tremendously impressed by the news of the rocket flight to the moon. They are proud of their scientists, engineers, technicians and workers, who were the first in the world to send to the moon a container with scientific instruments and an emblem with the coat of arms of the Soviet Union, thereby winning priority for our country. Our priority, the Soviet Union's priority, of the first successful rocket flight to the moon, is thus firmly established.

We realize, of course, that the triumph of our space conquerors is a feat of the entire Soviet people, a victory for the entire socialist camp. It is an outstanding contribution to the development of world science, an achievement of world significance.

The launching of the icebreaker *Lenin,* whose engines are now being powered by atomic energy, is likewise of symbolic importance. It is no mere coincidence that the Soviet people, who were the first in the world to start up an atomic power station, should also be the first to launch an atomic icebreaker. We have thereby again strikingly demonstrated that the Soviet people are fully resolved to use atomic energy for peaceful purposes.

Our atomic icebreaker *Lenin* will break not only the ice of oceans, but also the ice of the cold war. She will blaze the road to the minds and hearts of nations, calling upon them to turn from the competition between states in the arms race to a competition in uses of nuclear energy for man's weal, to warm his body and soul, to create everything that he needs. We are ready to cooperate with all nations in the peaceful uses of nuclear energy, and would be happy if this call were taken up by all governments.

The scientists of the Soviet Union who built the rocket and sent it to the moon have given me a replica of the emblem taken there by the Soviet rocket. I shall be happy to present this replica to the President of the United States, Mr. Eisenhower. May this emblem be a symbol calling on Soviet and American scientists, engineers and workers, on our peoples to join their efforts in creative work, in the struggle to improve relations between our countries, to win peace among all the nations of the world.

11

I should like to assure my dear compatriots and everybody else who has sent me friendly letters and telegrams in connection with my visit to the USA, that for my part I shall make every effort to justify your hopes. I do not doubt the good intentions of the President of the USA. In inviting me to visit the United States, he, too, evidently strives to find a common language for a settlement of controversial international questions and an improvement of relations between our countries.

Our main objective must be to secure peaceful conditions of life for all people on earth.

I thank you, dear comrades and foreign friends, for your good wishes.

N. KHRUSHCHEV

September 14, 1959

N. S. KHRUSHCHEV'S SPEECH AT ANDREWS FIELD

N. S. Khrushchev, Chairman of the USSR Council of Ministers, his family and his party arrived in the USA on an official visit on September 15.

At Andrews Field near Washington N. S. Khrushchev, replying to the welcome speech by U.S. President Dwight D. Eisenhower, said:

MR. PRESIDENT, LADIES AND GENTLEMEN:

Allow me at this moment, as I step on American soil for the first time, to thank Mr. Eisenhower for his invitation to visit your country, and to thank all of you for the warm welcome you have extended to us, representatives of the Soviet Union.

Russians say that "every good thing should be started in the morning." Our trip started this morning in Moscow, and we are happy that our first meeting with you on American soil is taking place on the morning of the same day. As you see, our countries are not so very far away from each other.

It was with great pleasure and gratitude that I accepted the invitation of the President of the USA to come to your country on an official visit, and I shall be happy to talk with statesmen, businessmen, intellectuals, workers and farmers, and to acquaint myself with the life of the industrious and enterprising American people.

For our part, we shall in the near future be happy to receive Mr. Eisenhower, the members of his family and his party in the Soviet Union. We shall accord the President a most cordial reception and afford him every opportunity of seeing the life of the Soviet people.

We have always held that mutual visits and meetings of government representatives are useful. Meetings and talks between statesmen of our two great countries—the Soviet Union and the United States—are of special importance.

All nations are deeply interested in preserving and consolidating peace, in peaceful coexistence. War augurs no good to anyone. Peace is of benefit to all peoples. That, in our opinion, is the cardinal prin-

13

Welcome parade in honor of the arrival of Khrushchev in Washington.

ciple which statesmen of all countries should act upon in order to
meet the hopes of the peoples.

We have come to you with an open heart and with good intentions. The Soviet people want to live in peace and friendship with
the American people. There is nothing to prevent the relations between our countries from being built up as relations between good
neighbors. The Soviet and American peoples, as well as other peoples, fought well together against the common enemy during the
Second World War and crushed him. In peacetime we have more
grounds and greater opportunities for friendship and cooperation
between the peoples of our countries.

On the eve of our meeting with you, Mr. President, Soviet
scientists, engineers, technicians and workers gladdened us by launching a rocket to the moon. The path from the earth to the moon has
thus been blazed and a container weighing 390 kilograms, with a

14

device bearing the coat of arms of the Soviet Union, is now on the moon. Our earth has now become somewhat lighter, and the moon several hundred kilograms heavier. I am sure that this historic achievement of peaceful Soviet science gladdens not only Soviet people, but also all the people who value peace and friendship between nations.

An atomic-powered icebreaker was launched in the Soviet Union a few days ago. We rejoice at this concrete expression of the desire of all peoples that nuclear energy be used for peaceful purposes only. We know, Mr. President, that you hold dear the idea of the peaceful utilization of nuclear energy, and note with satisfaction that in this sphere your aims coincide with ours.

We do not doubt that the splendid scientists, engineers and workers of the United States who are working to conquer outer space will likewise deliver their emblem to the moon. The Soviet emblem, as an old resident of the moon, will welcome your emblem, and they will live in peace and friendship just as you and we on earth must live in peace and friendship, and just as all the nations of our common Mother Earth, which rewards us so generously with her bounty, must live in peace and friendship.

Permit me in these first minutes of our stay in the United States to convey heartfelt greetings and very best wishes to the American people from the peoples of the Soviet Union, from the Soviet Government and from myself.

N. S. KHRUSHCHEV'S SPEECH AT WHITE HOUSE DINNER

President Dwight D. Eisenhower of the USA and Mrs. Eisenhower gave a dinner in honor of N. S. Khrushchev, Chairman of the Council of Ministers of the USSR, and Madame Khrushchova on the evening of September 15.

During the dinner President Dwight D. Eisenhower and N. S. Khrushchev exchanged speeches.

MR. PRESIDENT, MRS. EISENHOWER, LADIES AND GENTLEMEN:

I want to thank Mr. Eisenhower for his good wishes. We have come to the United States with the best of intentions, at the President's invitation. We want to reach an understanding on improving our relations. Our countries are very strong. They must not quarrel with each other. If small countries quarrel, they can do little more, to put it figuratively, than scratch each other. And in a day or two cosmetics will efface the traces of that quarrel. But if strong countries were to quarrel, such as the United States and the Soviet Union, it would not be our countries alone that would suffer enormous damage, but other countries as well would inevitably be drawn into a worldwide fray.

We are confident that our two states and our peoples can live in friendship and work in common for an enduring peace. You have mentioned the fact that it will soon be 150 years since diplomatic relations were established between the United States and Russia. I should also like to say a few words in this regard. I think that when the U.S. Ambassador presented his credentials to Emperor Alexander I, the Emperor did not trust him much, because the U.S. Ambassador represented a republic, while Alexander I was an absolute monarch. Yet, in spite of this, diplomatic relations were established between our countries. There was mutual understanding between the United States and Russia, and contacts between them grew stronger.

Our countries have never waged war against each other; indeed, they have never had any major quarrels, with the exception of the well-known events in the early years of Soviet power. Of course, I don't lay claim to a profound knowledge of history, but I feel sure that this is precisely how matters stand.

Now times have changed. Russia has changed. We believe that our socialist system is better than yours. You think that your system is better than ours. What are we to do? Should we extend the controversy over whose system is better to a fight between us on the battlefield? Would it not be better to let history settle the issue? I think that would be more reasonable. If you agree with that, we can build our relations on a basis of peace and friendship.

Yours is a rich and strong country. I have read many of your speeches, gentlemen of the Senate and House of Representatives present here. And although I have met you for the first time today, you are old acquaintances of mine, thanks to your speeches. (Animation.)

The time has come to stop and think, and to make every effort to improve the relations between our countries.

We want nothing from you and you need nothing of what we have. It is true that for the time being you are richer than we. But we want to be as rich tomorrow as you are now, and richer still the day after. (Animation.) And what is wrong with that? After all, we want to earn it all by our own labor, not to take wealth away from anyone. I must say that I was pleased with the meeting and exchange of views we had with the President today. When some of our jour-

16

nalists approached me after the meeting and inquired about my impressions, I told them that there would be a joint communiqué and that they should go by what that communiqué said. But I could not help telling them that I would inform my government that my impression was good and that, in my opinion, a good beginning had been made. God grant that the end may be better still.

I should like to propose a toast to the health of the President, to the health of his wife and to all of you esteemed ladies and gentlemen. *(Applause.)*

N. S. KHRUSHCHEV MEETS JOURNALISTS AT THE NATIONAL PRESS CLUB

N. S. Khrushchev met American and foreign journalists at the National Press Club in Washington on September 16.

N. S. KHRUSHCHEV'S ADDRESS

MR. CHAIRMAN, LADIES AND GENTLEMEN:

I am pleased to meet prominent U.S. journalists at the beginning of my visit. I have had more than one occasion to see that journalists

President Eisenhower laughs heartily as Soviet Premier Khrushchev gestures during a picture-taking session at the White House.

are very inquisitive people. They want to know everything about everything at once and have a very lively imagination. I have received so many questions that I would have to stay here six months to answer all of them. How about that, would you object if I were to stay here six months? Thank you in advance. But I must return to Moscow to receive your esteemed President in our country.

In addressing you, I will do my best to satisfy your curiosity and to tell you briefly about some problems connected with my U.S. visit.

In one of my talks with journalists in Moscow I called them my traveling companions. Indeed, many of you will be my companions on this tour of the United States. I should like you very much to be good, active and objective companions. For it will be largely up to you journalists to supply people with truthful information about our stay in the United States. You will hear my interviews and speeches and report them. I ask you ladies and gentlemen, to try to understand me correctly and to report correctly what I say. If I should happen to make a slip, ask me to repeat what I said and I will answer you gladly, because I don't want a misconstrued word to clash with what I meant to say and what I strive for.

I have been asked what results our visit may be expected to produce. We arrived in the U.S. capital only yesterday. It would be premature to try to anticipate the results of our trip. After all, even in forecasting the next day's weather, the meteorological service comes up against considerable difficulties, and political forecasts are no less difficult. But to judge by the first day of our meetings and interviews in Washington, I would say that the barometer points to "Fair."

We have almost a fortnight before us. We will acquaint ourselves with your country, with the life of your people, and will have talks with President Eisenhower on matters of interest to both parties. It has been long since I last met your President, whose outstanding qualities are highly appreciated in the Soviet Union. We kept in touch mainly through our Ambassadors or by exchanging messages. But, of course, such contacts cannot replace personal contacts and frank talk.

I am sure that you do not expect me to tell you all I have said, or intend to say, to the President. But I will have to tell you something, or you will not have a proper idea of the Soviet stand on the major international issues.

First of all, I wish to stress that we have come to you with the best of intentions and with an open heart. We have come with sentiments of friendship for the American people and a sincere desire to achieve better relations between our two countries and promote peace all over the world. That is the main object of our visit.

We should like to reach an understanding with your government on questions of vital importance. Such questions are many. But I should, above all, like to mention the questions of relaxing international tension and eliminating the cold war, of disarmament, a German peace treaty, world trade and better relations between our countries.

I think the main subject of our talks with the President will be the problem of eliminating the cold war and promoting peace, of easing international tension. Recently your President said that thought should be given to the question of how much longer the arms race and the state of tension in international relations could continue and whether the world had not reached a point where there might be an explosion. We fully share the dissatisfaction with the existing state of world affairs and the concern voiced in that statement.

If we turn to history, we will note easily enough that so far, unfortunately, wars and extermination of man by man have invariably accompanied human society. And although mankind had continuously advanced along the path of progress, wars became more destructive with every step forward. They took an increasing toll of human lives and their flames spread to larger and larger areas.

In the twentieth century mankind has already gone through two world wars, and the sacrifice made in these wars is in no way comparable to the past. Now that man has learned to control the energy of the atom and developed missiles capable of covering thousands of kilometers in a matter of minutes, the best aircraft, battleships and tanks used in the Second World War seem little more than toys compared with the latest means of waging war. In these circumstances it would be sheer madness to allow a new world war to mature.

To preserve peace and rule out war from the life of society for all time is the lofty goal which all peoples want to achieve. The present age has produced new means of mass annihilation, but it has also brought home to the peoples the necessity of preventing war and ensuring peace. It is to this lofty goal that the powerful peace movement has dedicated itself. We are convinced that in our day war is not inevitable. Man can and must be relieved from fear of its horrors.

19

The best and most dependable way of making war impossible is to put all states, without exception, in a position in which they will have no means of waging war, or, in other words, *to solve the disarmament problem.* To be sure, disarmament affects the most sensitive interests of states, the interests of their security, and invades the sphere of such secret information as any state finds difficult to part with, especially at a time of international tension and mutual suspicions.

Without anticipating what I intend to submit to the General Assembly the day after tomorrow, I can tell you that I intend to concentrate on the disarmament problem. The Soviet Government contemplates placing before the United Nations a proposal which we hope will play an important part in settling the most crucial problem of our time.

There are also other pressing international problems. You are aware, of course, that the Soviet Union attaches great importance to the conclusion of a peace treaty with Germany. It is high time, once and for all, to settle issues inherited from the Second World War, if we do not want to see the day when a third world war breaks out.

Why do we insist so strongly that a peace treaty be finally concluded with Germany? We do so for the simple reason that the absence of a peace treaty is poisoning the relations between dozens of countries. Unless the vestiges of the last war are removed, it will be impossible to provide for a durable peace in Europe. We cannot be sure that these vestiges will not fertilize the soil for a new war. I fully realize the importance of fertilizer in farming, but I am against fertilizer of that sort in politics.

We are deeply convinced that the situation must not be tolerated in which, fourteen years after the Second World War, the countries which fought against Germany have not yet concluded peace with that country, and, consequently, the occupation regime is still maintained in West Berlin.

There are Americans who sometimes reason as follows: Europe is far away from us; there are two German states on the territory of Germany, one of which is even an ally of the United States and, as all know, there is no harm in having an extra ally. So, they say, we can get along just as well without a peace treaty.

Pardon my saying so, but such reasoning is fit only for reckless people. Judge for yourselves, your country has twice in the lifetime of a single generation had to send its sons to battlefields in Europe to fight against Germany. And what will happen if your present ally, West Germany, provokes a third war? As matters stand today, it would no longer be a question of sending the breadwinners of American families to theaters of war far removed from American shores. The territory of any belligerent would become a theater of war. Modern means of annihilation are such that war may spread instantly to the entire globe.

You must understand that it is by no means for any fear of the German militarists that we remind you of the dangers of not having a peace treaty with Germany. We are strong enough to muzzle the revanchists and, if necessary, to bring them to their senses. But you will admit that there is no ignoring the fact that certain West German groups are nurturing plans of bringing the Soviet Union into conflict with other powers, of aggravating relations between them and keeping the world in a state of international tension.

It is known that the postwar development of Europe and Germany has led to the establishment of two German states. Both these states exist irrespective of our wishes or our attitude to them. We must reckon with that. Realistic policy is the most correct policy. The only thing to do is to accept the fact that there exist two German states, that is, to recognize the *status quo* which has taken shape in the German question, instead of dragging out the elimination of the vestiges of the war, and to conclude peace with the two German states.

To admit of just one possibility—the conclusion of a peace treaty with a unified Germany only, which, to be sure, would be tantamount, in effect, to dismissing the question of a peace treaty.

The conclusion of a peace treaty would also be instrumental in ultimately settling a question such as that of Berlin, which is causing continuous friction in the relations between the powers. It is alleged sometimes that a year ago the Berlin question did not exist and that the situation in Berlin was not bad. But must we really wait till a seemingly insignificant incident in Berlin starts the guns barking? We maintain that measures for the prevention of conflict should be taken in good time.

Neither the Soviet Union nor the German Democratic Republic has any hidden motives or secret designs on West Berlin. No one wants to annex West Berlin to the German Democratic Republic, any more than to change its social and economic order.

The communiqué released after the talks between the heads of government of the United States and the Federal Republic of Ger-

21

many late last month said that President Eisenhower had reaffirmed "the pledge of the United States and its allies to protect the freedom and welfare of the Berlin population." Very good, that formula accords with our own intentions. The Soviet Union has declared that the most reasonable thing to do in the present circumstances is to proclaim West Berlin a free city. We have proposed in the past, and propose now, that the independent existence of West Berlin be ensured through the most reliable guarantees known in international practice, with or without UN participation. That ought to assure the freedom and welfare of the people of West Berlin.

We take it as a good sign that at the Geneva foreign ministers' conference, the attitudes of the three Western Powers and the Soviet Union came somewhat closer together and a better understanding was achieved of each other's intentions and views. But there are still some outstanding questions on which agreement has to be reached. If I were to tell you that these questions will not be touched on during the forthcoming conversations, you would not believe me anyway.

We know that the Americans are a freedom-loving people and that they are prepared, as in the past, to stand up for their convictions, for the right to live as they choose. The same sentiments are dear to the Soviet people. Reserving this right for oneself, one cannot deny it to others, whatever one's opinion as to whose political and social system is better. The peoples must decide the question of how to live, what ideology, what views to adhere to on their own, without outside interference.

The Soviet Union is for the development of international relations along the principles of peaceful coexistence. These principles were bequeathed to us by Vladimir Ilyich Lenin, the great founder of the Soviet state. And we are faithful to these principles. We hold that differences in world outlook should not impair relations between countries. Close economic and cultural contacts should be established among all countries. That will help nations and statesmen to know and understand one another better. It will facilitate the establishment of mutual trust and peaceful cooperation.

The Soviet Union and the United States are faced with the choice either of having the latest achievements of scientific and technological thought—the discovery of the secret of the atom, the making of rockets and the penetration into outer space—placed at the service of man's peaceful future and prosperity, or of seeing them used for purposes of destruction and annihilation, so that, as a result, the earth will be covered with graves and ashes.

22

Khrushchev speaking at the National Press Club in Washington.

The Soviet people have long since made their choice in favor of peace.

Is this not conclusively attested to by such facts as the building in the Soviet Union of the world's first atomic power station, which for five years now has been supplying power for peaceful uses, or the launching into outer space of the world's first artificial earth satellites and the first artificial planet, made and fired into the universe by man's genius?

Is this not attested to by the outstanding success of Soviet scientists, engineers, technicians and workers who prepared and accomplished the world's first space trip from the earth to another heavenly body, the moon? A powerful container with scientific and measuring instruments and pennants displaying the Soviet coat of arms have been delivered to the surface of the moon. This peaceful feat of the Soviet people greatly extends the horizons of human knowledge and shows what glittering heights mankind will reach if it concentrates all its energy on peaceful pursuits, on the achievement of peaceful aims.

Before we left for the United States a mighty atom-powered icebreaker, the *Lenin*, was launched. She will soon begin to crush the thick ice of northern seas, clearing the way for peaceful ships carrying most peaceful cargoes for peaceful people.

We are certain that the American people, too, are for peace. But if our interests coincide in the key issue—the problem of guaranteeing peace—we should fall into step and work, joining our efforts and energy, for a decisive change in the international climate. Let us, therefore, see how we can establish Soviet-American cooperation.

As far as the Soviet Union is concerned, it is prepared to consider any proposals likely to promote the establishment of good-neighbor relations between the USSR and the USA. This, of course, calls for an effort by both parties, or, as people say in your country, both parties must meet each other halfway.

To be sure, this cannot be done overnight; it would be naive to expect that we could wake up one morning to find all controversial issues settled and all differences removed. The misunderstandings and prejudices born of the cold war are too numerous. But the Soviet Government believes that if we work together with a will, it will be quite possible to disperse the dark clouds in the relations between our countries.

Compare the present international situation with what it was, say, five or six years ago. There are unmistakable signs of a relaxation of the cold war. The cold war must be helped to disappear as quickly as possible. The press, which has apparently not for nothing been called a great power, could do a great deal towards this goal.

The Soviet people are happy to see that there have recently been signs of improvement in Soviet-American relations. Among other things, I have in mind the development of personal contacts between statesmen, such as the U.S. visits of A. I. Mikoyan and F. R. Kozlov, and Vice-President Richard Nixon's visit to the Soviet Union. The Soviet Exhibition in New York and the American Exhibition in Moscow were another big event. I had the pleasure of visiting your exhibition with Mr. Richard Nixon. There the two of us had heated and useful discussions.

We are also prepared to do everything we can for the expansion of world trade. It is high time to do away with the discredited policy of trade discrimination and thereby clear the atmosphere in international relations.

How can the present volume of Soviet-American trade, for example, be considered normal? All the commodities which our two countries exchange in a year could be loaded on two freighters. Yet our two countries account for more than half the world's industrial output. We may ask what purpose is achieved by the policy of trade discrimination, what object it serves. To take a sober view of things, it is a policy that only serves one purpose—that of maintaining distrust in the relations between our countries.

Trade is like a barometer. It shows the trend in political development—whether clouds are gathering as before a storm or whether it will be fair and fine. We sincerely hope the barometer will always point to "Fair," and this, we are deeply convinced, requires all-around expansion of international trade.

What else prevents us from achieving mutual understanding and trust?

It may seem strange, but in connection with this exchange of visits between the U.S. President and myself fears have been voiced that the Soviet Union, while declaring its readiness to put relations with the USA on a sound basis, is allegedly hatching some insidious scheme, seeking to sow discord between the United States and its friends and allies. There is no need for me to go into detail, because these allegations are utterly absurd. We have no intention of making anyone quarrel with anyone else. On the contrary, we are doing our best to have good relations not only with the United States, but also with its allies. We should like personal contacts between Soviet and U.S. statesmen to contribute, in turn, to a further improvement of relations between the Soviet Union and Great Britain, the Soviet Union and France and other U.S. allies.

An exchange of opinions between the Soviet and U.S. Governments will not, and cannot, do any harm to those who are sincerely interested in an improvement of the international situation. If, as a result of this exchange of opinions, the USSR and USA come to understand each other better and to show greater pliancy in settling controversial matters, both the large and the small countries of Europe, Asia and the other continents will benefit by it, and the cause of peace will benefit most of all.

We are not pursuing a policy of plotting with the strong against the weak. We want to reach an understanding with the strong and thereby to reach an understanding with all countries about eliminating the cold war. That would be an equal gain and an equal benefit for all countries.

I have already said that we came to your country with an open heart. We are here not to ask for anything or impose anything on you. Our purpose is to acquaint ourselves with your country and its great people, who have made a tremendous contribution to human progress, to meet your statesmen, public leaders and businessmen, to have useful talks on all matters that concern the peoples of our countries and all mankind.

It is my hope that the U.S. newspapers and magazines, radio and television will convey our friendly greetings to the American people, our wishes for peace and happiness to all Americans from all the Soviet people, from myself and from those accompanying me.

Thank you.

N. S. Khrushchev's address was listened to with great attention. His concluding words were received with vigorous applause.

QUESTION PERIOD

After N. S. Khrushchev had concluded his address, William Lawrence, Chairman of the National Press Club, suggested passing on to the question period.

The first question, relating to the J. V. Stalin personality cult, was considered by the speaker to be of a plainly provocative nature. In answering it, N. S. Khrushchev said:

I should like to ask those who have thought up this question: What was their aim, what were they after, what did they want, when they were inventing it, when thinking it up? You apparently want to place me in an embarrassing position, and are laughing beforehand. The Russians say, "He laughs best who laughs last." Gentlemen, inventing all sorts of absurd figments, though you may now be laughing and thinking how clever you are at inventing, see that you don't repent your own inventions afterward.

I will not be provoked and will not reply with unfriendly sallies against the many worthy representatives of the U.S. press gathered here. I will only add that a lie, however long its legs, can never keep pace with the truth. *(Applause.)*

QUESTION: Was it only a coincidence that the Soviet Union sent a rocket to the moon on the eve of your arrival here, and a related question: Does the sending of the emblem indicate any desire to claim possession of the moon?

KHRUSHCHEV: The coincidence of my trip to the United States with the sending of a Soviet rocket to the moon is a mere, but I would say a pleasant, coincidence. *(Laughter.)* If anyone among you doubts that it was a coincidence, I would suggest that he ask your scientists—let your scientists tell him about it. Try and tell your scientists to time the launching of a moon rocket to such-and-such a date, and see what comes of it. *(Laughter, applause.)*

And now, ladies and gentlemen, I should like to answer the second part of the question—whether the delivery of a pennant to the moon gives the Soviet Union cause for any sort of proprietary claim to the moon. Let there be no mistake—I have no wish to hurt anyone's feelings—but we are people of different continents and different ways of thinking.

Those who put the question in that way think in terms of private capitalist psychology, while I belong to the socialist system and am a man of a new world outlook and new concepts. In our country, the concept "mine" is withering away, while a new concept, "ours," is gaining ground. That is why we regard the launching of a space rocket and the delivery of our pennant to the moon as our achievement. And when we say "our," we imply all the countries of the world, that is, we imply that it is also your achievement and the achievement of all people living on earth. *(Applause.)*

QUESTION: What are the major possibilities for increasing trade between the United States and the Soviet Union, particularly in consumer goods? In brief, what particularly do you want to buy from us and what particularly do you wish to sell to us?

KHRUSHCHEV: What we want most particularly is an end to trade discrimination. That is the most important thing. All that you can make we can make too, and we have made some things before you. *(Laughter.)* We do not ask for anything. You are today turning out some goods in greater quantities than we, but that is due to historical circumstances. Your country took the path of capitalist development much earlier than ours, and you consequently developed your economy more than pre-Revolutionary Russia did. But you know that great changes have now occurred in the development of our economy. We are still some way off, some distance away from you. But we are now closing in like this *(animation in the audience as Khrushchev demonstrates with his hands how the distance between the U.S. economy and that of the Soviet Union is shrinking)*, and I think the day is not far distant when we will change places like this in that movement. We are catching up with you in economic progress, and the time is not far distant when we will move into the lead.

I want to tell you that I did not come to the United States with a long arm to dig my hand into your banks. That is yours. We have enough of our own. *(Laughter.)* I am not going to hold out my hat so that everyone may throw into it what he thinks he can spare. *(Animation.)* We are proud of our system, our people, our state and our achievements. We want to be good trading partners with you, and with all other countries. As for expanding trade between our countries, the way we see it, we should buy what we need and you should sell what you think you can.

I do not now propose to hold specific trade negotiations. I did not take along anyone from the Ministry of Foreign Trade quite deliberately, so that none would think that I had come with a long arm to rich Uncle Sam. *(Laughter.)*

If you show any desire to expand trade, then there will be Soviet representatives on hand to reach concrete agreement on the matter. They will then speak specifically of what you can sell and what we should like to buy from you.

QUESTION: In your opening remarks, Mr. Khrushchev, you spoke about avoiding outside interference in the affairs of other nations. How, then, do you justify Russian armed interference in Hungary?

KHRUSHCHEV: The so-called Hungarian question, you see, has stuck like a dead rat in the throat of some people—they are disgusted with it and yet cannot spit it out. *(Laughter.)* If you want to give our talk that particular twist, I can produce quite a few dead cats. They will be fresher than the question of the Hungarian events.

As regards Hungary, I have spoken about it quite exhaustively in public on many occasions. I was particularly pleased and gratified to answer before the Hungarian people when I was in Hungary as a guest, representing our valiant Soviet Union. It was shortly after the Hungarian events. All Hungary applauded us, and I know of no fuller or better way in which the Hungarians could have expressed their true attitude toward the Soviet Union. We have long since settled all matters with Hungary and are advancing triumphantly shoulder to shoulder. They are building socialism and we are building communism. Our goals coincide—our path is one and so is our goal.

I can add that I will not ask you any counter-questions of this kind, because I have come to the United States with other aims, because I've come with good intentions and an open heart. I have come here, not to dig up various questions so as to aggravate relations between our two countries, between our governments, but to improve existing relations, to remove, if I may say so, the road blocks that hinder a rapprochement of our countries. That is why I don't want to do anything that might conflict with that main objective—improvement of relations between our countries and cessation of the state of cold war—anything that might obstruct the establishment of friendship and the promotion of world peace.

QUESTION: While you are here, Mr. Chairman, will you seek to arrange with President Eisenhower a United States-Soviet civil air agreement to exchange airline operating rights?

KHRUSHCHEV: That is a very concrete question and, of course, it is not on the agenda of our conversations, because it is a minor question and a specific one. But we would be prepared to establish air communications between our two countries. Our country has air communications with many countries of Europe and Asia. If the U.S. Government should wish to reach such an agreement, I hardly think that we—the President and I, Chairman of the Council of Ministers—need handle it. Our Ministers can do it.

QUESTION: We are always anxious to get a little advance news too, Mr. Khrushchev. What is your time schedule for throwing a man to the moon?

KHRUSHCHEV: You used a rather unfortunate phrase when you said "throwing a man." We are not going to "throw" a man, because we value man highly and will not "throw" anyone. We will send a man into outer space when appropriate technical conditions have been developed. There are still no such conditions on hand. We don't want to "throw" anyone in the sense, so to say, of throwing him overboard. We value people.

QUESTION: Would Russia be willing to share with Canada and the United States, her Arctic neighbors, the information which Russian scientists have obtained in their extensive and successful Arctic explorations?

KHRUSHCHEV: I think so. All countries should cooperate in the matter. That would be useful. Generally speaking, we oppose all kinds of monopoly. (Laughter, applause.)

QUESTION: What is the purpose of your visit to Peking after your American tour?

KHRUSHCHEV: That is apparently the most "difficult" question. (Laughter.) Comrades—I beg your pardon, there are both "comrades" and "gentlemen" here. (Laughter.) Habit tells. Besides, our Soviet journalists are present here, whom it is our custom to address with the word "comrades." It is the usual form of address. Furthermore, I do not want to waive the supposition that among you, too, there are those who would not object to my calling them "comrades." *(Animation.)* And so, I am addressing you—gentlemen. *(Laughter.)* I think that journalists not only write, but also read. *(Laughter.)* If journalists do read, they should recall that on October 1, 1959, it will be ten years since state power was won by the American— here you are; now you will say, "See what Khrushchev is thinking about *(laughter),* we've caught him red-handed" *(laughter)*—since state power was won by the Chinese working class and China's working peasantry. It will be ten years since people's rule was established in China. The Chinese people solemnly celebrate this day and we, too, celebrate this holiday of our friends. We believe, for example, that there may come a time when a new era will be computed from the day of the October Revolution. But that is a thing of the future. The Chinese, too, treasure their victory and we respect their love of their achievements. When the Chinese People's Republic celebrated its fifth anniversary, I headed the Soviet delegation at the festivities in Peking. We have now been invited by the Chinese Government to send a delegation to the celebration of the tenth anniversary as well. It so happens that I must be back in the Soviet Union on September 28 and fly to Peking the next day. It will be a strain on me, of course, but I think it will also be a great honor to be among our friends in China. The Soviet delegation will leave for the Chinese People's Republic before my return to Moscow. In my absence it will be led by Comrade Suslov.

QUESTION: Mr. Chairman, can you summarize for us in your speech today, have you offered any specifically new proposals that have not been put forward before for easing world tension?

KHRUSHCHEV: We must first settle those questions that have already been brought up and await settlement. Thinking up new questions while the old ones have yet to be settled would mean evading the solution of cardinal problems. If I am told that I have not raised any new questions in my speech, I will agree. It would not be out of place at this point to recall the Russian saying: Repetition is the mother of learning. We will work hard to remove the obstacles hindering a rapprochement of peoples and to put out the sparks that may set off the flames of war. Those sparks must be stamped out by all means and pressing issues must be settled, so that peace can be assured for all nations.

QUESTION: There is great interest here, Mr. Khrushchev, in the situation of the various nationalities, including the Jewish population, in the Soviet Union. Can you say a few words for us on that score?

KHRUSHCHEV: In the Soviet Union there is no national question in the sense in which you understand it. All nationalities live in friendship and all have equal rights. In our country, the attitude toward anyone is not determined by his nationality or his religion. That is a matter for every man's own conscience. We look upon a man primarily as a man. In our country, all nationalities—Russians, Ukrainians, Turkmens, Uzbeks, Kazakhs, Byelorussians, Georgians, Armenians, Kalmyks, Jews—if I were to list all the peoples of the Soviet Union, it would take more time than has been set apart for this press conference—they all live in peace and harmony. We are proud of the fact that a multinational state such as the Soviet Union is solid and is making good progress. All the peoples of our country trust each other and are advancing shoulder to shoulder toward their common goal, communism. The position of our country's Jewish population, for example, is characterized, among other things, by the following fact: Jews hold a worthy place among those who made the successful launching of the moon rocket possible.

QUESTION: It is frequently attributed to you, Mr. Khrushchev, that at a diplomatic reception you said that you would bury us. If you didn't say it, you could deny it; and if you did say it, could you please explain what you meant?

KHRUSHCHEV: There is only a small section of the American people in this hall. My life would be too short to bury every one of you if this were to occur to me. (Laughter.) I did speak about it, but my statement has been deliberately misconstrued. It was not a question of any physical burial of anyone at any time but of how the social system changes in the course of the historical progress of society. Every educated person knows that there is now more than one social system in the world. The various states, the various peoples have different systems. The social system changes as society develops. There was the feudal system. It was superseded by capitalism. Capitalism was more progressive than feudalism. Capitalism created better conditions than feudalism for the development of the productive forces. But capitalism engendered irreconcilable contradictions. As it outlives itself, every system gives birth to its successors. Capitalism, as Marx, Engels and Lenin have proved, will be succeeded by communism. We believe in that. Many of you do not. But among you, too, there are people who believe in that.

At the reception concerned, I said that in the course of historical progress and in the historical sense, capitalism would be buried and communism would come to replace capitalism. You will say that this is out of the question. But then the feudal lords burned at the stake those who fought against feudalism and yet capitalism won out. Capitalism fights against communism. I am convinced that the winner will be communism, a social system which creates better conditions for the development of a country's productive forces, enables every individual to prove his worth and guarantees complete freedom for society, for every member of society. You may disagree with me. I disagree with you. What are we to do, then? We must coexist. Live on under capitalism, and we will build communism. The new and progressive will win; and the old and moribund will die. You believe that the capitalist system is more productive, that it creates better conditions for social progress, that it will win. But the brief history of our Soviet state does not speak in favor of capitalism. What place did Russia hold for economic development before the Revolution? She was backward and illiterate. And now we have a powerful economy, our science and culture are highly developed.

I don't recall just how many engineers we graduate annually—

V. P. YELUTIN*: Last year 94,000 engineers were graduated and 106,000 this year, or three times as many as in the United States.

KHRUSHCHEV: Some say in your country that if the USSR will have more scientists, we will perish. We are willing to "perish" in that sense, we are seeing to it that there are more scientists in our country, that all our people are educated, because communism cannot be built unless we do so. Communism is a science.

Thank you. *(Stormy, prolonged applause.)*

In conclusion William Lawrence, Chairman of the National Press Club, on behalf of the club's members, thanked N. S. Khrushchev for his address and replies to questions.

INTERVIEW WITH LEADERS OF THE U.S. CONGRESS
AND MEMBERS OF THE SENATE FOREIGN RELATIONS COMMITTEE

September 16, 1959

On September 16, N. S. Khrushchev visited the U.S. Congress at the invitation of Senator J. W. Fulbright, Chairman of the Senate Foreign Relations Committee. The meeting was attended by 25 Sen-

*Minister of Higher Education of the USSR.

ators—leaders of Congress and members of the Senate Foreign Relations Committee.

In his opening remarks, Fulbright welcomed N. S. Khrushchev, Chairman of the Council of Ministers of the USSR. "We are glad to see you here," he said, "and are glad that you are going to talk with the President on important matters pertaining to the relations between our countries. The Soviet Union and the United States are strong powers. The Soviet people and the Americans are gifted people. The possibilities of our countries are unlimited." Fulbright stressed that armaments reduction and peaceful coexistence would help to promote peace and security and to raise the living standards of all peoples. "I want to assure you," he went on, "that our people, like your own, do not want war. We must find ways of ruling out the possibility of war resulting from some accident and must provide ways of peaceful economic competition."

N. S. Khrushchev thanked Fulbright for his invitation to meet Congressional leaders and members of the Senate Foreign Relations Committee.

"I fully agree with everything you have just said," N. S. Khrushchev continued. "You, gentlemen of the Senate, hold a position of responsibility, and the trend in the policies of so powerful a state as the United States depends largely on you. I always follow your speeches with attention and know many of you from them. Now we have met in person. You will not be surprised if I say that I do not subscribe to everything you say in your speeches. There is a Russian saying: 'Break bread with me, but speak your mind.' But let us not now begin recollecting when and which Senator said something bad or something good. That is a thing of the past. Let us take guidance in political wisdom and think of the future, of how to guarantee peace and the security of nations.

"We Soviet people always think highly of the achievements of the American people, rejoice in these achievements, are a little envious at times, and want first to bring our economy level with yours, then gather strength and outstrip you. I think our peoples and future generations would be grateful to both of us if we shifted our efforts from the arms race to competition in developing economy and culture, and raising living standards. We are willing. I think this problem can be solved only if prejudices are given up and a new course is adopted without hesitation—a course of friendship and cooperation.

"I realize that it is not always easy to change the trend in relations between states, discard the old or obsolescent and adopt the new and progressive. Here is an example from everyday reality: Sometimes an elderly man puts on a new pair of shoes and wears them for a while, but then flings them off and puts on the old pair. The new pair hurts his corns, while he is accustomed to the old one which seems to fit better. It is sometimes the same in human society. Some people are apt to reject the new and try to preserve the old.

"Here is another example: You expect a daughter but your wife gives birth to a son, or while you expect a granddaughter, a grandson is born. You are disappointed, of course, but it cannot be helped, nature doesn't always comply with man's will. *(Animation.)*

"The peoples have always fought for progress. In all the developed countries, revolutions occurred in one form or another when the need arose to pass from feudalism to capitalism. When you fought for your independence against Britain, whose colony the United States was, the British king did not send you messages of greeting and you won your independence in an armed struggle. The Civil War which the North waged against the South was also a progressive struggle, and the name of Lincoln, who led that struggle for man's freedom, will live through the ages.

"A new social system, the socialist system, is being born now. At first socialism won in one country, Russia; now it has triumphed in many countries of Europe and Asia.

"You do not accept this system, but I have already said that when you want a grandson and a granddaughter is born instead, there is nothing you can do about it. Still less does the rise of a new system in any country depend on the will of other countries. If everybody recognizes the principle of noninterference in the internal affairs of other countries, which means recognizing the right of the people in each country to choose the political organization, the system they prefer, then universal peace will be assured. That is all we want.

"We have all we need for the expansion of our economy and do not covet the riches of other countries. Today we are successfully building communism. Other peoples who have taken the path of socialist development have by their experience also borne out the theoretical forecasts of scientific communism. We consider communism to be the best system for us. We do not ask for your approval. What we want is not to be interfered with.

"Changes in social formation in human society are not a process that occurs in all countries simultaneously. When and how the social system of a country changes is the affair of its own people. Recognize

34

Chairman Khrushchev and President Eisenhower in Washington.

this, and peace will be assured. If you do not recognize it, war will be unavoidable. If you are going to seek a forcible change in the system of other countries, the peoples of those countries will naturally have to defend themselves. And that will mean war!

"Allow me to take this opportunity of making a few critical remarks about you. I should like to state frankly that the decision of your Congress to appropriate funds for subversive activities in the socialist countries does not further peaceful coexistence and the cause of peace. It is an unwise decision. What is more, to use the manufacturer's phrase, it is not a profitable enterprise; the invested capital is yielding no interest in this particular instance. (Animation.)

"I don't want to sound didactic—the policy you make is your own responsibility. I don't know whether you permit your guests to express their views, but we in the Soviet Union welcome it when our visitors speak their mind, even if we disagree with them.

"Thank you. In conclusion, I want to stress once more that all we want is peace and friendship with the American people and with all the peoples of the world. Let us do a good thing, the responsibility resting on us is great and we must live up to the expectations of the peoples. And the peoples want just one thing—peace. If you like your capitalist system, carry on as you have done so far, and God be with you. As for us, we like the socialist system, so don't interfere with our living as we choose.

"There was a time when people were burned at the stake because they insisted that the earth revolved. But today you will not find a simpleton who would not believe it. Why will you not admit, then, that your present views of communism may be wrong? But, I repeat, that is your affair. Let us recognize the *status quo*—there exist socialist and capitalist countries in the world, so let us live in this existing world of ours on the basis of peaceful coexistence.

"Since I was the first to make some critical remarks about you, I thereby gave you a chance to do likewise. I am willing to hear your criticisms and to reply to them, and also to answer any questions you may ask." (Applause.)

Fulbright said that he liked N. S. Khrushchev's remarks. He said it was frank talk and they were pleased to have such a talk. Speaking of N. S. Khrushchev's remarks about Congress appropriating funds for subversive activities, Fulbright contradicted the remark, saying that "we interpret words differently." "We don't think it is so," said Fulbright, "we don't want to interfere in the internal affairs of other countries. On the contrary, we have, for example, given the Philippines a chance to win freedom. But I say that in passing."

Fulbright then accused some socialist countries of "trying to impose their regime on others by force."

"When discussing a meeting with your President," N. S. Khrushchev replied, "we agreed to talk about the relations between our two countries. Neither he nor I have been empowered to speak for any third country. If you have any complaints against a socialist country, negotiate with it, apply directly to its government. Go-betweens are undesirable in matters such as this. I represent the Soviet Union here and am willing to answer any question that concerns the Soviet Union."

"One more question," Fulbright said. "You are convinced that your system is better than ours—"

"Absolutely convinced," N. S. Khrushchev replied.

"But what happens," Fulbright continued, "if it suddenly develops that the capitalist system is better and that more and more people prefer capitalism to socialism? Will you put up with that, or will you use force to hold your positions?"

"Let us not read the tea leaves," N. S. Khrushchev said, "but if history were to confirm that the capitalist system really offers the best opportunities of developing the productive forces of society and of providing a better life for man—and we don't believe that a kopek's worth—I would be the first to vote against communism. If I really satisfied myself as to the superiority of capitalism over communism," N. S. Khrushchev said sarcastically, "then I would consider which way to turn and whether I should join the Republicans or the Democrats, though there is hardly any difference between them. It would be a difficult choice to make." (Laughter.)

"I can tell you which party is better," Fulbright put in, amidst general animation.

"Don't prompt me," N. S. Khrushchev continued. "I want to make my own choice. (Laughter.) I know which party you represent, but I'm not sure which of the two parties is better. I don't want to interfere in your internal affairs." (Animation.)

Fulbright asked another question—whether the Soviet Union was prepared to agree to any of its allies choosing a two-party system.

"Questions like that are decided by the peoples themselves," N. S. Khrushchev replied.

The next to speak was Senator Hayden, a veteran of the U.S. Senate and member of the Senate Appropriations Committee. He asked N. S. Khrushchev whether he favored the expansion of cultural and scientific exchanges between the USSR and the USA.

"Yes," N. S. Khrushchev replied, "we advocate the broadest possible cultural and scientific exchange between our countries. But as far as we know, it is not we who are holding things up. The counter-proposal of the American side for an agreement on cultural relations in 1960-1961, far from envisaging broader relations, is in fact aimed at reducing them."

G. A. Zhukov, Chairman of the State Committee on Cultural Relations, who was present, informed the audience that the U.S. counter-proposal provided for only two major events in the sphere of artistic exchange in 1960 and only one major event in 1961. None of the 17 Soviet proposals for technical exchange were accepted by the U.S. side. As regards the U.S. proposals for technical exchange, the Soviet delegation has already agreed to a number of measures with the proviso that the State Department, in turn, accept at least some of the Soviet proposals.

Senator Lyndon Johnson, Democratic majority leader, asked whether the Soviet Union would agree to cooperation between Soviet and U.S. scientists in exploring outer space.

"By all means," N. S. Khrushchev replied.

"Then why did you refuse to take part in the work of the UN Outer Space Committee?" Johnson asked.

"You know why," N. S. Khrushchev replied. "You wanted to place us in the position of a poor relation on that committee, but we will not have that. We offered you cooperation on a parity basis, but you turned it down. Then we refused to participate in the work of the UN Committee. You know perfectly well that at the moment only you and we alone can engage, in practice, in the exploration of outer space. Yet you wanted to push us out into the backyard on the UN Committee. We will never consent to be put in so humiliating a position. We refuse to be lectured in a committee in which you have a majority. Do not injure our self-respect and we will not injure yours. Then cooperation will be assured."

"I want to give the floor to a spokesman for the Congress minority and an experienced polemicist, Senate Republican Leader Dirksen," said Fulbright.

Everett M. Dirksen said he had two questions. First he asked whether there was "any hope" of the Soviet Union's lifting control over foreign correspondents' news dispatches.

"Every nation has its traditions," N. S. Khrushchev said, "and every country has its Constitution. In your country the newspapers see fit to print every possible slanderous fabrication and every possible comment, often provocative and nothing short of an outright appeal to war. But in the Soviet Union, anyone who took it into his head to write an article of that kind would be prosecuted, because we have a law prohibiting war propaganda. Your correspondents send any information or article from the Soviet Union quite freely unless it distorts the facts, unless it is grossly slanderous and insulting to the Soviet people, and unless it incites to war.

"Many of your correspondents send fairly sensible articles and our press even reprints some of them. But there are also correspondents who abuse the freedom of the press."

"Your correspondents working in the U.S. are not controlled," Dirksen observed.

N. S. Khrushchev replied that if any Soviet correspondent working in the United States were to send a false report, he would be instantly dismissed by his editorial office. Soviet journalists perform their mission honestly, while some of the Western correspondents working in Moscow have no scruples about writing stuff that if it were handed to the clerk in the telegraph office for transmission she would be outraged and would refuse to send such rot abroad. We have no censorship. There is only control to prevent abuse of the freedom of the press. We do not want to help foment hostility and hatred between peoples by adopting an overconciliatory attitude.

We want international friendship and cooperation.

Zhukov offered to provide Senator Dirksen with factual data on abuses of the freedom of the press by some foreign correspondents working in Moscow. Dirksen made no reply.

Dirksen next asked whether foreigners would be allowed unrestricted freedom of travel in the Soviet Union. He claimed that Soviet people could travel in the USA without any restrictions.

"Let us agree," N. S. Khrushchev said, "that for every kilometer which Soviet people travel on U.S. territory, we will let American travelers do two kilometers in the Soviet Union."

A. I. Adzhubei, Deputy to the Supreme Soviet, said that on one occasion he had even been refused permission to fly over the United States, to say nothing of traveling across its territory, although he had applied for a visa in person to Secretary of State Dulles. He added that Soviet correspondents coming to New York to cover the work of the UN General Assembly are allowed to use only specified streets.

"I have been told," N. S. Khrushchev observed, "that Soviet diplomats cannot even travel from Washington to New York without special permission. But I will not criticize your internal regulations. I only wish to ask you what you want. You say that you want to travel where you please. You want it for a very definite purpose. Don't try to force anyone's bedroom door if it is locked. That is indecent. What is this taste you have for peeping through keyholes? You want us to lift travel restrictions in the Soviet Union, do you? Then let us achieve agreement. Let us abolish military bases on foreign soil and withdraw troops from foreign territory to within national boundaries. I assure you that you would then be allowed to travel wherever you please. But you have surrounded us with military bases and want to travel freely in our country and scout our military bases. We call that military reconnaissance. That is why we restrict certain areas of importance to our country's defense."

"Our guest would be a most formidable antagonist in any parliamentary forum anywhere in the world," said Senator Russell, Chairman of the Senate Armed Services Committee, amidst general laughter.

"Not an antagonist, but a defender," N. S. Khrushchev remarked.

"You have a good knowledge of many things in this country," Russell continued. "But I am amazed to hear that you think we want to interfere in your internal affairs. I have been on the Senate Committee for 25 years but know nothing about appropriations for subversive work in other countries. I am convinced that today the people of the Soviet Union live better than ever before."

"Quite right," N. S. Khrushchev said.

"And will live still better," Russell went on. "We don't intend to interfere in your internal affairs, but I would like to ask this: You support national self-determination; in light of this, are you prepared to let the people of East Germany decide their destiny themselves by a plebiscite?"

N. S. Khrushchev reminded the audience that it had been agreed at the beginning of the interview not to touch upon matters relating to a third country.

"I am a Russian," he said, "and represent the Soviet Union here. You, however, are interested in German affairs. If you have any questions on that score, send them to the Prime Minister of the German Democratic Republic and he will supply you with the information you want. The address is well known—Grotewohl, Berlin. They'll get there." (Animation.)

"You are bearing out what I said about your being a fine polemicist," Russell commented, with some embarrassment. "I have one more question. You gave a vivid account of the launching of the Soviet moon rocket. We have had setbacks in launching rockets. What about you?"

"Why do you ask me?" N. S. Khrushchev said with a smile. "You had better ask Nixon—he answered your question when he said that the launching of our moon rocket had miscarried three times. He knows better how things are with us. (Laughter.) Nixon said he was using information from a secret source, but of course he didn't specify the source—you cannot disclose a secret such as that, because it is an invention.

"But if you like, I can answer that question, too. To be sure, launching a rocket into space is no simple matter. It takes a great deal of effort. I will tell you a secret—our scientists expected to launch a moon rocket a week ago. The rocket was prepared and put on the launching site, but when the equipment was being tested it was found to be not working smoothly enough. Then, to be on the safe side, our scientists replaced the rocket by another. It was that second rocket which was launched. But the first rocket is intact, and if you like, we can launch it too.

"That was how matters stood. I can swear on the Bible that this is so. Let Nixon do likewise." (General laughter, applause.)

Senator Russell thanked N. S. Khrushchev and said that the Soviet moon shot was an outstanding achievement of Soviet science, on which Americans sincerely congratulated Soviet scientists.

"Thank you," N. S. Khrushchev said. "We are satisfied with the results of the work done by our scientists."

Senator Theodore F. Green, a Senate veteran and ex-Chairman of the Senate Foreign Relations Committee, asked whether N. S. Khrushchev considered "free elections" possible in West and East Germany in the next six months.

N. S. Khrushchev reminded the audience that those taking part in the interview had agreed not to touch upon the internal affairs of a third country. Since, however, the German question comes within the competence of the Great Powers that fought against Hitler Germany, he said he was willing to comment on the matter.

"You are familiar with our attitude," N. S. Khrushchev said. "We think it necessary to reckon with the fact that there now are two sovereign states with different social systems on the former territory of Germany. Let the Germans decide for themselves how they should live in the future. It will be as they decide. I cannot answer you on behalf of Comrade Grotewohl or Herr Adenauer. Let them rather meet without an interpreter."

Senator Green then asked how elections were held in the Soviet Union and whether it was true that in the USSR nominations were made by only one party and votes could be cast only for one nominee.

"Not exactly," N. S. Khrushchev replied. "About 40 per cent of the deputies to the parliaments of the Soviet Union and Union Republics, and to the regional and district Soviets of Working People's Deputies are not Party members. There is indeed only one party in the Soviet Union. In the early period, when we still had antagonistic classes, other parties as well were represented in our parliament. But subsequently the structure of our society changed. Today we have no antagonistic classes, the interests of all the working people are represented by the Communist Party, the party of the working people. During the election campaign nominations are made as follows:

"Collectives of working people nominate various candidates, the number of candidates being unlimited. Every collective campaigns for its own nominee. Then representatives of the collectives of working people, elected by democratic procedure, get together and decide by vote which nominee should be left on the ticket as the fittest. And it is for him that the electors vote.

"You have a different election system. That is a matter of tradition. Every nation establishes the kind of system it prefers."

Senator Wiley, ex-Chairman of the Senate Foreign Relations Committee, asked the following question:

"On your way to this country, you doubtless set yourself a definite goal. What do you expect to accomplish by your U.S. trip?"

"I might address the same question to you, Senator," N. S. Khrushchev replied. "So far as we are concerned, we are willing to take any steps to ensure peace, particularly in the matter of disarmament. But reaching agreement requires a mutual desire to achieve useful results. Take the disarmament question. Are you prepared now to abolish military bases on foreign soil and withdraw your troops to within your national boundaries? We are!

"You claim that the socialist system in countries such as Poland and Hungary, where we have our troops for the time being, survives solely thanks to their presence there.

"Very well, would you like to put yourself to a test? You will have the opportunity of seeing how the Poles manage their affairs in the absence of foreign troops. You say that the Government of the German Democratic Republic is maintained only by our bayonets. Let us agree to withdraw your troops and ours to within the respective national boundaries and see what happens. Are you willing? *(The Senator keeps silent for a long time.)* Let us sign an agreement to withdraw troops. Let the soldiers go home. How happy their mothers and their girls will be to embrace them! Are you willing? *(The Senator says nothing.)* There you are. You yourself are hesitant to try it. How can I say, then, what results my trip will yield? I don't know how far you are willing to go, but a great deal depends on the U.S. Senate."

Fulbright, who was presiding, said that the Senators were happy to have met N. S. Khrushchev and discussed with him a number of questions of interest to them. He said he was not sure that anything had been solved by the meeting but thought there was now better mutual understanding, and that meant a lot.

N. S. Khrushchev thanked the Senators and left the premises of the Foreign Relations Committee of the U.S. Senate.

SPEECH BY N. S. KHRUSHCHEV
AT DINNER GIVEN FOR PRESIDENT DWIGHT D. EISENHOWER

> N. S. Khrushchev, Chairman of the Council of Ministers of the USSR, and Madame Khrushchova gave a dinner, on the evening of September 16, for President Eisenhower and Mrs. Eisenhower in the Soviet Embassy in Washington.
> During the dinner N. S. Khrushchev and President Dwight D. Eisenhower exchanged speeches.

MR. PRESIDENT, MRS. EISENHOWER, LADIES AND GENTLEMEN:

This is the second day of our stay in the United States. I don't know whether you are pleased with your guests, but the guests are very well pleased with their hosts. We like our stay in your country, but have no fear, I shall not ask for it to be prolonged. *(Animation.)* My time is limited. I will fly to China literally the day after my return from the United States. There will be festivities there on the occasion of the tenth anniversary of the People's Republic. It is not to make a secret deal that I will fly there, but to celebrate the big national holiday of People's China.

My friends and I have had a fine day today. You are real exploiters, I must say, and have made a good job of exploiting us. *(Animation.)* Mr. Lodge has been empowered to do so, and he has worn us out completely. *(Laughter.)* I don't know whether the exploiters are satisfied with us, but on this particular occasion the exploited are satisfied with their exploiters. *(Laughter.)*

We had an interesting time at your agricultural research center. You can be proud of it. We saw livestock and poultry there—they are excellent. And I did not feel in the least that they had any objection to our representing a socialist country in a capitalist one. They realized the necessity of coexistence. *(Laughter.)*

My next visit today was to the National Press Club. Journalists are impetuous, quick-witted people. You and I, Mr. President, are able to appreciate each other's plight when meeting journalists. *(Laughter.)* In any case, I am hale and hearty, as you see, and I think that speaks well for the meeting. As for what they will report, we will know that tomorrow. It is something I cannot guess. There were different people there, and they will probably report differently. *(Animation.)*

Then we toured the city of Washington. I bear Mr. Lodge no grudge on this point. We saw little because time was short. But we did see the best section of the city. It is a wonderful city. We saw the Lincoln Memorial and paid homage to that great, most human of humans in U.S. history, whose memory as a champion of freedom will live through the ages.

Then there was the talk with the members of the Senate Foreign Relations Committee. I don't know whether the Senators were

Send-off at the railway station in Washington.

pleased with me. I cannot speak for them. But I am pleased, and think that makes a half success. *(Animation.)* If the Senators are also pleased with me, I would take that to be a complete success, but I don't know if they are.

I believe I speak for all my companions when I say that we are very pleased with this evening and with your presence, Mr. President, the presence of your wife and your colleagues, at so distinguished a dinner. I feel sure—perhaps because I want it very badly—that our coming at your invitation, Mr. President—for we would not have come to you otherwise—and your forthcoming visit to our country will help to thaw international relations; the ice of the cold war has not only cracked but has indeed, begun to crumble.

I think that through joint effort we will reach the goal of actually melting the ice and establishing normal living conditions for our peoples and good, friendly relations between our countries.

I raise this glass of champagne and invite all the guests to follow suit. I propose this toast to the President of the United States. I don't know whether I have the right, whether I have your permission, but we regard you as our good friend. You have shown how thoroughly scrupulous you are—I don't quite know whether the term is suitable to give an exact idea of how you performed your duty when you were Allied Commander-in-Chief during the Second World War. When you come to our country, you will feel the warmth which our people will express. But I should like to ask you, when you feel that warmth, not to draw a line between the people and the government as some people try to do. That is a very bad line to draw, because in our country the government expresses and does what the people think and want.

If the people express sympathy, it follows that the government is of the same opinion. It would never even occur to me that there is any need to test this unity. During your stay in the USSR you will be able to satisfy yourself about the solid unity of our people and government. We need only wink to understand each other. Let those who doubt come to us and see this unity for themselves.

I raise this glass of champagne and invite you to drink to the health of the President; to your health, Mrs. Eisenhower; to yours, dear guests, ladies and gentlemen; to all present here. Although this wine is cold, may our relations grow warmer, may the atmosphere mellow, so as to melt the ice of the cold war and create favorable conditions for the peaceful coexistence of states, of our peoples. Your health! *(Applause.)*

N. S. Khrushchev and his party arrived in New York on September 17. Richard C. Patterson, representative of the municipal authority, welcomed N. S. Khrushchev at the station.

Replying to his greetings, N. S. Khrushchev said:

MR. REPRESENTATIVE OF THE MAYOR OF NEW YORK:

Allow me to thank you for your warm words on my own behalf and on the behalf of my family, as well as those accompanying me.

I was very glad to receive the invitation to visit New York. I express to you my gratitude for this invitation.

I would like to use this opportunity and convey wishes of best success to the citizens of New York in their work, success in their private lives and wish them happiness and well-being.

It is generally known that New York is a major industrial city, a leading business center of the United States. In the past I myself was a worker and am therefore especially glad to have the opportunity of greeting the working people who create material values for society.

I am certain that the meetings and talks which I will have in New York with representatives of various sections of the population will facilitate a better understanding between our countries. This will facilitate the adjustment of friendly relations between our states and the strengthening of peace throughout the world.

I thank you for your attention.

N. S. KHRUSHCHEV'S SPEECH AT THE LUNCHEON GIVEN BY ROBERT WAGNER, MAYOR OF NEW YORK

Robert F. Wagner, Mayor of New York, gave a luncheon in honor of N. S. Khrushchev, Chairman of the USSR Council of Ministers, on September 17.

The Mayor made a speech of welcome. Henry Cabot Lodge, the President's special representative, also made a speech.

N. S. Khrushchev delivered a speech as well.

N. S. KHRUSHCHEV'S SPEECH

Thank you, Mr. Mayor, for the honor you have shown me today. I very nearly called you Robert Petrovich Wagner. In my youth when I worked at a factory, our manager was an engineer by the name of Robert Petrovich Wagner. (*Animation, applause.*) But, of course, I am not confusing you with that other Wagner; you only have the same names and surnames. (*Laughter.*)

I should like to thank you most sincerely for this wonderful reception and, in particular, for the memorial medallion of your city that you have presented to me, and for the message to the peoples of the Soviet Union as a sign of respect and friendship between our countries. (*Applause.*)

I should like to take this opportunity again to address words of profound appreciation to the President of the United States, Dwight Eisenhower. We made his acquaintance immediately after the war, when he visited our country. The military services rendered by General Eisenhower as Allied Commander-in-Chief in Western Europe are valued highly in our country. We fought well together with you against Nazi Germany. (*Stormy applause.*) It is only due to President Eisenhower's invitation that I have the opportunity of being with you today.

My respect for Mr. Eisenhower has grown still more since this step. His decision to invite Khrushchev to America was not an easy one. Few Americans would have dared to take such a step. To do so one had to be a big man and, what is more, to understand big politics. (*Applause.*) I am informed that some of the American political leaders are opposed to this decision by the President. The President's wisdom lay precisely in the fact that despite this, he went through with what he had decided. It showed that he was more far-sighted than those who, as we say in Russia, cannot see farther than their own noses. (*Laughter, applause.*) A statesman must not only know what is taking place today, but must show concern for the future and work for its sake. (*Applause.*)

I would now like to thank you as well, Mr. Mayor of the City of New York, because while President Eisenhower invited me to America, you invited me to New York, because without your invitation I could not have come to your great city. This invitation from you might have come, of course, merely as a sign of courtesy to the President. But evidently you also had a well-meaning interest in seeing what sort of a person Khrushchev was. (*Laughter, applause.*) To see what he was like. And so here I am before you and your colleagues. (*Stormy applause.*)

Last but not least, I should like to thank Mr. Lodge, the President's special representative, who is performing a difficult function and torturing me with a stiff program. *(Laughter, applause.)* But he is also torturing himself. *(Laughter, applause.)* I am glad of that, because it is easier to bear torture together. *(Stormy applause.)*

Ladies and gentlemen, I have never gone in for diplomacy but I have a good idea of diplomatic language in relations between governments. If I tell you frankly what I think, let the diploma'd diplomats not judge me too severely for possible deviations from protocol. *(Animation, applause.)*

You have probably noticed that I attentively followed Mr. Lodge's and Mr. Wagner's speeches, and applauded both. That is why I should like to make things clear. After all, some might think that Khrushchev has been converted to your capitalist faith. *(Laughter, applause.)* Lodge and Wagner defend the capitalist system, while I applaud them. What am I? Among Communists I applaud Communists, and among capitalists I applaud capitalists. It follows that I applaud both to play up to them. *(Animation, applause.)*

Let us agree upon the following beforehand. I do not think there is any need for me to exert myself to try and make Communists out of you. That would be a waste of energy, and I need energy for more important matters. *(Applause.)* But if anyone still nurses the hope that I shall adopt the capitalist attitude, I want to tell you straight from the shoulder that that is also a vain hope. *(Stormy applause.)* Were I a supporter of capitalism, I would of course try to come to your country, for after all the United States is the main root of the world capitalist system. *(Animation.)* But I am convinced that our system is much more solid and much better.

We Russians have a proverb which says that every snipe praises its own bog. You extol the capitalist bog; as for us, I shall not, naturally, say that socialism is a bog, but you can, of course, speak of our system much as I speak of yours. But, as a matter of fact, the proponents of capitalism are now beginning to be ashamed of praising it. They are saying that it is no longer the capitalism that Marx wrote about, but people's capitalism.

God knows, I see no difference between the capitalism Marx wrote about and the capitalism Lodge spoke of today. *(Animation.)* I speak bluntly, so that you should know who you are dealing with. Such clarity improves relations: We like socialism, while capitalism does not suit us. If you like capitalism—and I know that you like it —carry on, and God bless you! But remember that a new social system, the socialist system, has come into being. It is already treading on your heels, and we are reckoning on overtaking and outdistancing you.

Let's better speak of what ought to unite us, rather than magnify what might disunite us. *(Stormy, prolonged applause.)*

Let's compete peacefully and let the peoples judge which system is better, which offers greater scope for the development of the productive forces, which provides better for man's well-being. We must respect the choice of the peoples. We must respect their right to live as they choose. We must base relations between governments on the recognition that different social systems have an equal right to exist. We must ensure peaceful coexistence and thereby strengthen peace throughout the world. *(Applause.)*

I say to you in all sincerity that we want to live with you in friendship and peace. *(Stormy, prolonged applause.)* At one time our people watched with admiration, and I would even say with envy, how rapidly America developed after liberating herself from colonial dependence. That was a revolutionary upsurge and an exploit. Your country swiftly built up its strength and outstripped all countries in economic development. You still have the highest standard of living. You are still the richest country and the most powerful of the capitalist countries, of the capitalist countries—I want to specify that. *(Animation.)* Just to be accurate, of course. *(Applause.)*

But by the time we also had a revolution you had evidently forgotten the days of your own revolution and sent your troops to Russia to help the Russian landlords and capitalists to suppress the people. You may remember what came of it—our people gave the interventionists a kick in the pants. We kicked out your troops, and the French, and the British, together with the White Guards. After that you recognized us. True, you required sixteen years of deliberation before doing it. But it was impossible not to recognize the new that had come into being without so much as a by-your-leave and had begun to live by its own will. When you recognized us, we were, of course, in a different position than today. But now there is all the more reason for us to ensure peaceful coexistence.

Now, too, some of you may not like our system. But what can you do? Try to use force to change the situation in our country? You know yourselves what that would lead to!

But now that I have met you I can see that, like us, you too do not want war. *(Applause.)* So let us come to terms on how we are to secure eternal peace. *(Stormy applause.)* Let us broaden our contacts. Let more delegations come to you from us and to us from you.

The only thing is that your State Department is said to be afraid of this and wants to cut down on contacts rather than extend them. We have sent them a few interesting proposals, but they are turning them down. That is bad. Does that imply that you want to return to the iron curtain? (*Animation.*)

We are for broad contacts, for the promotion of cultural and scientific relations, for an exchange of scientific literature, for co-operation with the United States and with all other countries regardless of their social system. (*Applause.*)

In your speeches you spoke of our joint struggle against Nazi Germany. I set great store by the assistance you rendered us in that struggle. Allow me, on behalf of the Soviet Government and people, to convey our gratitude to the American people for that cooperation in the fight against the common enemy. The assistance you rendered us under lend-lease played its role. (*Applause.*)

You are informed, of course, of the contribution of the Soviet people to victory over the common enemy. That contribution was the very largest. It played a decisive role in defeating the German invaders. In the last war the Soviet people suffered the heaviest losses for the sake of victory over fascism.

I had the pleasure today to shake hands with Admiral Kirk and Mr. Harriman, who had been ambassadors of the United States in Moscow during the war years, and also with the present U.S. Ambassador in Moscow, Thompson, who worked at that time in the American Embassy in Moscow, making every effort to ensure victory over the common enemy. (*Applause.*)

Mr. Harriman visited us in the Soviet Union some time ago and we had a pleasant friendly talk. We conversed with him in a friendly way. Some may ask how that could be, Harriman being a big capitalist, and I not the hindmost of Communists. Yet there we were, having a friendly talk. (*Animation.*) But that only confirms that there is a question that can bring everybody together—workers, and peasants, and merchants, and capitalists. It concerns all people living on earth. It is the question of ensuring peace. For the sake of resolving this question we are in duty bound to seek and find a common language. (*Applause.*)

In conclusion, I should like to thank the Mayor of New York City for inviting us to take part in the exhibition that you are planning to hold in 1964. For the moment I can only give you my personal opinion (you have a poor idea of our democratic system, the Chairman of the Council of Ministers cannot in our country take such a decision before the government examines the question), but I think your invitation will be favorably received. When you send us this proposal officially, we shall discuss it, and I expect that we shall consider it an honor to participate in the exhibition you are planning for 1964. *(Applause.)*

I have come to the end of my speech. I thank you for your attention and for your patience. After all, I spoke extemporaneously, and being speakers yourselves you well know that when you speak without notes your speech turns out longer than you wanted. I have therefore wearied you somewhat. Thank you again for your attention. Good-bye, ladies and gentlemen. *(Stormy applause.)*

N. S. KHRUSHCHEV'S SPEECH
AT THE DINNER GIVEN IN THE ECONOMIC CLUB OF NEW YORK

Members of the Economic Club of New York gave a dinner in honor of N. S. Khrushchev, Chairman of the Council of Ministers of the USSR, on the evening of September 17.

In his introductory speech Herbert Woodman, President of the Club and President of the large Interchemical Corporation, pointed out that today everybody recognizes the historic significance of the exchange of visits between Khrushchev and Eisenhower. The Soviet people, the Club President declared, may be justly proud of their economic achievements. At the same time, Woodman praised the capitalist system in every way possible, claiming, for example, that the struggle against monopolies was, allegedly, under way in the USA. Henry Cabot Lodge, the President's special representative, spoke in the same vein.

After that the floor was given to N. S. Khrushchev.

MR. CHAIRMAN, GENTLEMEN:

Before proceeding with the address which I prepared prior to coming to your club, I should like to say a few words on some of the points brought up here by the Chairman, Mr. Woodman, and by Mr. Lodge.

Mr. Woodman said that never in the history of your club has there been such a large number of people as today, wishing to attend a meeting with a guest. Before our meeting began I jokingly told Mr. Woodman that in some parts of my country, where the people have never seen, say, a camel, large crowds assemble when a camel appears. Everybody wants to take a look at it, and some even wish to pull its tail. *(Laughter, applause.)*

Forgive me my joke, but I should like to draw something of a parallel. The flower of the capitalist world of New York, and not

51

only of New York, is gathered here. And suddenly a Communist appears in such select company, a company to which you are accustomed. Understandably, the wish arises to take a look at him, and to pull him by the tail if he proves to have one. *(General hilarity, burst of applause.)*

I don't know if Mr. Marshall MacDuffie is present here. I saw him today at the luncheon given by the Mayor of New York. During the first years after the war, when I was Chairman of the Council of Ministers in the Ukraine, Mr. MacDuffie came to the Soviet Union as representative of UNRRA, the American war relief organization. I was on very good terms with him and with the late La Guardia, the former Mayor of New York and head of UNRRA. Marshall MacDuffie came to us again when I was already working in Moscow. In one of our conversations he told me then that it would be very useful if I were to visit America. I asked him why. MacDuffie replied that some Americans thought I had horns. If they were to see I had no horns, that would be a great achievement. *(Laughter, applause.)*

I did not make that up. Ask MacDuffie, he will confirm our conversation. I think that now all of you here can see for yourselves that I really have no horns. *(Laughter, applause.)* Having convinced yourselves of this, the victory will be half won if you convince others. People will realize that Communists are human beings like everybody else. The only difference between us is the difference in our views on the political structure and social system of states. And we must achieve agreement on the point that each people must choose for itself what system to maintain.

As far as I know, you do not let your competitors look into your account books. Don't look into our accounts, then, for we have our own communist system of bookkeeping. *(Animation.)* Let's better live in peace. There are cases with you too, aren't there—though they may be rare—when competing corporations come to an agreement not to attack each other. Why then, to use your language, should not we, representatives of the communist corporation, and you, representatives of the capitalist corporation, agree on peaceful coexistence? Let each abide by his own views. *(Prolonged applause.)*

I know that you like capitalism, and I don't want to dissuade you. I would simply do no more than humiliate myself if I were to take advantage of the hospitality of the biggest capitalists and begin moralizing to you about the superiority of communism. That would be a senseless thing to do before this audience. Let history be the judge! *(Prolonged applause.)*

Leaving the session hall of the United Nations General Assembly after delivering the speech on general and complete disarmament.

Why then did Mr. Lodge so zealously defend capitalism here? He did it so zealously, and that is only natural. If he did not defend capitalism so fervently, he would not hold such an important post in your country. *(Laughter, applause.)* The only question I have is what made Mr. Lodge plead the benefits of capitalism with such ardor today? Is it possible that he wished to talk me into adopting the capitalist faith? *(Laughter.)* Or perhaps, Mr. Lodge is afraid that if a Bolshevik addresses capitalists he will convert them and they will espouse the communist faith? I want to reassure you: I have no such intentions—I know with whom I am dealing. *(Laughter, prolonged applause.)*

If Mr. Harriman will allow me, I shall tell you about our exchange of jokes in a conversation we had in Moscow. I said in jest that Mr. Harriman was "jobless" after having been ousted by Rockefeller from the post of governor of your state *(animation)*, and that now he was at loose ends. Whereupon Comrade Mikoyan observed

53

that a job for him could be found in the Soviet Union *(laughter, applause)*, and I said: "If you like, I offer you the position of economic adviser to the Chairman of the Council of Ministers of the USSR, with a good salary and a good country house." *(Laughter, applause.)* You, of course, realize that this was said in jest.

That is my reply to Mr. Lodge.

I cannot grasp why he tried to convince me that you are businessmen. I know it myself. If you were not managing important affairs you would not be occupying such high positions and would not be here today.

I am accompanied by Comrade Yelyutin, the Minister of Special Secondary and Higher Education. He will confirm that we are training many specialists. But if any of you wanted to share in building communism in our country, we would take his measure and find him a suitable job; the greater the benefit his work would bring, the more he would be paid for it. *(Laughter, applause.)* We know how to value people, and the greater the benefit their work yields, the higher the pay for their labor. Such is the principle of socialism.

You will excuse me for this digression. I only wanted to explain to Mr. Lodge that there was no cause for him to worry about his capitalists. So far as I can see, none of them will become Communists. And do not worry about me, either. I shall remain a Communist and shall not join any of your corporations. *(Laughter, applause.)* As people say, we shall come out even. *(Applause.)*

Ladies and gentlemen, it gives me great pleasure to meet businessmen in the Economic Club of New York. My visit to the United States gives me the opportunity of getting a better knowledge of the life of your great country and of establishing personal contacts with your people, with all sections of it, including you gentlemen of the business world.

I think that you too would find it interesting to make a closer acquaintance with us Soviet people representing the socialist system, and, so to say, to get first-hand information on how we live, how we run our household and how we build our economy.

I know that businessmen are wont to talk without diplomatic niceties, with utter frankness. That is why I take the liberty of telling you in all frankness what may not perhaps be to the liking of some of you, but would yet be good for you.

Some people—blinded, to put it mildly, by their dislike of socialism and communism—dream in their sleep, as the saying goes, of the ruin of the countries that have taken that path of development.

In his dreams a person usually sees his cherished desires, and all too often the awakening brings him disappointment: He opens his eyes and finds the same faces and the same environment that surrounded him when he plunged into his vain dream.

Some people frequently dream that socialist Russia is the same as it was before the Revolution. But let's compare the rates at which the Soviet Union has been developing since we overthrew the old, rotten system, and the rates of development in the United States during the same period. Compared with the 1913 level, output in the Soviet Union has increased 36-fold, and only fourfold in your country. Why does our economy and culture develop more rapidly than yours? I am not imposing my ideology upon you, though I do not conceal my allegiance to the Communist Party and my political views—they are known to you. But the figures show convincingly that the source of our rapidly growing strength is the socialist revolution, which enabled our country to take a road of development along which the locomotive of Soviet economy is racing at an ever increasing speed. Old Russia could never have even dreamed of such a pace.

Possibly you disagree with me. But can you explain, then, what miracles brought those results about? What miracles, I ask you?

In old Russia 76 of every 100 people over nine years of age were illiterate. Nearly 80 per cent of the children and teenagers had no opportunity of going to school, whereas today all our children go to school and there are practically no illiterate people in the country. We now have 40 times more specialists with a special secondary or higher education than in pre-Revolutionary Russia, and our higher schools train almost three times as many engineers as American universities and colleges. Last year, for example, we trained 94,000 engineers, while you trained 35,000.

We have now worked out and begun a titanic seven-year plan of economic development. I shall name just one figure to give you an idea of its scale: Our capital investments alone will amount to approximately 750 billion dollars in these seven years. Fulfillment of this plan will bring us close to the level of economic development in the United States.

Where do we get the funds for all this? Where do we get the accumulations? All this can only be explained by the advantages of the socialist system, for, as we know, miracles don't happen.

Some people may, as before, doubt the feasibility of our plans. But that is ostrich policy; when an ostrich sees that its rival is overtaking it, it is said to hide its head in the sand. Our development will not cease if you close your eyes to reality.

Already I can disappoint the people who are playing ostrich. Do you happen to know how we are fulfilling the first year of the seven-year plan?

Our plan for 1959 envisaged a 7.7 per-cent rise in industrial output. Actually, we have increased output by 12 per cent in the first eight months of this year. There is reason to believe that we will produce more than 10 billion dollars worth over and above this year's plan. This means that, far from planning any impossible rates of economic development, we have, on the contrary, provided favorable conditions for industry, so as not to overtax the economy, and to receive additional accumulations through overfulfillment of the plan and to make the work of our enterprises more rhythmical. Consequently, we shall be able to overtake the USA in economic development, first in volume and then per head of population, more rapidly than projected in our plans.

Before my departure, Comrade Kosygin, Chairman of the State Planning Committee, reported to me on the plan prepared by the committee for 1960, which has, in the main, been worked out in detail. True, it is still a tentative plan, but it has already been coordinated with all the Union Republics, and is therefore close to the form in which it will be approved. It will probably be approved soon after my return from America, at the close of October or early in November. The figures of this plan are not without interest. For example, in 1960 we shall be able to produce two million more metric tons rolled stock than initially projected for the second year of the seven-year plan. With regard to oil, we are planning to increase output by more than 14 million metric tons in 1960 alone. This, too, is not bad for our economy.

Excellent prospects are opening up for our gas industry. For the time being, America ranks first in the world for output and known reserves of gas, but in recent years we have been making increasing use of natural gas. Our geologists have discovered such huge gas deposits as will suffice for decades to come. This enables us to expand the extraction and consumption of gas still more and to surpass you in this respect as well.

These, gentlemen, are only a few words about our potentials. We have everything we need. Our people are solidly behind their government, full of enthusiasm. They strive to do their duty to the best of their ability and thereby strengthen their socialist system still more.

Possibly some people thought I would come to the United States to solicit for the development of Soviet-American trade, without which, it is alleged, the seven-year plan cannot be fulfilled. I want to say in all frankness that I have not come here to beg. We have always, ever since the inception of the Soviet state, urged the development of international trade. And we are by no means raising this question today because lack of such trade will prejudice the fulfillment of the seven-year plan. Whoever thinks so is making a big mistake.

We attach considerable importance to the development of international trade, acting upon the same rule as many people in your country, too, if we are to believe the motto reproduced on a postage stamp recently issued in the United States: "World peace through world trade."

We agree with this approach. True, when I said approximately something of the kind some time ago, indicating that trade is important as a means of relaxing international tension, I was criticized by some people in America. Your newspapers wrote at that time that Khrushchev spoke of trade only because for him trade is no more than politics. But if we are really to speak about who has turned trade into a political weapon, it is an American institution you all know that invented a special list of embargoes, which you, businessmen, are compelled to observe when trading with the Soviet Union. Let's not argue, however. History will establish who associated trade with politics, and in what way.

I want to emphasize that the Soviet Government has always advocated, and continues to advocate, equitable, mutually beneficial international trade without any discrimination whatsoever—the trade spoken of by Benjamin Franklin, whose words "Commerce among nations should be fair and equitable" are engraved above the front entrance of the U.S. Department of Commerce.

The establishment of all sorts of embargo lists in trade is something we oppose and shall always oppose as unreasonable practice. If you do not wish to trade in so-called strategic, or any other goods, you don't have to. That is your affair. But do not introduce discrimination against any country or group of countries. This practice disrupts normal international trade and leads to political complications. Indeed, history tells us that governments resort to such restrictions only when they contemplate a military campaign against the country subjected to discrimination. Let us then clear the path to normal trade relations between all countries, irrespective of their social systems.

We are trading on a basis of equality with many countries. Suffice it to say that last year the volume of Soviet foreign trade exceeded the 1938 level sevenfold and amounted to 34,589 billion rubles.

Our trade relations with Britain are shaping up quite well. Trade is expanding with businessmen in West Germany. It should be noted that the Government of West Germany also has a correct understanding of the interests of its country in this matter and cooperates in the development of trade contacts rather than obstructs them. We welcome this. Good economic relations are shaping up between us and Italy. Relations with France are not bad. Why then must America stand apart? However, that is up to you. The question of trade is a question of profit. If you find it unprofitable to buy from us, or to sell us some goods, do as you think best.

But bear one thing in mind. It sometimes happens that too choosy a girl lets time slip, stays a spinster too long, and is left empty-handed. *(Laughter.)* Such maidenly indecision is doubly out of place in business, where the rule "First come, first served" perpetuated in an English proverb, operates more than anywhere else. We too have a rather good saying to that effect: "He who comes late gets a picked bone." *(Animation.)*

In justifying the stagnation that has persisted in Soviet-American economic relations for almost 10 years, some public leaders—politicians rather than businessmen—allege that this situation is normal and even of advantage to the Western world. They seriously maintain that by refusing to trade with us the United States retards the economic development of the Soviet Union and weakens its defensive might.

However, I think there are few people in this hall who believe this. You all know through the press about the Soviet sputniks and rockets, about the growth of our economy, which has never been so rapid as in the past ten years. If any of you still have even the slightest doubts on that score, you are welcome to come to the Soviet Union and see for yourselves, as your colleague, Mr. Harriman, has done recently.

By the way, we spoke with Mr. Harriman on a number of questions, including the question of trade. I told him, and I can now repeat it, that the law banning trade with the USSR, which was passed in the United States as a repressive measure against the Soviet Union, has led to results directly opposite to what its authors anticipated.

We have even derived a certain benefit from the trade policy which the United States pursued with regard to the Soviet Union. We have had to develop production of machines that we did not have before and intended to buy from you, and now are not dependent on anyone in this respect. Thus, the artificial dwarfing of trade with the Soviet Union has strengthened rather than weakened us.

Look at the tremendous successes achieved in our economy in those ten years, look how our technology and science have developed! We discovered the secret of using the energy of hydrogen before you did. We were ahead of you in developing the intercontinental ballistic rocket, which, in fact, you do not have to this day. Yet, when you come to think of it, the intercontinental ballistic rocket is truly a condensation of creative human thinking.

So, what sense is there in your restrictions? Continuation by the United States of the policy of trade discrimination against the Soviet Union is simply a piece of senseless obstinacy. (Animation.)

From time immemorial lively trade has been considered a good omen in relations between countries. In the situation obtaining today international trade acquires still greater importance as a kind of barometer of the relations between countries. Then may the pointer of this barometer move at least towards "Variable," and once it passes that line we are sure that—given the effort of both sides—it will soon point to "Fair weather."

You are all well informed of the fact that we are offering you economic competition. Some describe this as our challenge to the United States. But speaking of challenges, one might say perhaps— and it would even be more precise—that it was the United States that first challenged the whole world. The USA developed its economy to a higher level than in any other country. For a long time nobody ventured to dispute your supremacy. But the time has now come when a country has appeared which accepts your challenge, which takes into account the level of development in the United States, and in turn challenges you. You may rest assured that the Soviet Union will hold its own in this economic competition: It will overtake you and leave you behind.

But what harm is there in that? No matter who wins in this competition—you or we—both the Soviet Union and the United

States will gain by it, because our peoples will have peace and live still better than today.

Incidentally, competition as we Soviet people understand and practice it by no means excludes cooperation and mutual assistance, and we are ready to extend this rule to the United States, if you will agree to it. After all, haven't we cooperated with you in the past? Some thirty years ago, when our country started building a large-scale industry, good economic contacts were established with leading U.S. firms. Ford helped us build the motor works in Gorky. Cooper, a prominent American specialist, acted as consultant during the building of the hydropower station on the Dnieper, which in those days was the biggest in the world. Your engineers helped us build the tractor works in Stalingrad and Kharkov. Americans, along with the British, were consultants during the construction of the Moscow subway. We were grateful to your specialists for their cooperation, and many of them returned home with Soviet decorations and letters of thanks, to say nothing of material remuneration. *(Animation.)*

What is there to prevent us from renewing and developing economic cooperation at the present, qualitatively new stage, when it is not only we who could learn from you, but you, too, who could learn a lot from our engineers, designers and scientists? Such cooperation would most certainly be of mutual benefit.

Your and our economic successes will be hailed by the whole world, which expects our two Great Powers to help the peoples who are centuries behind in their economic development to get on their feet more quickly. I shall say nothing now about whose fault that is —you know it perfectly well. Let us better decide on a just and humane way of helping these countries out of the plight in which they find themselves.

The position of the Soviet Union in this matter is clear. Although our country has not made a single ruble through the exploitation of the natural resources and labor of other countries, we are ready to continue assisting the countries of Asia and Africa that have won their independence. Yet it would be only fair if the countries that utilize the natural resources and the labor of other countries loosened their purse-strings more.

Gentlemen, I read the allegation in your newspapers that the policy of peaceful coexistence which we are offering to you actually means the establishment of a "divided world." Nothing could be farther from a correct understanding of the ideas of peaceful coexistence than such an interpretation. In reality, we want to secure exactly the opposite: Peaceful coexistence and competition imply increasing economic and cultural intercourse between nations. And, conversely, rejection of peaceful coexistence and competition signifies the disruption of all intercourse between countries and the further fanning of the cold war.

Every person who does not want deliberately to shut his eyes to hard facts will recognize that the only sensible way for international relations to develop in our time is that of settling outstanding international issues by negotiation. Our visit to the United States and President Eisenhower's coming visit to the Soviet Union will, we hope, allow us to hold a frank exchange of views on existing controversial issues and facilitate agreement between us. *(Applause.)*

To live in peace as good neighbors or to drift to another war— such is the choice that now confronts the Soviet Union, the United States of America and the whole world. There is no third choice if, of course, we discount the fantastic possibility of either one of us wanting to move from the earth to another planet. I do not believe in the latter possibility: The Soviet people are doing quite well on earth, and you, too, I should imagine, do not intend to book passage for the moon. My information is that it is not very cosy there at the moment.

Big possibilities are concentrated in your hands, gentlemen. You are influential people. That is why, in addressing you today, I should like to voice the hope that U.S. businessmen will use their influence in the right direction and support peaceful coexistence and competition between us, just as some prominent representatives of your economy are already doing. I have respect for Mr. Cyrus Eaton, for example, who is showing courage and foresight.

True, they say that there are people who do not like the fact that certain American businessmen are supporting the idea of peaceful coexistence. These businessmen are even criticized for it in the press. But, as the saying goes, "He who wants to have eggs must put up with the cackle of hens." *(Laughter.)*

Naturally, gentlemen of the business world, I am not urging you to adopt our world outlook. I think that you, too, do not expect to win me over to the capitalist faith—we are obviously past that age. You evidently believe in the victory of your system, and I am confident in the victory of socialism.

I can see some of you smiling—a person who is convinced that his own views are right is usually ironical in his attitude to the other party, who is just as firm in his views. But although I lay no claim to being a prophet, I can say that some people will apparently have to swallow a bitter pill when they realize that they have incorrectly evaluated the situation and erred in their calculations. If they are men of action and intelligence, then judging by the experience of the socialist countries, they will be given the opportunity of applying their knowledge, their energy and their abilities when the American people go over to a new social system.

You will forgive me this joke; I had no intention of offending and, still less, of insulting anybody. I just wanted to express my thoughts about the future as I see it.

In conclusion, allow me to wish that each of you make his contribution to improving the relations between our countries and bettering the international situation. Thank you. *(Prolonged applause.)*

After N. S. Khrushchev finished his speech, he answered a number of questions.

QUESTION PERIOD

The first to take the floor was the editor of the American magazine *Look*. His question was considered by the speaker to be of an obviously provocative nature and meant to divert the attention of the gathering from the basic points put forward by the head of the Soviet Government in his speech, which was received with great

Delegates to the United Nations General Assembly greeting Khrushchev.

interest by the numerous guests assembled in the largest room of the Waldorf-Astoria Hotel. The questioner did not seem to understand how the thesis of peaceful coexistence of capitalist and socialist countries could be reconciled with the propositions of scientific communism about the inevitable triumph of communist ideas throughout the world.

KHRUSHCHEV: The fact that you ask such questions and the fact that some gentlemen are laughing before hearing my reply show how little they know of the substance of the matter. People who are well-grounded in history know that when human society was completing the transition from feudalism to capitalism there also was a struggle between the old and the new. Like other nations, the American people also fought for a transition to the more perfect social form of that day. You fought against slavery and feudalism, you fought for progress, against the old system which impeded the development of the productive forces, and in the end you were victorious. But at the time the American people established a republic, czarist Russia was still a semi-feudal country where serfdom prevailed. Your economy progressed rapidly, while the economy of czarist Russia lagged considerably behind the American economy in its development. And that was only natural, because the social system which triumphed in your country was more progressive than the system that preceded it. Nevertheless, republican America coexisted peacefully with monarchist Russia. They did not wage war against each other.

Why is it, then, that at this time, when mankind has come to a new stage of development, you refuse to accept the idea of the peaceful coexistence of capitalist and socialist countries? This, of course, does not alter the substance of the matter.

REMARK FROM THE BALCONY: That does not answer the question!

KHRUSHCHEV: You may not like the substance of the matter, but such is the history of human development. I might only add what folk say in such cases: If a girl who has had a baby still wants to be regarded as a girl, and even goes to court to be recognized as such, this does not alter the case. Even if the court were to grant her that recognition, she would never again be a girl all the same. (General laughter, applause.)

I am told that you are the editor of a magazine. That is evidently so. What do you want? Do you want me to give you a guarantee that the American people will live eternally in the conditions of a capitalist society? Do you want a prescription for preserving capitalism from extinction? I am no doctor and cannot offer prescriptions of that kind. The question of what system you will have in your country depends neither on me, nor on you. It depends on the American workers, on the American people. They will decide what system to choose. Do not, therefore, expect to get any sedatives, Mr. Editor, I cannot give them to you. No one can halt the inexorable march of history! I just want to emphasize that we are for noninterference in the internal affairs of other countries. Hence, the situation in your country is your own responsibility! *(Prolonged applause.)*

M. KELLY *(researcher and consultant in industrial management)*: I am interested in the Soviet Government's attitude toward cultural and scientific exchange between the United States of America and the Soviet Union. Could you say something about that?

KHRUSHCHEV: I can tell you that I have discussed the question yesterday with the Senators on the Foreign Relations Committee. The Soviet Union is persistently advocating broader cultural and scientific exchange with all countries, including, of course, the United States of America. I told the Senators that we were surprised the State Department was not meeting us halfway and was contemplating to curtail somewhat the exchange in all fields—the exchange of cultural, scientific, student and other delegations. So you will have to take this question to the State Department and ask them why they have adopted the line of curtailing, rather than extending, our cultural relations. *(Animation, applause.)*

HERBERT WOODMAN: Thank you, Mr. Khrushchev, for your reply. The State Department is represented here, and we hope to hear something from them on the question. *(Animation, applause.)*

KELLY: Allow me to ask one more question. Does the Soviet Union intend to extend publication of data on scientific research done by Soviet scientists? Lately we have had frequent contact with Soviet scientists and admire their achievements. Is there any intention of publishing more of their papers? It would promote international cooperation among scientists.

KHRUSHCHEV: I like this question—you can feel a practical approach in it. Just what papers do you mean? It is hard for me to reply, because you have put the question in general form. In the Soviet Union we strive to publish all works of great scientific value, with the exception of classified matter related to defense. Other countries, including the United States, do the same thing. We are well aware that a country which makes a secret of all scientific research thereby retards the development of its own science. We have no wish to harm ourselves. Our socialist society is free of competition and we do not have to fear that the publication of information by one research institute will cause damage to another, as is often the case in relations between capitalist firms carrying on research. That is our advantage over the capitalist system.

KELLY: You are right, my question was too general. Allow me, therefore, to ask you to speed up as much as possible the publication of information about research done by Soviet scientists under the International Geophysical Year.

KHRUSHCHEV: Thank you for specifying. When I return home I shall look into the matter and try to speed up the publication of the materials you speak of. I can see no secrets in the matter. *(Stormy applause.)*

WOODMAN: Why don't our broadcasts to the Soviet Union reach the listener? (*The representative of the tobacco firm went on to urge that all sorts of publications from capitalist countries be distributed in the Soviet Union and that reception of broadcasts from the Voice of America and similar radio stations be organized on as wide a scale as possible in the Soviet Union.*)

KHRUSHCHEV: Gentlemen, please understand me correctly. I have come here at the invitation of the President. In our very first talks with Mr. Eisenhower we decided not to touch upon questions related to the internal competence of our two countries.

(Cries of an obviously provocative nature are again heard from the balcony. But some people below as well join the voices from the balcony.)

KHRUSHCHEV: Gentlemen, since you have invited me, I would ask you to hear me out attentively. If you do not want to, I can stop talking. I did not come to the USA to beg. I represent the great Soviet state, a great people who have made the Great October Revolution. And no sallies, gentlemen, can drown out what has been achieved and done by our great people, and what it is planning to do. *(Noise in the hall, rebuking the authors of the remarks and cries.)* I will reply to all your questions if you stop trying to shout me down.

The question of how and what our people should hear is the affair of our people, the affair of the Soviet people. These questions are decided, and will always be decided, by the Soviet people themselves and their government, without foreign interference.

You are displeased that the Soviet people refuse to listen to the anti-Soviet broadcasts of the Voice of America, but you yourselves "jam" some good American voices. We Soviet people, and many other people as well, like the wonderful voice of America, for example, with which Paul Robeson sings. Yet you must know, of course, that for many years your government did not let him go to countries that invited him to sing. Why did you jam that voice? Paul Robeson has a splendid voice and we like to listen to him. But we have no desire to listen to the false voice with which you want to talk to us. It would be different if your voice were friendly, wholesome. We will not jam such a voice. We are ready to listen to it. *(Cries of approval.)*

WOODMAN: Thank you, Mr. Chairman of the Council of Ministers of the USSR, for your speech, for patiently listening to all our questions in spite of being very tired, and for answering them so comprehensively. Tell us, if we show that it will be better in our country than in yours, will you go on fighting capitalism just the same? I should like to assure you that the members of our Economic Club are willing to compete with the Soviet people in peaceful pursuits.

(Amid cries of approval from the entire audience, Nikita Sergeyevich Khrushchev shakes hands warmly with Mr. Woodman. Then he returns to the rostrum.)

KHRUSHCHEV: Gentlemen, everybody will be winners in the peaceful competition that we are offering you. If the cause, the system which you represent, gives people more blessings and creates better living conditions for them, if it gives more scope to the productive forces of society than socialism, I shall come to you and ask you for a job. *(General laughter, applause.)* But at the moment, gentlemen, do not offer me "causes," because the cause I serve, the great cause of communism, is the best and the noblest cause of all! Why then should I change it for something else! *(Animation.)* To speak seriously, I have come to your country to establish friendship with the American people. The Soviet people want this friendship, they desire greater cooperation with the American people. They want a strengthening of peace throughout the world.

Thank you. *(Prolonged applause.)*

N. S. Khrushchev's speech and his replies to questions were received by those present with great attention and on numerous occasions were interrupted by applause. They made a great impression on the representatives of American business circles.

On September 18, Mr. Herbert Woodman addressed the following letter to N. S. Khrushchev:

Dear Chairman Khrushchev:

While you are still in New York, I want to express to you the great appreciation of the Economic Club of New York for your address at the meeting last night. It was an epoch-making event in the history of the club. I also want to express my great personal pleasure in having had the opportunity to meet and talk with you.

I sincerely hope that there was no real misunderstanding as a result of the apparent discourtesy on the part of a few members of the audience during the question period. In so large a group it seems almost inevitable that there will be a few people who are forgetful of their manners. I feel sure you realized how very few they were. The membership of the club and the vast preponderance of guests were greatly interested in what you had to say and were genuinely appreciative of your willingness to answer questions after such an extremely long and strenuous day.

This morning I have received many comments about the meeting. They have, without exception, been to the effect that it was an extremely interesting and rewarding experience. Once again, I thank you both personally and on behalf of all who were present.

Sincerely,
HERBERT WOODMAN

Dear Mr. Woodman:

I thank you heartily for your letter in which you speak so highly of my speech in the Economic Club of New York.

Like you, I am well aware that the individuals who tried to cast a shadow on our meeting with their unfriendly cries do not represent the opinion of either the businessmen who gathered at the Economic Club or the American people, and for that reason failed to receive any support at such a distinguished and responsible meeting. Just like you, I pay no attention whatsoever to them.

We have had a good businesslike meeting and in many respects it has helped to improve mutual understanding and strengthen friendly relations between the United States of America and the Soviet Union.

With sincere respect,
N. KHRUSHCHEV

September 19, 1959

SPEECH BY N. S. KHRUSHCHEV
AT THE SESSION OF THE UN GENERAL ASSEMBLY

N. S. Khrushchev addressed the session of the UN General Assembly on September 18. Below we publish the full text of the Declaration of the Soviet Government he submitted to the General Assembly of the United Nations.

MR. PRESIDENT, ESTEEMED DELEGATES:

My visit to the United States at the invitation of the President, Mr. Dwight Eisenhower, has coincided with the beginning of the session of the United Nations General Assembly. Permit me, first of all, to express my sincere thanks to the Assembly delegates and to the Secretary General for this opportunity to speak from the lofty tribune of the United Nations. I appreciate this honor all the more since the Soviet Union is today submitting to the General Assembly highly important proposals on the most burning issue disturbing the peoples—the disarmament problem.

History knows no other international organization in which the peoples reposed such hopes as in the United Nations. Born in the grim days when the rumble of the last battles of the Second World War had not yet died away and when the ruins of devastated towns and villages were still smoking, the United Nations, expressing the thoughts and aspirations of millions upon millions of tormented people, proclaimed its main purpose to be that of delivering succeeding generations from the scourge of war. Today the United Nations embraces more than eighty states. Its ranks have been joined by many of the states which, in the past war, were in the camp hostile to those who had laid the foundations of this organization.

More than fourteen years have elapsed since this international forum was created. Yet the purpose for which the organization was founded still has not been achieved. The peoples still live in constant anxiety about peace, about their future. And how can they not feel this anxiety when, now in one part of the world, now in another, military conflicts flare up and human blood is shed? The clouds of a new war danger, at times thickening into storm clouds, loom over a world which has not yet forgotten the horrors of the Second World War.

The tension in international relations cannot continue forever: Either it will reach a point where there can be only one outcome—war—or, by their joint efforts, the states will succeed in ending this tension in time. The peoples expect the United Nations to redouble

N. S. Khrushchev speaking at the 14th session of the UN General Assembly on September 18.

its efforts toward creating an atmosphere of trust and mutual understanding among states and consolidating world peace.

In international affairs success in solving controversial problems is possible provided the states concentrate on what brings states closer together rather than on what divides the present-day world. No social or political dissimilarities, no differences in ideology or religious beliefs must prevent the member-states of the United Nations from reaching agreement on the main thing: that the principles of peaceful coexistence and friendly cooperation be sacredly and unswervingly observed by all states. If, on the other hand, differences and social dissimilarities are pushed to the fore, it is bound to doom to failure all our efforts to preserve peace. In the twentieth century one cannot undertake crusades to wipe out unbelievers with fire and sword, as the fanatics of the Middle Ages did, without running the risk of confronting humanity with the greatest calamity in its history.

The United Nations is itself an embodiment of the idea of peaceful cooperation between states with different social and political systems. Indeed, see how many states there are belonging to different social systems, what a multitude of races and nationalities, what a diversity of philosophies and cultures are represented in this hall!

But since the states differ in their evaluation of controversial issues, since there are divergent views on the causes of the present international tension, we have to be prepared for the elimination of disagreements requiring persistent effort, patience and statesmanship on the part of the governments. The time has come for the efforts of the United Nations in strengthening peace to be supplemented by the efforts of the heads of government of all states, by the efforts of the broad masses of the people who stand for peace and international security. Everything indicates that the time has come to open a period of international negotiations, conferences and meetings of statesmen in order that the pressing international problems may one after another be solved.

For the principles of peaceful coexistence to become undividedly established in the relations between states, it is necessary, in our opinion, to put an end to the cold war. The peoples cannot allow the unnatural states of cold war to continue any longer, as they cannot allow epidemics of plague and cholera.

What does ending the cold war mean and what must be done to accomplish it?

First of all, an end must be put to calls for war. There is no getting away from the fact that belligerent speeches also continue to be made by some short-sighted statesmen. Is it not time to put a stop to saber-rattling and threats against other states?

The cold war is doubly dangerous because it is going on in the conditions of an unbridled armaments race, which, growing like an avalanche, is increasing suspicion and distrust among states.

Nor must it be forgotten that the cold war began and is proceeding at a time when the vestiges of the Second World War have not yet been eliminated by any means, when a peace treaty with Germany has not yet been concluded and an occupation regime is still maintained in the heart of Germany, in Berlin, on the territory of its Western sectors. The elimination of this source of tension in the center of Europe, in the potentially most dangerous area of the globe, where large armed forces of the opposing military alignments are stationed in close contiguity, would furnish the key to normalizing the climate in the world. We appeal to the Governments of the United States, Britain and France to exert every effort to reach agreement on real steps to achieve this.

Who can deny that in ending the cold war and normalizing the international climate great importance is attached to developing, in every way, contacts between the peoples? We are for extending the practice of mutual visits by statesmen, and also by representatives of political, business and public circles, for developing international economic, cultural, scientific and technical cooperation.

I should like to say that the United Nations will fulfill its noble mission far more successfully if it is able to rid itself of the elements of cold war which often handicap its activities. Isn't it the cold war that has produced the intolerable situation wherein the Chinese People's Republic, one of the biggest powers in the world, has for many years now been denied its lawful rights in the United Nations?

It is inconceivable, after all, that anyone could seriously think that a dependable and lasting solution of major world problems can be achieved without the participation of the great People's China, now approaching its glorious tenth anniversary.

Permit me to voice the following thoughts on this subject in all frankness. Everyone knows that when a person dies he is eventually buried. No matter how dear the deceased, no matter how it hurts to part with him, life compels everyone to face up to the realities: A coffin or a tomb is made for the dead man and he is taken out of the house of the living. So it was in ancient times and so it is today. Why then must China be represented in the United Nations by the corpse of reactionary China, that is, by the Chiang Kai-shek clique? We consider that it is high time for the United Nations to deal with a corpse as all peoples do, that is, carry it out, so that a real representative of the Chinese people may take his rightful seat in the United Nations. (Applause.)

After all, China is not Taiwan. Taiwan is only a small island, a province, that is, a small part of a great state, China. China is the Chinese People's Republic, which has for ten years now been developing rapidly, which has a stable government recognized by the entire Chinese people, and legislative bodies elected by the entire people of China. China is a great state whose capital is Peking. Sooner or later Taiwan, as an inalienable part of the sovereign Chinese state, will be united with the whole of People's China, that is, the authority of the Government of the People's Republic of China will be extended to this island. And the sooner it is done, the better.

The restoration of the lawful rights of People's China will not only enormously enhance the prestige and authority of the United Nations, but will also be a notable contribution to improving the international climate generally.

I should like to hope that the United Nations will find the strength to get rid of all cold war accretions and become a really universal organ of international cooperation working effectively for world peace.

It may, however, be asked: Abolition of the cold war, consolidation of peace, and the peaceful coexistence of states is, of course, a supremely noble and attractive goal, but is it attainable, is it realistic? Can we at this time, in present-day conditions, place the relations between states on a new basis?

From this rostrum I emphatically declare that the Soviet Government considers the achievement of this goal not only urgent but also entirely realistic. The Soviet Union is convinced that the necessary conditions are now in evidence for a *radical* change for the better in international relations, for the *complete* abolition of the cold war in the interests of the whole of humanity.

Let us consider, if only briefly, the most important of the events of recent months bearing on the problem of reducing international tension.

The convocation in May 1959 of the Geneva foreign ministers' conference, in which plenipotentiary representatives of the two German states for the first time took part, was in itself the expression of a new spirit in international relations, the spirit of realism and mutual understanding. The results achieved in Geneva are, of course, not yet such as could be considered sufficient for the practical solution of pressing international problems. But it is already something that the detailed and frank discussion of the problems on the Geneva conference agenda made it possible, as noted in the final communiqué of the conference, to bring the positions of the sides on a number of points closer together. In this way a fairly good foundation was laid for further negotiations which can lead to agreement on the questions that remain outstanding.

It is especially heartening that important steps have been taken to develop Soviet-American relations. No one is likely to doubt that the evolution of the international situation as a whole depends in no small measure on how relations develop between the United States and the Soviet Union, the two strongest powers in the world. That is why even those first shoots of something new which have appeared in Soviet-American relations of late meet with the most heartfelt approval all over the world. The ice in Soviet-American relations has undoubtedly begun to break, and of this we are sincerely glad.

Among the events making for improvement in Soviet-American relations, the exchange of visits between the heads of government of the USSR and the United States can prove a turning point. We have had, and will continue to have, an exchange of opinions with the President of the United States on problems of Soviet-American relations and on pressing international problems. We believe that Mr. Eisenhower wishes to contribute to removing the tension in relations between states.

At one of his news conferences the President of the United States expressed a readiness to negotiate realistically with the Soviet Union on a reasonable and mutually guaranteed plan for general disarmament or disarmament in the field of special types of weapons, to make a real beginning toward solving the problems of the divided Germany, and to help in otherwise reducing tension in the world. Permit me to express the hope that our exchange of views with President Eisenhower will be fruitful.

We belong to those who hope that the exchange of visits between the leading statesmen of the United States and the USSR and the forthcoming meetings and conversations will help to pave a straight way to the complete ending of the cold war, provided, of course, there is a mutual desire to achieve that. That is how we regard our visit to the United States and the coming visit of President Eisenhower to the Soviet Union.

Many other facts could also be adduced which exemplify the new favorable trends in world affairs.

Signs that relations between states are becoming warmer are not, of course, a result of chance favorable circumstances.

The world, we think, is really entering a new phase of international relations. The grim years of the cold war cannot fail to leave a mark on everyone. The ordinary people and political leaders in many different countries have done much thinking and have learned much. Everywhere the forces actively supporting peace and friendly relations between the nations have grown immeasurably.

It would, of course, be unjustified optimism to assert that the atmosphere of distrust and suspicion in the relations between states is already a thing of the past, that peace in the world is already secure, and that there is no need for further persistent efforts by all the states. Unfortunately, that is as yet by no means the case. Circles which obstruct a relaxation of international tension and sow the seeds of new conflicts are still active and influential in many countries. These people uphold the old, moribund state of affairs, they cling to the legacy of the cold war.

But the course of events, especially of late, shows that attempts to hinder relaxation of international tension, to put spokes in the wheel, can only lead to the discomfiture of those who persist in such attempts, for the peoples will not support them.

We live at a time when mankind is marching ahead with giant strides, and we are witnessing not only the rapid development of industry, science and engineering, but also rapid changes in the political appearance of large areas of the world. Once backward peoples are coming free of colonial dependence, and new independent states are arising in place of former colonies and semi-colonies. Permit me to extend warm greetings from the bottom of my heart to the representatives of those states present in this hall. (Applause.)

At the same time it should be admitted that not all the peoples who have a right to be represented in the United Nations have their representatives here as yet. The Soviet Union, like all freedom-loving nations, warmly wishes success to the peoples who still live in colonial dependence but who are fighting resolutely for their national liberation from the colonial yoke.

The last strongholds of the obsolete colonial system are crumbling, and crumbling badly, and this is one of the salient factors of our time. Take a look at the map of Asia and Africa and you will see hundreds of millions of people who have freed themselves of centuries-old oppression by foreigners, of foreign exploitation.

Coming generations will esteem highly the heroism of those who led the struggle for the independence of India and Indonesia, the United Arab Republic and Iraq, Ghana, Guinea and other states, just as the people of the United States today revere the memory of George Washington and Thomas Jefferson, who led the American people in their struggle for independence.

I deem it necessary to say here, from the rostrum of the United Nations, that the Soviet Union has the sincerest sympathy and the profoundest understanding for all peoples who, on different continents, are upholding their freedom and national independence. It is my opinion that this position of ours fully accords with the principles of the United Nations Charter, which is predicated on recognition of the right of the peoples to a free and independent existence and development.

Who but the United Nations should be the first to extend a helping hand to peoples liberating themselves, to ensure their inalienable right to be masters of their own destiny and to shape their life without any pressure or encroachment from without? And is it not the duty of the United Nations to contribute to the utmost to the economic advancement of the new states rising from the ruins of the colonial system, to help them speedily build up their national economies? This can only be achieved by the provision of large-scale economic assistance without any political or other strings attached. And that is the position taken by the Soviet Union on the question of economic aid which we are rendering and intend to render in the future to many countries. This position, we feel, fully accords with the principles of the United Nations Charter.

The Soviet Union would also be prepared to join with other powers in rendering economic assistance to the underdeveloped countries, as they are called, by using part of the resources that would be made available in the Soviet Union and other countries by the conclusion of an international agreement on disarmament and reduction of military budgets. We have already stated our readiness to assume such an undertaking, and I am empowered by my government to reaffirm it from the rostrum of the General Assembly.

There is another highly important source which, in our opinion, should be drawn upon extensively to provide assistance to economically underdeveloped countries. The peoples of many of these countries have won political independence, but they are still cruelly exploited by foreigners economically. Their oil and other natural wealth is plundered, it is taken out of the country for next to nothing, yielding huge profits to foreign exploiters.

In common with the representatives of many other states, we consider that in the question of economic aid one cannot put on a par those who do not take part in the exploitation of former colonial countries, and never did, and those who continue without any scruples to squeeze wealth out of the underdeveloped countries. It would be right and just for the foreign exploiters to return at least part of the riches they have amassed by exploiting the oppressed peoples, so that these funds, returned in the form of aid to the underdeveloped countries, be used for the development of their economy and culture, for raising the living standards of their peoples.

The Soviet Union has been rendering and will continue to render genuine, disinterested assistance to the underdeveloped countries. Rest assured of that.

What preposterous survivals in these days are the various artificial obstacles to the full-blooded, all-round development of international trade! The entire system of discrimination in trade has long deserved to be buried, and without any honors.

As you know, the Soviet Union has consistently advocated maximum development of international trade on a basis of equality and mutual benefit. It is our deep conviction that trade provides a good basis for developing peaceful cooperation among states, for

75

strengthening mutual confidence among nations. We consider that this position accords completely with the United Nations Charter, which obligates all member states to develop friendly relations among nations on the basis of respect for the principle of equality and self-determination of the peoples.

We, all of us, are faced with many outstanding international problems. Not all of them are equally important or urgent. Some of them concern the relations between individual countries, others affect the interests of the peoples of a number of countries and continents. But there is one problem whose solution is awaited with hope by the people of all countries, large and small, whatever their social system and way of life—the problem of disarmament. Whether mankind heads toward war with its disastrous consequences or whether the cause of peace prevails depends largely on whether or not the correct solution is found to that problem. The peoples long for peace, they want to live without fear for their future, without fear of losing their loved ones in the flames of another war.

For centuries the peoples have dreamed of getting rid of the destructive weapons of war. The demand for disarmament has been advanced and pressed by humanity's finest minds, the greatest public leaders and statesmen, the parties closest to the working people. But instead of disarmament the world has for many decades now been convulsed by the armaments fever.

Who can honestly say that the arms race has helped to solve a single, even the simplest international problem? On the contrary, it only complicates and tangles the solution of all issues in dispute.

Never before in the history of mankind has the armaments drive proceeded at such a pace and with such dangers as are involved today, in the age of the atom, electronics and the conquest of outer space.

Only recently rapid-fire automatic weapons, tanks, long-range artillery and aerial bombs were regarded as the most terrible, the most powerful instruments of annihilation. But can they stand any comparison with the weapons available today? We have reached a stage where it would be difficult to devise a weapon more powerful than the hydrogen bomb, whose potential is practically unlimited. If all the instruments of destruction mankind has possessed in the past were put together, they would amount in power to only an insignificant fraction of what the two or three Great Powers possessing nuclear weapons have at their disposal today.

I shall not be disclosing any great secret when I say that the explosion of one—only one—big hydrogen bomb releases a tremendous energy of destruction. Recently I read some remarks by the American nuclear physicist W. Davidson, stating that the explosion of one hydrogen bomb releases more energy than all the explosions effected by all countries in all the wars in the history of mankind. And, by all indications, he is right. Can one disregard the fact that the destructive power of the weapons of war has reached such colossal proportions? And can one forget that there is not a spot on the globe today that nuclear and rocket weapons cannot reach?

It is hard to imagine the consequences for mankind of a war with the use of these monstrous instruments of destruction and annihilation. If it were allowed to break out, its toll would run not into millions, but into tens and even hundreds of millions of human lives. It would be a war that would know no distinction between front and rear, between combatants and children. Many large cities and industrial centers would be reduced to ruins, and great monuments of culture, created by the efforts of man's genius over centuries, would be lost irreparably. Nor would this war spare future generations. Its poisonous trail in the form of radioactive contamination would long continue to cripple people and claim many lives.

The situation in the world today is a dangerous one. Various military alliances are in existence and the arms race never stops for a moment. So much inflammable material has accumulated that a

Speaking at the UN.

single spark could touch off a catastrophe. The world has reached a point where war could become a fact owing to some stupid accident, such as a technical fault in a plane carrying a hydrogen bomb or a mental aberration in the pilot behind the controls.

It is well known, moreover, that the arms race is already a heavy burden on the peoples. It is causing rising prices on consumer goods, depressing real wages, harmfully affecting the economy of many states, disrupting international trade. Never before have so many states, such masses of people, been drawn into war preparations as at present. If we consider, in addition to the military, the number of people directly or indirectly connected with the production of arms and involved in various forms of military research, we shall find that over 100 million people—and, moreover, the most capable and energetic workers, scientists, engineers—have been taken from their peaceful pursuits. A vast fund of human energy, knowledge, ingenuity and skill is being spilled as into a bottomless pit, consumed by the growing armaments.

The annual military expenditures of all states today total approximately 100 billion dollars. Is it not time to call a halt to this senseless squandering of the people's means and the people's energies for the preparation of war and destruction?

The Soviet Government, guided as it is in its foreign policy by the principle of peaceful coexistence, stands for peace and friendship among all nations. The aim of our domestic policy—its one aim —is to create a life worthy of the best ideals of mankind. Our seven-year plan is pervaded with the spirit of peaceableness, of concern for the welfare and happiness of the people. The aim of our foreign policy—its one and invariable aim—is to prevent war, to ensure peace and security to our country and to all countries.

Some people in the West expected that the cold war would sap the material resources of the Soviet Union and the other socialist countries, would undermine their economy. But their calculations have been wrong. Even though it has to bear a certain armaments burden, the Soviet Union is able to ensure the rapid development of its economy and the ever fuller satisfaction of the growing requirements of its people. Of course, the people's material requirements would be more amply met if the arms burden were removed.

The Soviet Union is a resolute and consistent champion of disarmament. In our state there are no classes or groups interested in war and armament building, in the conquest of foreign territories. Everyone will agree that to accomplish the great tasks we have set ourselves to improve the well-being of the Soviet people, to carry out our economic construction plans—we need peace. In common with the other states who cherish peace, we would like to gear all our economy and resources to peaceful purposes in order to provide our people in abundance with food, clothing, housing, etc. With the arms race going on, however, we cannot undividedly devote our efforts to peaceful construction without endangering the vital interests of our people, the interests of the country's security.

All peoples need peace. Following the conclusion of the Second World War, the Soviet Union submitted concrete disarmament proposals to the United Nations. We proposed the complete prohibition of atomic weapons, a substantial reduction of armed forces and armaments, and a steep cut in arms expenditures. We urged the dismantling of military bases on foreign territory and the withdrawal of armed forces from foreign territories.

We have proved our desire to solve the disarmament problem by deeds, and not just words. Time and again the Soviet Union has taken the initiative and undertaken concrete steps toward ending the arms race and getting down with all speed to practical disarmament measures. Immediately after the end of the war, our country carried out an extensive demobilization of its armed forces. The Soviet Union has given up all the military bases it had after the Second World War on the territory of other states.

You will recall that in the past few years the Soviet armed forces have been reduced, unilaterally, by a total of over two million men. The Soviet forces in the German Democratic Republic have been reduced considerably, and all Soviet troops have been withdrawn from the Rumanian People's Republic. We have also made a substantial cut in our military expenditures.

In 1958 the Soviet Union unilaterally suspended tests of atomic and hydrogen weapons in the hope that the other powers would follow this noble example. It is only to be regretted that these hopes were not justified. Now the Soviet Government has decided not to resume nuclear explosions in the Soviet Union if the Western Powers do not resume atomic and hydrogen weapon tests. Only if they resume tests of nuclear weapons will the Soviet Union consider itself free of this commitment.

The disarmament problem has been under discussion for over fourteen years now in the United Nations and at other international meetings, but no practical results have yet been achieved. What is the reason? I should not like to rake over the past, to go into an analysis of the obstacles and differences that arose in the course of the disarmament talks, much less to bring accusations against anyone. That is not the important thing now. The important thing, we are profoundly convinced, is to remove the main road blocks piled up in the way of disarmament, to try to find a new approach to the solution of the problem.

The record of the disarmament talks shows plainly that the question of control has been put forward as one of the main obstacles to agreement. We were and are for strict international control over the implementation of the disarmament agreement, when it is reached. But we have always been against the control system being divorced from actual measures of disarmament, against the control organs becoming, in effect, organs for the collection of intelligence information while there would in fact be no disarmament.

We are for genuine controlled disarmament, but we are against control without disarmament. The opponents of disarmament can easily make any measure conditional upon control provisions that other states will be unable to accept in the conditions of a universal arms race. The countries which, for one reason or another, advance such far-reaching control demands would themselves most probably be disinclined to accept these demands if it came to carrying them out.

There is yet another difficulty. So long as disarmament is conceived as only partial and some armaments are to remain after the conclusion of the disarmament agreement, it would still leave states the material possibility of attacking. There would always be the fear that with these remaining types of armaments and armed forces an attack could still be committed. The knowledge that such a possibility would remain hampered the disarmament negotiations in no small measure.

Many states feared that the disarmament measures would affect precisely those types of armaments in which they have the greatest advantage and which they believe to be particularly necessary to themselves. Naturally, under these conditions, in an atmosphere of cold war and mutual suspicion, no state, speaking seriously and not for propaganda, could reveal its military secrets, the organization of its defense and war production, without prejudicing the interests of its national security.

All the delegates will, I am sure, agree that the collective reason of all states, as well as of the United Nations, must be focused on finding a new approach to the solution of the disarmament problem.

The task is to find a lever which would make it possible to stop mankind from sliding into the abyss of war. What is essential now is to rule out the very possibility of wars being started. So long as there exist large armies, air forces and navies, nuclear and rocket weapons, so long as young men on the threshold of life are first of all taught the art of warfare and general staffs are busy working out plans for future military operations, there is no guarantee of stable peace.

The Soviet Government, having comprehensively considered the situation, has come to the firm conviction that *the way out of the deadlock should be sought along the lines of general and complete disarmament.* With such an approach, the possibility of any military advantages being created for any states is completely ruled out. *It is general and complete disarmament that will remove all the barriers raised during the discussions on partial disarmament and clear the way for the establishment of comprehensive, complete control.*

What does the Soviet Government propose?

The essence of our proposals is that over a period of four years all states should effect complete disarmament and thereafter no longer possess any means of waging war.

This means that land armies, navies and air forces would cease to exist, general staffs and war ministries would be abolished, military training establishments would be closed. Tens of millions of men would return to peaceful constructive labor.

Military bases on foreign territory would be dismantled.

All atomic and hydrogen bombs in the possession of states would be destroyed and their further production discontinued. The energy of fissionable materials would be used exclusively for peaceful economic and scientific purposes.

Military rockets of all ranges would be eliminated and rockets would remain only as a means of transportation and of the conquest of outer space for the good of all mankind.

The states would retain only strictly limited contingents of police (militia) agreed upon for each country, equipped with small arms and designed exclusively to maintain internal order and protect the personal security of citizens.

So that no one could violate his obligations, we propose the establishment of an international control body comprised of all states. A system of control over all disarmament measures should be set up which should be instituted and should function according to the stages by which disarmament is to be effected.

If disarmament is comprehensive and complete, then upon its consummation control will also be general and complete. States will have nothing to conceal from one another: None of them will possess weapons that could be used against another, and no restraints will be imposed on the controllers' zeal.

This solution of disarmament questions would ensure the complete security of all states. It would create favorable conditions for the peaceful coexistence of states. All international issues would then be resolved not by force of arms but by peaceful means.

We are realists in politics and understand that working out such a broad disarmament program will take some time. While such a program is being elaborated, while matters are being agreed, we must not sit with folded arms and wait.

The Soviet Government considers that the elaboration of a program of general and complete disarmament should not hold up the settlement of so acute and entirely ripe a question as the discontinuance of nuclear weapon tests for all time. All the prerequisites for settling it are now in evidence. We hope that an appropriate agreement on the discontinuance of tests will be concluded and put into effect without delay.

The danger of a nuclear-rocket war which threatens the peoples calls for bold, far-reaching solutions to ensure peace.

A decision to effect general and complete disarmament at an early date and the implementation of that decision would usher in a new state in international life. The agreement of states to undertake general and complete disarmament would be convincing, practical proof of the absence of any aggressive designs on their part and of a sincere desire to base their relations with other states on friendship and cooperation. With the destruction of weapons and the abolition of armed forces, no material possibilities would remain for states to pursue any policy other than that of peace.

On achieving complete disarmament, mankind would feel as does an exhausted desert traveler, tormented by fear of dying from thirst and exhaustion, when after long weary wanderings he reaches an oasis.

General and complete disarmament would allow enormous material and financial resources to be switched from the manufacture of weapons of death to constructive purposes. Human energy could be directed to the creation of material and spiritual values beautifying and ennobling man's life and work.

The implementation of a program of general and complete disarmament would make it possible to shift enormous sums to the building of schools, hospitals, homes, roads, to the production of foodstuffs and manufactured goods. The money released would allow taxes to be substantially reduced and prices lowered. This would have a beneficial effect on the living standards of the population and would be welcomed by millions of ordinary people. The funds spent by the states for military needs over the last decade alone would suffice to build over 150 million houses which could comfortably accommodate many hundreds of millions of people.

General and complete disarmament would also create entirely new opportunities for aid to the countries whose economies are still underdeveloped and who need assistance from the more developed countries. Even if only a small part of the money released by the termination of the military expenditures of the Great Powers were devoted to such aid, it could open up literally a new epoch in the economic development of Asia, Africa and Latin America.

All the artificial obstacles to the development of international trade which today exist in the form of discriminatory restrictions, embargo lists, etc., would disappear. The industries of such nations as the U.S.A., Britain, France, West Germany and other highly developed countries could at last receive large orders from other states. The utilization of the funds released by disarmament would provide the widest employment opportunities. That is why the claims that disarmament would bring on a crisis or economic recession in the highly developed industrial countries of the capitalist world are unfounded.

When no country has the actual means of undertaking military action against other countries, international relations will develop in a spirit of confidence. Suspicion and fear will vanish, all nations will be able to treat each other like genuine good neighbors. The doors will open wide for economic, commercial and cultural co-operation among all states. For the first time the secure and stable peace that all peoples so eagerly desire will become a reality.

Convinced that by the joint efforts of all the countries united in the name of the peaceful principles of the United Nations Charter these great aims can and must be achieved, *the Government of the Union of Soviet Socialist Republics submits for the consideration of the United Nations a Declaration on General and Complete Disarmament containing concrete proposals on the subject.*

It goes without saying that if for any reason the Western Powers do not evince a readiness at present to embark on general and complete disarmament, the Soviet Government is prepared to reach agreement with other states on appropriate measures for partial disarmament and the strengthening of security. The chief of these, in the Soviet Government's opinion, are:

1) The creation of a control and inspection zone with a reduction of foreign troops on the territory of the West European countries concerned;

2) The creation of an atom-free zone in Central Europe;

3) The withdrawal of all foreign troops from the territory of European states and the dismantling of military bases on foreign territory;

4) The conclusion of a nonaggression pact between the member-states of NATO and of the Warsaw Treaty;

5) An agreement on the prevention of surprise attack by one state on another.

The Soviet Government thinks it appropriate to recall its disarmament proposals of May 10, 1955, containing concrete ideas concerning partial disarmament measures. It is convinced that these proposals are a good basis for agreement on this vitally important problem.

This is not the first time the Soviet Union has advanced the idea of general and complete disarmament. As far back as the period between the First and Second World Wars the government of our country came forward with a comprehensive program of complete disarmament. At that time the opponents of disarmament were wont to assert that the Soviet Union had put forward these proposals because it was an economically and militarily weak country. If in those days this false thesis could perhaps delude some, it is now evident to all that talk of any weakness of the Soviet Union is absurd.

The new proposal of the Soviet Government is prompted by the sole desire to ensure truly lasting peace among nations.

We say sincerely to all countries: In contrast to the "Let us arm!" slogan, still current in some quarters, we put forward the slogan "Let us completely disarm!" Let us rather compete in who builds more homes, schools and hospitals for the people; produces more grain, milk, meat, clothing and other consumer goods; and not in who has more hydrogen bombs and rockets. This will be welcomed by all the peoples of the world.

Gentlemen, the United Nations, whose General Assembly I today have the honor of addressing, can and should play a large part in international affairs. Its importance derives from the fact that nearly all the nations of the world are represented in it. They have united to consider jointly the pressing problems of international relations. If two or more states are unable to agree among themselves, the United Nations should help them. Its role in such cases is to smooth the rough edges in relations between states, which can lead to disputes, to tensions and even to wars. By performing its cardinal function of strengthening world peace and security, the United Nations will win the respect it should enjoy, and its prestige will grow.

But I have to say in all frankness that at present the United Nations in some cases, unfortunately, does not perform these functions. Sometimes, by a wrong approach in the UN, needless tension is actually created between states.

Why does this happen? Because not all UN member-states treat with due respect this organization in which mankind reposes such hopes. Instead of constantly reinforcing the prestige of the United Nations, so that it may really be the most authoritative international organ to which the governments of all countries could apply whenever in need of getting some vital problem solved, some states seek to use it in their own narrow interests. Naturally an international organization cannot work effectively for peace if there is within it a group of countries which seek to impose their will on others. That kind of policy will undermine the foundations of the United Nations. If things should continue to develop along these lines, which might be called factional, this would lead to deterioraiton of relations between states instead of improving them. From an organ expressing the interests of all its members, the United Nations would become the organ of a group of states, pursuing the policy of that group and not the policy of safeguarding world peace. This would in the initial stage engender disrespect for the United Nations and then might lead to its break-up, as happened to the League of Nations in its day.

The distinguishing characteristic of a properly functioning international organ is that questions ought to be settled there not by a formal count of votes but by a reasonable and patient quest for a just solution acceptable to all. After all, one cannot expect countries against whose will an unjust decision is taken to agree to carry it out. It leaves a bitter taste in the mouth. Recall how many such instances there have been in the history of the United Nations! Therefore, the United Nations should pass only such decisions as all will vote for, seeing in them an expression of the common will and the common interest. Such decisions would be recognized as the only correct and the only possible ones both by our generation and by future historians.

Naturally, a group of states which at a given moment commands a majority can put through the decision it wants. But this is a Pyrrhic victory. Such "victories" injure the United Nations, they disrupt it.

It should also be borne in mind that in the voting of one question or another the majority in the United Nations is a variable quantity. It could change against those who today so often bank on the voting machine. As the Russian saying goes, "You reap what you sow." And so, the wisest and most far-sighted policy is one of seeking jointly for mutually acceptable decisions stemming exclusively from concern for safeguarding world peace and noninterference in the internal affairs of other nations.

When the Security Council was being established in the UN, the idea of agreed decisions was made the basis of its work. And a special responsibility for the maintenance of peace was laid upon the Great Powers, whose representatives are permanent members of the Security Council. It was found necessary, in order to avoid complications in international relations, to establish the principle of Great Power unanimity in the Security Council, known as the veto power.

Some people are against the veto. But if there were no veto there would be no international organization, it would fall to pieces. The veto principle obliges the Great Powers to reach a unanimous decision on all matters before the Security Council that ensures the effective maintenance of peace. It is better to seek unanimous decisions of the Great Powers than to settle international issues by force of arms.

Gentlemen, I have tried to state frankly some ideas concerning the international situation and also concerning our understanding of the tasks of the United Nations. We are sure that the proposals we have set forth on the instructions of the Soviet Government will be received with sympathy by the majority of the people of all countries and by the delegates sitting in this hall.

86

I should like to assure the delegates to the General Assembly that in the Soviet Union the United Nations will continue to have a most active participant in all endeavors to rid mankind of the burden of armaments and to consolidate world peace. Thank you, gentlemen. *(Stormy applause.)*

DECLARATION OF THE SOVIET GOVERNMENT

Agreement among the states on the limitation and destruction of the weapons of war has for many years been the cherished dream of mankind. Public leaders and statesmen, and the parties closest to the working people, advanced and pressed the demand for disarmament long before mankind experienced the horrors of world wars.

All nations, large and small, irrespective of their social systems and way of life are interested in the adoption of effective disarmament measures. There are no peoples today who do not feel a deep anxiety in the face of the rivalry of states in armaments, a rivalry which has become truly unprecedented, especially in the field of developing ever more destructive and lethal weapons; and they have no more fervent desire than to put an end to this rivalry which is fraught with grievous consequences for the destiny of the world.

GENERAL AND COMPLETE DISARMAMENT IS THE WAY TO DELIVER MANKIND FROM THE SCOURGE OF WAR

The armaments race has impressed itself upon men's minds as a specter that is always the forerunner of war. So it was when Europe, convulsed by the armaments fever, moved step by step toward the First World War. And so it was again in the thirties, when in a number of countries everything was subordinated to the slogan "Guns before butter" and the arsenals were again packed to bursting. Everyone knows what came of it. The peoples were plunged into the Second World War, which brought them misfortune and suffering that caused everything that mankind had endured in the darkest periods of its history to pale into insignificance.

The war ended, but people still did not gain peace of mind. Practically the very next day after the roar of the last battles subsided, the world was again seized by the armaments fever which was,

87

this time, far more dangerous to mankind, since the preparations were for nuclear war.

Never before has the armaments race been fraught with such danger as today, in the age of the atom, electronics and the conquest of outer space.

However terrible such earlier instruments of annihilation as rapid-fire automatic weapons, tanks, long-range artillery and aircraft bombs many have seemed to be, they stand no comparison with atomic and hydrogen weapons and rockets. If all the instruments of destruction mankind possessed over the centuries were put together, they would amount to only an insignificant fraction of what the two or three nuclear powers have at their disposal today.

Indeed, it is known that the explosion of a single large modern hydrogen bomb releases a destructive energy surpassing that of all the explosives manufactured in the whole world in four years of the Second World War.

The introduction of atomic and rocket weapons into the armaments of armies, the training of servicemen in their use, and the adaptation of the strategy and tactics of warfare to the new weapons have already progressed so far that the next military conflict among the powers threatens to turn into a war with the employment of all the instruments of destruction at the belligerents' command. Outer space, unattainable to man just a couple of years ago, can now be used, like the seas and air before, for delivering a nuclear attack against any point of the globe.

Both World Wars began between countries which were neighbors and had a common frontier. But now war can break out between countries which are many thousands of kilometers apart, and can draw whole continents into its orbit.

In such a war, if it is not averted in time, distances would be measured in thousands and tens of thousands of kilometers, time in minutes and seconds, and losses in millions and tens and hundreds of millions of human lives. It would be a war that would know no distinction between front and rear, between active armies and civilian populations, between soldiers and children.

The appearance of military alliances which girdle almost the entire globe and which bristle with armaments against each other has produced a situation where a small spark, an incident of seemingly local significance, would be enough to touch off a war conflagration. And if up to now the concatenated system of military commitments

88

has not been put into motion, if the brakes have held out, there is and can be no guarantee that it will not happen in the future.

Never before have so many states and such masses of people been drawn into war preparations as at present. There are tens of millions of men under arms, and when to these are added those who are directly or indirectly connected with the production of armaments, military research and other activities designed to supply and service the armies, it emerges that hundreds of millions of people have been taken from the labors of peace. A vast fund of human energy, knowledge, ingenuity and skill is being spilled as into a bottomless pit, consumed by the growing armaments.

The armaments race has extended to countries which economically cannot carry the burden of armaments, while militarily their very existence is jeopardized by it. Military bases on foreign territory, armed forces stationed thousands of kilometers from their own frontiers are palpable proof of that.

Moreover, the stockpiling of mass destruction weapons in the arsenals of some powers and the advancement of air, naval and rocket bases toward the frontiers of other states compel the states against which these war preparations are being conducted to adopt the measures necessary to strengthen their security and safeguard a life of peace for their peoples. The Soviet Union and all the socialist countries, and also many other states who cherish peace, would wish to gear all of their economy and resources to peaceful purposes in order to provide their people abundantly with food, clothing and housing. But they cannot undividedly devote their efforts to peaceful construction without mortally endangering the vital interests of their peoples and their very existence. The arming of one side compels the other side to act likewise. The quantities of mass destruction weapons keep growing and with them grows the danger of a military explosion.

Today atomic and hydrogen bombs are not only stored at ultra-secret depots. They are carried by bombers that make flights over the territory of many West European countries. The situation is developing in such a way that super-powerful and super-long-range weapons could be discharged not only on the orders of governments, but at the will of the individuals at the control panel of those weapons. But a state on whose territory a nuclear load is dropped, whether by evil intent or owing to a technical fault or other accident, is hardly going to investigate how it happened, but will be obliged to react to it as to a military attack, as to the unleashing of war. Can it be permitted that the question—peace or war—should be left to the mercy of blind chance? Is not all this added proof that the road of armaments can be followed no further? The Soviet Union by no means accepts armaments rivalry as a fatal inevitability, eternally bound to accompany the relations between states. In its foreign policy the Soviet Government has been acting upon the conviction that it is possible to prevent the development of human society from continuing along the road which has led to two world wars, that it is possible to ensure that its history shall no longer be, as hitherto, a record of sanguinary wars.

Weapons are created by the hands of man. Those same hands can destroy them.

It is about fourteen years now that the disarmament problem has been under discussion in the United Nations. Before that, it was discussed for many years by the League of Nations and the disarmament conference it convened. However, there are to this day no practical results, in the sense of any decisions agreed among the states.

Much could be said about the reasons for this unfortunate state of the disarmament question. However, the important thing now is not to rake over the past and aggravate the polemics, but to remove the chief obstacles that frustrated all previous attempts to reach agreement on disarmament.

The record of many years of disarmament negotiations shows that the question of control over disarmament was put forward as one of the main obstacles to such agreement.

The Soviet Government stands, and always has stood, for strict international control over the fulfillment of agreements on disarmament measures, when such agreements are achieved. All Soviet proposals for banning atomic weapons and tests, and also for the reduction of conventional armaments and armed forces, were invariably accompanied by specific proposals for effective control on an international basis. But the Soviet Government has always been against the control system being made a program of measures divorced from any actual disarmament, and all the more against the control organs becoming organs for the collection of intelligence on the armaments of states while there would in fact be no disarmament.

However, besides the complications introduced into the control problem artificially, there are also real difficulties attaching to the establishment of control under present conditions. They will be seen clearly enough if we take, for instance, the problem of banning and eliminating nuclear weapons.

90

It is well known that the same fissionable materials can be used at appropriate enterprises both for the production of nuclear weapons and for peaceful purposes. This means that in the present circumstances, with atomic energy being ever more widely used in the economy, there is a possibility of part of the fissionable materials being secretly channeled to the production of weapons.

To be completely free—in the existing atmosphere of distrust—of suspicion of this or that state secretly using atomic materials for military purposes, it would be necessary to grant foreign controllers access to a great number of enterprises in every country, amounting, in fact, to a variety of foreign guardianship over an important branch of its economy. But on account of this same reason and the distrust prevailing among the states, no state can show itself willing to admit foreign controllers and inspectors to its enterprises, especially to those engaged in military production.

It is obvious that in the present state of affairs, with the continuing armaments race, tension in international relations and lack of confidence, the conditions necessary for establishing comprehensive controls are not in evidence.

So long as distrust prevails among the states, the opponents of disarmament can easily make any disarmament measure conditional upon such control provisions as other states will be unable to accept. For that matter, the states which for, one reason or another advance such far-reaching demands as to the powers of the control bodies actually would not have any inclination themselves to accept such control provisions if it came to carrying them out.

That being the position, to put forward deliberately exaggerated demands as regards control, and, all the more, to put control before disarmament, making it a preliminary condition of any disarmament measures, is tantamount to blocking all approaches to the solution of the problem.

The Soviet Government considers that the time has come to evaluate the situation soberly and to recognize that since the approach so far applied to the solution of the disarmament problem has failed to produce results, the logical conclusion must be drawn from that fact. That conclusion, in the opinion of the Soviet Government, can only be that *it is the duty of all states, as also of the United Nations, to find without delay a new way to go about solving the disarmament problem, the burning problem of our time.*

What is this new way? What must be done to put an end to a position where a huge proportion of the wealth taken by man from nature, created by the genius of scientists, the skill of engineers, the efforts of millions and millions of working people is squandered on instruments of death and destruction? What must be done to prevent tens of millions of men in the prime of their creative energies from being taken from productive endeavors for service in the armed forces, for the preparation of a devastating war?

By now the majority of statesmen and public leaders, as well as the broad masses of the population in all countries, have already come to realize that a new world war would be a terrible tragedy for all, and for some countries with relatively small territories and a high density of population, a disaster threatening their very existence.

The task now is to find a lever by grasping which it will be possible to stop mankind from sliding into the abyss of a nuclear-missile war.

With the present nature of international relations and the present level of military technology, when any military conflict can lead to a nuclear-missile war, a radical solution of the problem of security for all states involves precluding the very possibility of wars being started. So long as there exist large armies, air forces and navies, nuclear and missile weapons, so long as young men on the threshold of life are first of all taught the art of warfare and general staffs are busy working out plans of future military operations, there is and can be no secure peace among nations in the present situation. Not equilibrium in armaments, which every state tries to interpret and turn to its own advantage, but a position where the states will not have the material means of waging war—that is the most effective and solid guarantee of peace that meets not only remote ideals but the urgent demands of the people.

After thoroughly assessing the present international situation and the experience of previous disarmament negotiations, the Government of the Soviet Union has arrived at the conviction that the surest way to a practical solution of the cardinal international problem of our day—the disarmament problem—is the way of *general and complete disarmament of all states*.

By general and complete disarmament the Soviet Government means the renunciation by all states without exception of the maintenance of any armed forces save for minimum internal security contingents (militia, police) equipped with small arms and designed to maintain order within each country.

This means that land armies, navies and air forces will cease to exist; general staffs and war ministries will be abolished; military training establishments will be closed. Tens of millions of men will return to peaceful constructive labor.

The foreign military bases now existing on the territory of a number of states, which injure the sovereignty and security of those states and do untold harm to the cause of international confidence and cooperation among all nations, will be dismantled.

All atomic and hydrogen bombs in the possession of states will be destroyed and their further production discontinued. The energy of fissionable materials will be used exclusively for peaceful economic and scientific purposes.

Military rockets of all ranges will be eliminated and rockets will remain only as a means of transportation and of the conquest of outer space for the good of all mankind.

Guns, tanks, shells, torpedoes will be melted down to provide more metal for peaceful construction. Warships and military aircraft will be scrapped.

The stockpiles of chemical and bacteriological weapons accumulated by some states—poison gases and asphyxiants, cultures of lethal germs, potential sources of dangerous epidemic diseases—all this will be destroyed conclusively, without a trace and for all time.

Such is the program of disarmament which the Soviet Government submits for the consideration of all states, and first of all of the UN members, and proposes that its implementation be started without delay.

This is a radical program, but precisely therein lies the guarantee of its feasibility under present conditions. The existence of opposing alignments in which dozens of states are bound by mutual military commitments, the fantastically rapid development of military technology—all this requires bold, far-reaching solutions to ensure peace.

The proposal for complete and general disarmament differs from all other disarmament proposals in that its realization absolutely rules out any inequality of conditions, the possibility of any military advantages for any state or states.

No one is likely to deny that if the radical decision were taken to carry out within a short fixed term complete and general disarmament of all the states, and if it were put into practice, the entire international situation would change fundamentally. The relations between states, including countries belonging to different social systems and to opposing military-political alignments, would be put on an utterly new basis.

Fear of possible aggression on the part of this or that state would, in effect, be eliminated. The readiness of states to undertake general complete disarmament would be convincing practical proof of the absence of any aggressive designs on their part and of their sincere desire to base their relations with other states on the principle of peaceful coexistence; and with the destruction of armaments and the abolition of armed forces, no physical possibility would remain for states to pursue any policy other than a peaceable one. The destruction of the war weapons would provide a still firmer basis for peaceful coexistence between states, since any other line in the development of international relations would be completely precluded.

Under general and complete disarmament the distinction between the victors and vanquished of the last war would be obliterated. The importance and international influence of the powers would be determined not by their military might but by the degree of their participation in creating the material and spiritual values that enrich mankind. It would not be the number of divisions, bombers or rockets, not the tonnage of surface or submarine navies, nor stockpiles of atomic and hydrogen bombs, but achievements in the production of material wealth, in the improvement of people's conditions of life and work, in the struggle for the prolongation of man's life span, that would then serve as the measure of the prestige of states and their contribution to the history of mankind.

Of course, even after the fulfillment of the general disarmament program differences between states, particularly between states with different social and economic systems, will remain. These differences will not, however, be resolved through military clashes, but only by peaceful economic competition, by the struggle of ideas and by other peaceful means as prescribed by the United Nations Charter.

Under the conditions of general and complete disarmament the difficulties connected with control will also disappear. Under these conditions the states will have nothing to conceal from each other. There will be every possibility to carry out any checks, any inspection if any doubt arises about the good faith of this or that state in the fulfillment of its disarmament obligations.

In other words, a decision to effect general complete disarmament would at last allow a way to be found out of the vicious circle of distrust between the states, which now fetters them in their negotiations of partial disarmament measures and prevents even one real step forward being made in this field.

When general complete disarmament becomes a fact, different and much more favorable conditions will also arise for solving many complicated political problems which still remain outstanding, among them European problems.

Lastly, general complete disarmament would open before all countries new vistas in the field of their economic development.

There would arise opportunities hitherto unseen to rapidly improve the living standards of all nations by putting to good use the money which is now being spent by the states for the maintenance of armed forces and the manufacture of weapons.

Opponents of disarmament not infrequently try to discredit the very idea of disarmament by alleging that the discontinuance of weapons manufacture would be bound to cause economic difficulties and deprive of employment many people now engaged in the military industries. But to put the matter in this way is a deliberate deception.

Do not the lethal weapons being manufactured at present consume fabulous sums of public money which could be used to build homes for the people, new schools for their children, free hospitals for those who need medical treatment, and for instituting or increasing pensions for the aged and disabled? Would not the utilization of these funds for peaceful purposes create the broadest employment opportunities?

There can be no doubt that general and complete disarmament would permit the creation of conditions for such material and spiritual progress in all countries as would exceed by many times the existing rates of their development. The billions that would pour in a mighty torrent into the civil economies as a result of the discontinuance of military expenditures would be utilized in new and far more favorable conditions than those obtaining now. The artificial partitions by which states are presently isolating themselves from one another, protecting their achievements in science and technology out of military and strategic considerations, would gradually disappear. Scientists in all countries would be able to work exclusively for the good of man, for the improvement of his life. Unhampered exchange of experience would stimulate scientific, technical and economic progress in each individual country and all countries taken together.

Were all states to pool their efforts and allocate the funds necessary for launching an all-out offensive against such enemies of man as cancer and some other dangerous diseases still difficult to cure, these would be brought under control in a short time. General disarmament would create the prerequisites for such pooling of efforts in the fight for man's health.

One of the results of the growth of confidence among the states in the conditions of general and complete disarmament would be the broad development of international trade. The artificial obstacles to the development of this trade which are now created by certain powers in the form of discriminatory restrictions, embargo lists, etc., would disappear. The industries of such countries as the USA, Britain, West Germany and France would be able finally to avail themselves of the ample opportunities for obtaining large orders from other states. Mutually beneficial trade would have a favorable effect on the economy of the trading nations.

General and complete disarmament would also create entirely new opportunities for aid to the countries whose economies are at present still underdeveloped and need assistance from more advanced countries. Even if only a small part of the funds released by the termination of the military expenditures of the Great Powers were devoted to such aid, it could usher in a new era in the economic development of Asia, Africa and Latin America.

It will suffice to cite the following example:

The construction of the Aswan High Dam and the Nile hydro-electric installations connected with it, which has been started in the Egyptian part of the United Arab Republic, is probably the largest construction project being carried out at present in any of the under-developed states of Africa or Asia. If general and complete disarmament is put into effect and the highly developed industrial countries allocate, say, 10 per cent of the funds thus saved for assistance to underdeveloped countries, such allocations from the budgets of two powers alone—the USA and the Soviet Union—would be enough to build several such dams annually.

The direct military expenditures of the member-states of the NATO military bloc in 1958 alone reached the sum of 60 billion dollars. If one-tenth of this sum were used for assistance to under-developed countries, it would make possible the annual construction of more than ten metallurgical plants similar to those now being built in India.

Such are the potentialities for assisting the economic rise of the underdeveloped countries in conditions of general and complete disarmament. The Soviet Union stands for utilizing these potentialities to the fullest.

This is not the first time the idea of general and complete disarmament has been put forward. The Soviet Government advanced proposals on this score as far back as the period between the two World Wars. The interests of rival groups of powers which sought to direct the military might of the aggressive states against the only socialist state then in existence prevented the adoption of this Soviet proposal, and this led to disastrous consequences for the world.

The opponents of the proposals for general and complete disarmament were wont to allege at that time that the Soviet Union made those proposals because it was an economically and militarily weak country. If in those days this false thesis could perhaps mislead some, it is obvious to all now that talk about any weakness of the Soviet Union is absurd and that the new Soviet proposal for general and complete disarmament is prompted by the sole desire to promote truly lasting peace among the nations.

The Soviet Union, the Chinese People's Republic, all the socialist countries are emphatically opposed to war and the manufacture of the weapons of war. But it would be wrong to think that states with a different social system have no reason to sincerely and unreservedly support the proposal for general and complete disarmament. Destruction of the weapons of war cannot and will not run counter to the national interests of any state. No government, if it really cares about the future of its country and its people, can take a negative stand on the proposal for general and complete disarmament.

There are more than a hundred states on the political map of the world. These states have attained different levels of economic development, they have different social and political systems, they differ in their people's living conditions and standards of culture. But despite all the diversity of conditions under which people in different countries live, there is one thing they have in common: the desire to prevent another war, to establish eternal peace in the world. When no state has the actual wherewithal to launch hostilities against other states, the development of international relations will be marked by sincere confidence.

Convinced that by the joint efforts of all the states united in the name of the peaceful principles of the United Nations Charter all these great aims can and must be achieved, the Government of the USSR submits for consideration by the United Nations the *proposal for general and complete disarmament.*

PROGRAM OF GENERAL AND COMPLETE DISARMAMENT

The program of general and complete disarmament should include the following measures:

Disbandment of all armed forces (land, naval and air) and the prohibition of their re-establishment in any form;

Destruction of arms and ammunition of all types, both in the armed forces and in stockpiles;

Scrapping of all warships, military aircraft and all other types of war materiel;

Complete prohibition of atomic and hydrogen weapons—discontinuance of the production of all types of these weapons, their elimination from the armaments of the states, and destruction of stockpiles of same;

Complete discontinuance of the production of rocket weapons of all types and ranges, including space rockets for military purposes, and their destruction;

Prohibition of the production, possession and storage of chemical and bacteriological weapons, and destruction of stockpiles of these weapons;

Dismantling of all types of military bases on foreign territory —land, naval and air, and of all rocket-launching installations;

Abolition of military production at war plants and of war production facilities in general industry;

Discontinuance of all military training and musters, both in armies and in public organizations, and the enactment of law abolishing military service in any form—compulsory, voluntary, through recruitment, etc.;

Abolition of war ministries, general staffs, military training institutions, and of military and para-military establishments and organizations of all kinds;

Discontinuance of allocation of funds for military purposes in any form, both out of the state budget and by public organizations and private persons;

Prohibition by law of war propaganda and military indoctrination of the youth, and the enactment of laws providing for the strictest punishment for violation of any of the above measures.

The states should retain only strictly limited contingents, agreed for every country, of police (militia), equipped with small arms and designed solely to maintain internal order and protect the personal security of citizens.

To supervise the punctual implementation of the measures of general and complete disarmament there shall be established an international control body comprised of all states. The personnel of the control body shall be recruited on an international basis with due regard to the principle of equitable geographical distribution.

The international control body shall have at its disposal all facilities necessary to exercise strict control. The functions and powers of that body shall correspond to the nature of the disarmament measures being carried out.

The Soviet Government proposes that the program of general and complete disarmament be carried out as soon as possible—within a period of four years.

In the first stage it is proposed to carry out the following measures:

Reduction, under appropriate control, of the strength of the armed forces of the USSR, the USA and CPR (the People's Republic of China) to the level of 1,700,000, and of those of the United Kingdom and France to 650,000 each.

Reduction of the strength of the armed forces of other states to levels to be agreed at a special session of the United Nations General Assembly or at a World Conference on General and Complete Disarmament.

Reduction of the armaments and war materiel at the disposal of the armed forces of states by such proportions that the remaining quantity of armaments corresponds to the determined level of armed forces.

In the second stage it is proposed to carry out:

Completion of the abolition of the armed forces retained by the states.

Dismantling of all military bases on foreign territory. Troops and military personnel shall be withdrawn from foreign territory to within their own national frontiers and disbanded.

In the third stage:

All types of nuclear and rocket weapons shall be destroyed.

The materiel of the air force shall be liquidated.

Prohibition of the production, possession and storing of chemical and bacteriological weapons shall come into force. All stocks of chemical and bacteriological weapons in the possession of states shall be removed and destroyed under international control.

Scientific research for war purposes and the development of weapons and war materiel shall be prohibited.

War ministries, general staffs, all military and para-military establishments and organizations shall be abolished.

All military training and musters shall be terminated. States shall prohibit by law military training of the youth.

In accordance with their respective constitutional procedures states shall enact laws abolishing military service in any form—compulsory, voluntary, through recruiting, etc.—and prohibiting the re-establishment in overt or covert form of any military or para-military establishments or organizations.

Allocation of funds for military purposes in any form, both out of state budgets and by public organizations, shall be discontinued. The funds released by the implementation of general and complete disarmament shall be used to reduce or entirely abolish taxes on the population, to subsidize the national economies and to render extensive economic and technical assistance to underdeveloped countries.

To control the implementation of the measures of general and complete disarmament, an international control body is to be set up. The scope of control and inspection shall correspond to the stage of the phased disarmament.

After the consummation of general and complete disarmament, which must include the abolition of all types of armed forces and the destruction of all types of weapons, including weapons of mass destruction (nuclear, rocket, chemical, bacteriological), the international control body shall have free access to everything subject to control.

The control organization may set up a system of aerial observation and aerial photography over the territories of states.

During the implementation of the program of general and complete disarmament, up to the time of disbandment of all armed forces, the states shall maintain between the various services of their armed forces the ratio which existed between them at the time the disarmament treaty entered into force.

The program of general and complete disarmament shall be carried out by the states in strict conformity with the time limits specified in the treaty, and its implementation cannot be suspended or made dependent on the fulfillment of any conditions not provided for by the treaty.

Against the event of any state attempting to circumvent or violate the treaty on general and complete disarmament, the treaty should

100

include a provision to the effect that any violation of it shall be subject to immediate consideration by the Security Council and the General Assembly of the United Nations in accordance with their powers.

It goes without saying that the Soviet Government wishes to view the existing situation realistically, and if for any reason the Western Powers do not evince a readiness at present to embark on general and complete disarmament, the Soviet Government is prepared, as before, to reach agreement with other states on appropriate partial measures for disarmament and the strengthening of security. The chief of these, in the opinion of the Soviet Government, are:

1) Creation of a control and inspection zone with a reduction of foreign troops on the territory of the West European countries concerned;

2) Creation of an atom-free zone in Central Europe;

3) Withdrawal of all foreign troops from the territory of European states and dismantling of military bases on foreign territory;

4) Conclusion of a nonaggression pact between the member-states of NATO and of the Warsaw Treaty;

5) An agreement on the prevention of surprise attack by one state on another.

The Soviet Government thinks it appropriate to recall its disarmament proposals of May 10, 1955, containing concrete ideas concerning partial disarmament measures. It is convinced that these proposals constitute a good basis for agreement on this vitally important problem.

As to the question of the cessation of nuclear weapons tests, the Soviet Government stands, now as before, for immediate termination of these tests for all time.

The Soviet Government expresses its deep conviction that the proposed radical solution of the disarmament problem would ensure a fundamental change in the development of international relations, establish an atmosphere of confidence between the states and create the conditions for a peaceful life for the peoples. The Soviet Government calls upon the governments of all countries of the world, and particularly the Governments of the Great Powers—which have the most powerful armed forces, which are permanent members of the Security Council, and which bear a special responsibility to the peoples for world security—to proceed jointly and without delay to the implementation of general and complete disarmament.

N. S. KHRUSHCHEV'S STATEMENT BEFORE HIS
DEPARTURE FROM NEW YORK

N. S. Khrushchev and his party left New York on September 19 for Los Angeles.

Before his departure N. S. Khrushchev made the following statement:

Ladies and gentlemen, we visited New York and spent two days here at the kind invitation of the Mayor, Mr. Wagner. And although that is a short period, we were very pleased to have a glimpse, if only cursory, of your city, to meet its residents, its civic leaders and businessmen. It may be said that in a way I am also a representative of my country's business world, because under our socialist system the Government of the Soviet Union directs not only the political, but also the economic life of the state.

I have become convinced that the absolute majority of officials and businessmen in your city, and particularly the ordinary working people, treated us—representatives of a different, socialist world—with great regard.

I was a miner in the past and feel best of all, like a fish in water, when I am among working people. Regrettably, in your city I have had no opportunity of coming into contact with the ordinary people —the workers, who are the backbone of the life of the city, the producers of its wealth. It was not because the city authorities wanted to prevent such contact. They explained that they feared provocative acts by a handful of hooligans who might have taken advantage of such contact to stage a provocation, although these elements are, of course, only a drop in the ocean among the friendly population of New York. The people of New York came out into the streets in large numbers and gave us a friendly welcome. We appreciate it, and are grateful to them.

Our visit to your country and the return visit to the Soviet Union by President Eisenhower will evidently mark the beginning of an improvement and expansion of relations between our countries. We are indebted to the President for his kind invitation and will, in turn, do everything to receive him appropriately in our country.

I should like to thank the Secretary General of the United Nations Organization, Mr. Hammarskjold, who invited me to address the General Assembly and gave a dinner last night at which I met representatives of many member-countries of the United Nations.

I also thank the delegates at the UN General Assembly for the attention with which they listened to my address at the meeting. In that address I made very important disarmament proposals on behalf of the Soviet Government. If these proposals are supported by the governments of other countries, it will mark the start of a new era in international relations and lay the foundation for enduring friendship and cooperation among nations.

I assure you that the Soviet Government and I will do all in our power to strengthen peace and friendship among nations.

As I leave your great city, I should like to convey greetings and best wishes for happiness and prosperity to the people of New York.

Good-bye, ladies and gentlemen!

N. S. Khrushchev and his party arrived in Los Angeles on September 19 at 12:09 P.M., local time.

SPEECH OF N. S. KHRUSHCHEV AT LUNCHEON
HELD AT THE TWENTIETH CENTURY-FOX STUDIOS

On September 19 Eric Johnston, President of the Motion Picture Association of America, and Spyros P. Skouras, owner of the Twentieth Century-Fox Studios, gave a luncheon in honor of N. S. Khrushchev.

Spyros P. Skouras, the owner of Twentieth Century-Fox Studios, made a speech in which he warmly greeted N. S. Khrushchev on his arrival in Hollywood. He also expressed his opinion on a number of questions concerning the film exchange between the USA and the USSR. Skouras used the opportunity to return again to the topic already used time and again by American speakers concerning the "merits" of the capitalist way of life.

N. S. Khrushchev spoke in reply:

MR. JOHNSTON, MRS. JOHNSTON:

I am also addressing you, my dear brother Greek! *(N. S. Khrushchev turned at this point to Spyros P. Skouras, President of the Twentieth Century-Fox Film Corporation, who spoke before him.)* Yes, ladies and gentlemen, Russians have from times of old called the Greeks brothers, because the Russians took part in the war against the Turks to liberate Greece. You should also know that back in ancient times the Russians adopted the religious, Christian rites of the Greeks. So you and we are also in a way brothers in Christ. *(Animation, applause.)* You might say to me that I'm an atheist. But then I am speaking not only for myself, but also on behalf of our entire people, among whom there are both atheists and believers—Christians, Moslems and people of other religions.

Americans always begin their speeches by saying "Ladies and Gentlemen." Allow me, too, to begin that way.

Ladies and Gentlemen *(applause)*,

I thank Mr. Johnston for the invitation to this meeting.

I am very glad to meet the flower of the U.S. stage and screen world represented in this hall. I think the comrades who have come with me to the United States and are accompanying me share my joy.

I must say that I had planned to speak along somewhat different lines, but Mr. Spyros Skouras here has led me off my tack. *(Laughter, applause.)* I hadn't meant my speech to follow the direction which Mr. Skouras laid down in his speech, for some people might have suspected me of having come here to make propaganda for our way of life and of wanting to win over all of you fine Americans to our side. By the way, I should like that. Anyone wishing to come to our country is welcome, we'll treat him to Russian pies. *(Laughter, applause.)* But since you've brought up the subject of how ordinary people work their way up, allow me to answer you.

Mr. Skouras said he had risen from the ranks. What were you in Greece? (Skouras says that he began working for hire at the age of 12.)

That naturally produces an impression, and I wish to express my respect for you. But I'm not amazed. Would you like to know what I was? I began working when I learned to walk. Till the age of 15 I tended calves, then sheep, and then the landlord's cows. I did all that before I was 15. Then I worked at a factory owned by Germans and later in coal pits owned by Frenchmen. I worked at Belgian-owned chemical plants, and now I am Prime Minister of the great Soviet state. *(Stormy applause, Voice: "We knew that.")*

KHRUSHCHEV: What if you did? I'm not ashamed of my past. All honest labor, whatever its nature, is worthy of respect. *(Applause.)* Work, as such, cannot be dirty. It's only the conscience that can be. *(Applause.)* All honest labor is worthy of respect.

SKOURAS: How many Prime Ministers are there in Russia?

KHRUSHCHEV: And how many Presidents do you have? *(Laughter, applause.)* Anyway, I'll answer you. We have the Government of the Soviet Union and I have been made Chairman of the Council of Ministers. We also have 15 Union Republics and each republic has its government. In other words, there are 15 Prime Ministers. Besides, we have Prime Ministers of the Autonomous Republics. How many do you have? *(Laughter, applause.)*

SKOURAS: We have two million presidents of companies. *(Laughter.)*

KHRUSHCHEV: We have Comrade Tikhonov here with us. Please rise. Is anyone here in America richer than this man? What is he? He was a worker, then became a metallurgical engineer. And now he is Chairman of the Dnepropetrovsk Economic Council. He is in charge of huge iron-and-steel works. He is in charge of huge chemical works. The Dnepropetrovsk Economic Council supplies more than

N. S. Khrushchev chats with Mr. Eric Johnston, President of the National Motion Picture Association, during a luncheon given by the Twentieth Century-Fox Film Corporation in Hollywood.

half the iron ore mined in the Soviet Union. Isn't that enough, Mr. Skouras? *(Laughter.)*

SKOURAS: That's a monopoly!

KHRUSHCHEV: Yes, it is a monopoly, but a monopoly of the people! Comrade Tikhonov has no capital of his own. All that he manages belongs to the people. *(Applause.)* So it's no use arguing about who has greater opportunities, you or we, because you can't beat us there.

We have Professor Yemelyanov here with us. He is an atomic scientist of ours. What was he? An ex-worker, he graduated from an institute and became a metallurgical engineer. Now he is an eminent scientist in the field of atomic energy. There you have two of our presidents, and we have millions of presidents just like them.

As you see, gentlemen, you had better put aside the question of ordinary people working their way up. That's the best thing you can do. *(Animation, applause.)* I might quote the Russian saying in this regard. It says, "You cannot catch old sparrows with chaff." *(Laughter.)*

America is a fine country and its great people are a worthy people. Time was when America was admired by all peoples of the world. It has taught everyone a lesson in industrial development. It is the home of assembly-line production, which is the most progressive and efficient industrial process. After the Revolution we set out to learn from the Americans. We sent our engineers to you for training. They studied in your colleges and universities and were employed as ordinary workers at Ford's and alsewhere. The man in charge of our automobile industry today is Engineer Strokin, a Minister of the Soviet Government. He is one of our best automobile engineers. He used to work for Ford, and Ford thought highly of him; he suggested that Strokin stay and work for him. If Grandfather Ford were alive, he could have told you what his pupil is worth.

Colonel Cooper, an American engineer, was awarded the Order of the Red Banner of Labor for services as consultant for the Dnieper Hydropower Project. Hundreds of American engineers worked in our industries at the time of the First Five-Year Plan. We thank you for it and bow low before you for your help. *(Applause.)* You may be proud of our successes, just as a good teacher, or professor, is proud when his effort is rewarded by his pupil being worthy of his preceptor. We learned from you, and you need not be ashamed of your pupils, you should be proud of them, because now we want to catch up with you. *(Animation, applause.)* It follows that our people are bright pupils, not dunces. *(Laughter, applause.)* In the First Five-Year Plan years, when you helped us build our first tractor plant, it took us two years to get it going properly, because we had no experience. When Ford helped us build the Gorky Automobile Plant, we ruined quite a few machines before learning to make automobiles. But now we, your ex-pupils, have sent a rocket into outer space and a Soviet pennant has now reached the moon. *(Stormy applause.)* Not bad pupils, are we? *(Animation, applause.)* Yet there are still some people in your country who keep harping that people in the Soviet Union are little short of slaves. But what sort of slave system is that? How could a slave system have assured such unprecedented progress in science and art as we have made in our country?

The reason why Roman civilization, as well as Greek civilization, declined, esteemed Mr. Skouras, was that it was a civilization built on slave labor, which shackled man's energy, will and freedom. Science and the arts can attain full bloom only if there is the fullest freedom of the individual and of society. *(Applause.)*

You and we have different ideas on this matter. You say that profit, or business as you call it, is the prime mover of people's energy, of their intellect and initiative. We say a different thing:

107

The prime mover is man's conscience, his awareness of the fact that he is free and working for himself, for his kin, for the society in which he lives, that the means of production belong to society and not to some individual who grows rich by exploiting other people's labor.

You are against our concept and we are against yours. Well, what's to be done about it? Carry on under capitalism, with your corporations and whatever else you have. Don't seek salvation for "God's lost sheep"—the Soviet people, who have chosen the path of socialist development. You'll only gain by it if we come a cropper and return to the fold of capitalism. Why should you worry if you think we are on the wrong path? *(Laughter.)* You have done your civic duty. You have told us that we are following a path which you think leads us to a pitfall. That will do, thank you for warning us. But I say to you that I see no pitfall ahead but a clear vista, the future happiness of mankind. Some of you may believe that I don't understand certain simple things. That is their affair, of course. But I, too, am entitled to tell such people that they have not yet risen to an understanding of the new that is communist construction.

Where are we to seek a way out of the present situation? Shall we settle the matter in a free-for-all? That, indeed, is how disputes were settled in the past. But formerly things were much simpler; people would come to grips and tear out handfuls of each other's hair, beard and whiskers, and then new beards and new whiskers would grow in their place. But now you know that if a new rough-and-tumble ensued, there would be nothing left to grow; as we say in Russia, "It's too late to cry over lost hair after your head is cut off." *(Laughter, applause.)*

That is why, ladies and gentlemen, we say: Let us live in peace. *(Stormy applause.)* Let time judge who is right and who is wrong. Time is the best judge. This is our attitude. I have come to you so that we may achieve a better understanding of each other, so that you may get a better idea of what our people are like. I am not a delegate sent to conduct diplomatic negotiations, I am the guest of your President, the guest of your great country. And that is why I want to discuss things in a way that will enable us to find reasonable solutions and settle controversial issues with the object of banishing war and establishing peace and friendship between the peoples of our countries and between all peoples. *(Stormy applause.)*

I think that the argument with my brother Greek on this matter is over and that each retains his own opinion. I respect your opinion,

108

so you, too, leave mine alone. *(Animation.)* Carry on under capitalism, "and God help you," as the saying goes. *(Laughter, applause.)* And we, for our part, will carry on under socialism and build communism. At the moment you are ahead of us in the economic field, we still have to put in a great deal of work and sweat to catch up with you. Very good, we will put our backs to it but we will catch and pass you, and forge ahead. I am convinced of that. You may laugh at it for the moment, but you'd do better to wait till we pass you and say, "Good-bye, Messrs. Capitalists, our train is moving on." *(Animation.)* By the way, a group of U.S. economists who studied our country's potentialities in the competition with your country have estimated that in production the Soviet Union will overtake the United States by 1970. I repeat, it isn't I who say so but American economists. If you like, I will let you read their report. That is, if you haven't read it yet. I must say that nowadays I read less fiction and fewer political books, because I have to read mostly statements made by U.S. Senators, economists and journalists. *(Laughter.)*

Ladies and gentlemen, I had not meant to make a political speech here. It was Mr. Skouras who introduced class complications from the outset. *(Laughter.)* I did not want that, I wanted to say nice things to you. I wanted to tell you we were very happy to meet you. In the Soviet Union, you know, we have the deepest respect and affection for intellectuals. And you are not only intellectuals, but toilers of the most refined, I might say the most delicate, of arts— subtle artistry. That being so, you require gentle treatment, loving care and warmth, like orchids, which need the right humidity, light and warmth. In our country, we cannot think of making any progress without producing an intelligentsia of our own, without developing our culture in every way. There would be no point in building a new society without that.

I recall certain incidents of our Civil War, my meetings and conversations with intellectuals of the former, czarist Russia. I was in the Red Army when we beat the White Guards and drove them into the Black Sea. My unit was stationed in the Kuban region, and I was quartered in the house of an educated family. The landlady was a graduate of the St. Petersburg Institute for young ladies of gentle birth. As for me, I suppose I still smelled of coal when I was living in her house. There were other educated people in that house —a lawyer, engineer, teacher and musician. We Red Army men mixed with them. When they met me, a Communist, they saw that, far from eating human flesh, I was starving, to put it plainly. Sometimes I even had no bread, but I never tried to take any away from them or, indeed, ask for anything. They came to respect me. The mistress of the house saw that we Bolsheviks were not at all the sort of people our enemies made us out to be. Members of the old intelligentsia convinced themselves more and more that Communists were honest people who sought no personal gain and dedicated themselves to the common weal. We were still unpolished, uneducated workers at that time, but we wanted to receive an education, to learn to govern the state, to build a new society, and we devoted all our energy to it. I remember the landlady asking me: "Tell me, what do you know about ballet? You're a simple miner, aren't you?" To tell the truth, I didn't really know anything about ballet at that time, because I hadn't seen any ballet then and, moreover, had never seen a ballerina. *(Laughter.)* I had no idea what it was all about, so to speak. *(Laughter.)* But I said to her, "Just wait, we're going to have everything, ballet too." Frankly speaking, if I had been asked at that time just what we were going to have, I might not quite have known what to say, but I was certain that there was a better life ahead. It was Lenin's Party that had instilled this certainty in our hearts.

And now I wish to ask you what country has the most highly developed ballet. Would it be your country? No. Why, you don't even have a state opera and ballet theater. Your theaters subsist solely on the hand-outs of wealthy people. But in our country it is the state that appropriates funds for the development of art. The whole world recognizes that Soviet ballet is the most extensively developed. We are proud of it. When our ballet company toured the United States, you rewarded it with well-deserved applause and praise. And what about our dramatic theater, what about our stagecraft? I won't brag but will merely ask you to consult your conscience and tell me whether our theater is on the decline or on the rise. And what about our movies? You and we have different tastes. But it is a fact, isn't it, that our films win prizes at international festivals. They are awarded to our films by impartial people who know their business. One of the prizes at a recent world festival went to the screen version of *The Fate of a Man,* a story by M. A. Sholokhov, the outstanding writer, who is here with us. The film is a masterpiece.

We also give our intelligentsia substantial material support. At any rate, they don't have to go to the doctor to be treated for undernourishment; in fact, they often seek medical advice against excessive weight. *(Laughter.)* That isn't a bad indication. Professor Markov here, who is a prominent doctor, will bear me out. *(Applause.)*

Our art workers receive not only the remuneration that they earn. The best of them are also decorated or awarded Lenin Prizes. That is a token of the deep respect in which they are held by our people and government. Come and see our country, and speak to our art workers! And what about literature? We are proud of it. Meet Mikhail Alexandrovich Sholokhov, a Don Cossack. He has brought fame to our country by writing *And Quiet Flows the Don, Virgin Soil Upturned* and other excellent works.

Now I will answer a question put by my Greek friend. By the way, Mr. Skouras, I hope you are not offended that I take this liberty in speaking to you? It is just to show my good feelings for you. If you are offended in any way, I'm willing to apologize and to take no more liberties.

SKOURAS: I am honored to have the Premier of a great nation argue with me.

KHRUSHCHEV: I am not arguing, I am simply discussing matters with you. I am the guest and cannot argue with my host. *(Laughter, applause.)* Besides, it was you who started the argument, if that is what you call it. *(Laughter, applause.)* You referred here to the aid extended to Soviet people after the Civil War, during the terrible famine of 1921-1922, when ARA, the American Relief Administration, was set up to aid the starving population. The committee was headed by Herbert Hoover. We remember that well, and we thank you.

But I feel I must raise a "but" on this score. The "but" is that our people remember not only the fact that America helped us through ARA and that as a result thousands of people were saved from starvation in the Volga Region. They also remember that in the hard time after the October Revolution, U.S. troops led by their generals landed on Soviet soil to help the White Guards fight our Soviet system. And they were not the only ones to land. The Japanese landed too, the French landed in Odessa and the Germans advanced as far as the Soviet Caucasus. The armed forces of bourgeois Poland seized Kiev. The British, too, landed their forces to fight us. Many European capitalist countries, as well as the United States and Japan, sent their troops into an offensive against the young Soviet state in an effort to strangle our Revolution.

You can imagine what our plight was at that time. We were ruined by the First World War and then by the Civil War. Our

111

mines lay idle and our factories were at a standstill. We were starving, we had nothing to wear and we went barefoot. But what happened? In spite of all these terrific difficulties, we beat your troops, pushed all invaders into the sea and defeated the White Guards.

Why do I recall all this? For the simple reason that if you and your allies had not landed troops at that time, we would have made short shrift of the White Guards and would have had no Civil War, no ruin and no famine. And you wouldn't have had to help Soviet people through ARA, whose work you have just mentioned.

But even so, even in these circumstances, we thank the Americans for the help they gave us.

Your armed intervention in Russia was the most unpleasant thing that ever occurred in the relations between our two countries, for we had never waged war against America until then; our troops have never set foot on American soil, while your troops have set foot on Soviet soil. You see how it is, ladies and gentlemen. Please excuse me for these comments. I assure you that I had planned to make a very short and unemotional speech. But I cannot be silent when someone treads on my pet corn, even if he does so after putting a pad on it. I cannot put up with it. I want to be a worthy partner who gives a worthy explanation in defense of his country, his people, his state and our ideology.

In conclusion, I want to express once more my heartfelt thanks for the invitation to visit your country, and to say that my companions and I are pleased with our stay in America. But, on the other hand, I cannot help voicing my disappointment, voicing some surprise, at a certain circumstance.

We have always regarded the United States as a strong, well-organized state whose people have a highly-developed culture. Here we are now, in your city, where you have the cream of the artistic world—film stars, as you say in your country. Also living here are industrial workers, ordinary Americans, people of a vast variety of trades. We should have liked to meet them, to see how they live, and how they work and rest. Now just think of it, I, a Soviet man, the Prime Minister of the Soviet Union, have come to you as a guest; when I was on my way here, an itinerary was drawn up for me and a program of what I could see here and what places I could visit. It was planned, among other things, that I would visit Disneyland. But I have just been told that I cannot go to Disneyland. *(Laughter.)* Why not? I asked. Is it by any chance because you now have rocket-launching pads there? *(Laughter.)* "No," they tell me, "you can't go

112

there because"—just listen to this!—"The American authorities cannot guarantee your safety if you go there."

What is it? Has cholera or plague broken out there that I might catch? *(Laughter.)* Or has Disneyland been seized by bandits who might destroy me? But your policemen are such strong men, they could lift a bull by the horns. Surely they could deal effectively with bandits! Then I said I should like to go to Disneyland just the same and see how Americans spend their leisure. *(Applause.)* "Do as you like," they answered me, "but in that case we cannot guarantee your safety." What was I to do—go and commit suicide? *(Laughter.)* This is the situation I, your guest, find myself in! It is more than I can understand. I won't know how to explain it to my people. Come to our country if you like, we will go with anyone, you may walk in our streets and parks, and I guarantee that a foreign guest will hear nothing from Soviet people but words of respect and welcome. What am I to say to the organizers of my U.S. tour? I thought you had a well-organized household. Putting me in a closed car and stewing me in the sun is not the right way to guarantee my safety. I thought I could walk freely in your country and meet Americans. But I am told it's impossible. This development causes me bitter regret and I cannot but express my disappointment.

You might say, "What a restless guest." But I keep to the Russian maxim, "Break bread with me, but speak your mind." And that should in no way affect our friendly relations.

Please forgive me for speaking somewhat vehemently or heatedly. But the temperature here is to blame for it, to some extent. *(Laughter.)* Besides, Mr. Skouras had warmed me up to it. *(Laughter, applause.)* Please forgive me if I have said anything not quite pleasing to your ear, if I have let slip anything that has jarred you a little. The sentiment that guided me in speaking here before you was one of friendship and respect for you, for your people and for your President, Mr. Eisenhower.

Thank you for your attention. Thank you, dear friends, thank you, Mr. Johnston. *(Stormy, prolonged applause.)*

SPEECH BY N. S. KHRUSHCHEV AT RECEPTION GIVEN BY THE MUNICIPAL AUTHORITIES AND THE ASSOCIATION ON INTERNATIONAL AFFAIRS OF LOS ANGELES

On the evening of September 19 the municipal authorities and the Association on International Affairs of Los Angeles held a reception in honor of N. S. Khrushchev.

113

In his introductory speech Norris Poulson, the Mayor of Los Angeles, allowed himself to repeat the already time-and-again-refuted, distorted version of one of N. S. Khrushchev's speeches and permitted himself to make tactless attacks against the guest. This behavior of the mayor aroused surprise and disapproval on the part of many present at the reception. Later it was condemned in a number of articles in the American press and in numerous letters and telegrams from ordinary Americans.

N. S. Khrushchev made a speech at the reception which was received with great attention and often interrupted by applause.

MR. MAYOR, LADIES AND GENTLEMEN:

Allow me to thank you for the hospitality accorded us and for the invitation to take part in this gathering. We are pleased to meet representatives of the business world and the intellectuals of the city of Los Angeles.

We highly appreciate the opportunity we have been given of acquainting ourselves with the life and achievements of the great American people. Of course, one must travel a good deal in so vast and varied a country as the United States of America to form a more or less correct idea of it. But they say that if you want to get a true idea about the United States you cannot do it without visiting sunny California. Today, when we had flown here from the Eastern seaboard of the United States and seen Los Angeles (from our car, of course), the truth of this opinion was brought home to us.

In the middle of the last century California won fame for its gold mining, and now you figuratively call it the "Golden State." But it might be called the "Golden State" even if there had been no gold dust in its bowels. Fertile land, a warm and mellow climate and landscapes of unique beauty, combined with enormous outlays of human labor—something which is evident at every turn—have made California a rich land. Orchards, vineyards and cotton fields border upon one of the country's greatest industrial centers, Los Angeles. As one sees your city, one is seized by a feeling of respect for the enterprise and indomitable will shown by the American pioneer settlers and their descendants in combating the forces of nature.

You people of California, the development of which began much later than that of other U.S. areas, should probably understand the enthusiasm of Soviet people who are now building new big cities, the world's largest hydropower stations and industrial plants in the erstwhile wildernesses of Siberia and Kazakhstan, settling and cultivating what were almost uninhabited tracts of land. To enable you to judge the scale of that effort, I can tell you that in the expanses of Siberia and Kazakhstan the Soviet people have in recent years developed virgin land whose total area is more than double the entire agricultural area of California. To be sure, there is some difference in the natural conditions of our two countries. Your pioneers had to develop the new lands of California in a scorching sun. Soviet people, on the other hand, are developing the riches of Kazakhstan and Siberia in a bracing cold of forty degrees below zero Centigrade. Anybody who finds it hot here may come to our country. He can cool himself there.

I should like to deal briefly at this meeting with the aims of our U.S. visit. We gratefully accepted the U.S. President's invitation to visit your country, to acquaint ourselves with the life of your people and to discuss with the President a number of questions that are of interest to both our countries.

There is one question which is equally important to the Soviet and American peoples and to all other peoples—the question of ensuring peace. Everybody realizes that the welfare and prosperity of nations and states depend on the course which international relations will take in the next few years—whether it will be toward strengthening peace or whether the war danger will go on increasing.

What is it that today prevents states from joining their efforts and bending them to ease international tension? First of all, it is the atmosphere of the cold war, which weighs heavily on relations between countries, in particular, those between the USSR and the USA.

One can at least understand it when strained relations between countries are due to real antagonisms, such as, for example, territorial disputes or economic claims. But it is a feature of the cold war that it involves countries which have no direct antagonisms of that kind.

I have been told that in Los Angeles one can observe an atmospheric phenomenon known as "smog," which occurs when in bad weather smoke and soot get mixed with fog, with the result that breathing becomes difficult. It seems to me that smog is in many respects like the cold war.

The cold war is called "cold" because so far it has produced no flames, fortunately enough. But it is accumulating a great deal of inflammable material that may flare up from any chance spark. The cold war produces more than enough soot. To normalize cooperation between states, it is indispensable by joint effort to put an end to the cold war and get rid of the prejudices, dislikes and mutual distrust engendered by it. The sooner we end the cold war, the better it will be for our peoples and for all mankind.

I should like to believe that the exchange of visits between President Eisenhower and myself will contribute toward the cold war fading into the past for good, with a warmer climate setting in in the relations between countries, a climate similar to that of California or to the no-less-blessed climate of the South Coast of the Crimea, where I recently spent my vacation.

As everyone knows, the cold war has given rise to quite a number of international problems that are now awaiting solution.

The most important and pressing problem is that of disarmament. Weighing the negative consequences of the arms race, one does not primarily think so much of the human labor, knowledge and ingenuity spent to no sensible purpose, nor of the heavy economic burden it imposes even on the mightiest powers, as of the danger of a military explosion that inevitably attends the arms race.

There are now many people who realize the extremely grave danger arising from the arms race. Indeed, it is an open secret that modern means of annihilation have been stockpiled in such quantities that they can cause terrible destruction and take an enormous toll of human lives.

Until the recent past long distances and oceans served as natural barriers to military conflicts expanding and crossing from continent to continent. Both the First and the Second World Wars chiefly devastated Europe and some regions of Asia and Africa. Today the situation is different. The distances between the remotest points on the globe are now measured in tens of minutes, and the most devastating means of extermination—nuclear weapons—can be carried to any area of the globe.

We in the Soviet Union often wonder why, despite our desire to reach agreement on disarmament with the Western Powers, we are being forced to take part in the arms race. Perhaps the object of the arms race is to achieve military superiority over the Soviet Union. But whatever you may say, experience shows that the arms race cuts both ways.

The arms race is not benefiting either the Soviet or the American people; and no matter how you look at it, it is becoming more and more absurd and dangerous. The armaments curve has crept so far upward that today the need for an earnest and honest understanding on disarmament is greater than ever.

Those present here probably know that at yesterday's UN General Assembly meeting, the Soviet Government put forward cardinal proposals on disarmament. The gist of these proposals is that they call for the general and complete disarmament of states within the shortest possible time—roughly four years—for the destruction of all types of armament, nuclear weapons and missiles among them, the disbandment of all armed forces and the abolition of war ministries and general staffs. The states would keep only small, agreed-upon police (militia) forces intended for the maintenance of internal order and public safety, and equipped only with small arms.

To appreciate in full measure the significance of our new proposals, one should also bear in mind that these proposals remove one of the main difficulties that arose in all the previous disarmament talks, namely, the problem of control, for, given complete disarmament, the states will have nothing to conceal from each other and control can accordingly be complete and comprehensive. It will be control and not military reconnaissance because, in the absence of armies, reconnaissance becomes pointless.

By making these proposals, we want to solve the disarmament problem completely and for all time, to put the states in conditions in which they will have no material means of waging war. Indeed, it is hard to imagine that having neither aircraft, tanks, rockets nor any other modern weapons, the Americans and Russians would fight each other with, say, forks or table knives. We have invariable faith in the good aspirations of man and think that human beings are not born to kill each other, but to live in peace and friendship. You know that the prime commandment of the Christian religion is, "Thou shalt not kill."

We know, of course, that the idea of disarmament has many opponents and that our new proposals will not be to everybody's liking. But we should like to believe that these proposals, made in good faith and representing the utmost of what a Great Power can bring itself to do, especially in the present state of international tension, will bring a favorable response from the United States. We should also like to hope that as a result of our talks with President Eisenhower, the Soviet and U.S. Governments will gain a better understanding of each other's attitude to the disarmament question and will subsequently join their efforts in solving this most formidable and most vital problem of our time. And surely, if our two countries find a common language and arrive at a common opinion on ques-

117

tions of disarmament, it will be safe to say that the greater part of the difficulties are over and done with.

Our peoples fought shoulder to shoulder against the common enemy in the grim days of the Second World War. And since our peoples were together in the most crucial periods of history, what surer indication can there be that fundamental and lasting interests draw the two countries to cooperation and friendship?

In this connection, I recall what President Eisenhower said in Geneva in 1955. "The American people," he said, "would like to be friends with the Soviet peoples. There are no natural differences between our peoples or our nations. There are no territorial conflicts or commercial rivalries. Historically, our two countries have always been at peace."

The peoples of the USSR and the USA have much in common. The meetings I have had convince me that the American people value and love peace. I have discovered many other traits that bring our two peoples closer together. They are industry, the quest for the new, the urge for knowledge and technological progress and, lastly, such good human traits as frankness, a sense of humor, good will and love of country.

We are happy, of course, that of late a fresh note has come into Soviet-American relations. Mutual visits and meetings of Soviet and American statesmen, livelier cultural, scientific and technological contacts, exchanges in the fields of agriculture, education, public health and exhibitions, and expanding travel are all shoots of the new element in Soviet-American relations. Los Angeles is the heart of the American cinema. The cinema is the most popular of arts and exerts a tremendous influence on the life of society. If it takes the right direction, it can serve as an important medium for promoting peace and friendship among peoples, for spreading humane ideas and good will. But if it takes the wrong direction, it will become a medium for whipping up hatred and may seriously prejudice the cause of friendship, peace and progress. What ends this powerful art will serve depends on the film workers. We attach great importance to the development of the cinema in our country, to the making of films that educate people in the lofty ideals of international friendship, humanism, peace and progress.

Los Angeles faces East. The Pacific washes both the Los Angeles waterfront and that of the Soviet city of Vladivostok. In meeting representatives of your city, I should like to re-emphasize

118

the Soviet Union's readiness to develop all-round contacts and establish friendly cooperation with the United States of America.

Strictly speaking, I had expected to conclude my speech with this. But the speakers who preceded me raised some points which I cannot leave unanswered. *(Laughter, applause.)*

I turn to you, Mr. Mayor, my host. You said in your speech that we wanted to bury you. You are treating my companions and myself to an excellent meal and we thank you for it, but I will speak my mind just the same. Is that the custom in your country? *(Applause.)*

I want to ask you why you must take up again what I dealt with in earlier speeches following my arrival in America. I suppose mayors, too, read the press. *(Laughter, applause.)* In any case, the chairmen of city Soviets in our country read the newspapers unfailingly. If they did not read the press, they might not be elected for another term. *(Laughter, applause.)*

Ladies and gentlemen, some people don't seem to want to get off the hobby-horse of the cold war and the arms race. If they refuse to get off it and hang on to the saddle, where will it take them and what will they get? If such people want the arms race and war, let them stay on their horse. Then everybody will see clearly that there can be no question of disarmament. On the contrary, the arms race will gain in intensity. If you are unwilling to accept disarmament and want to continue the arms race, we will have no choice but to go on making rockets, which in our country are being turned out by the assembly-line method.

Gentlemen, think well what that may lead to. You know that I have come here with good intentions, but it appears that some of you would like to reduce the matter to a joke. I repeat that it is a question of extremely serious things—the question of peace or war, the life or death of people. We offer you a hand of friendship. If you don't want it, say so.

(Voice: "We want it!")

KHRUSHCHEV: In that case we must show a sensible approach to the question under discussion. We mustn't play with words. We hold much too important posts, and playing with words may have most deplorable consequences for our peoples. *(Prolonged applause.)*

Ladies and gentlemen, since your Mayor doesn't seem to have read what I said in Washington, I should like to make it clear once more what I said there.

I have already said that the words "We will bury capitalism" should not be taken literally, as is done by ordinary gravediggers who carry a spade and dig graves and bury the dead. What I had in mind was the outlook for the development of human society. Socialism will inevitably succeed capitalism. According to our doctrine, it will be so and according to yours, it won't. History will decide which is right and which is wrong. I say it again—I've almost worn my tongue thin repeating it—you may live under capitalism and we will live under socialism and build communism. The one whose system proves better will win. We will not bury you, nor will you bury us. Carry on to your hearts' content, and God be with you. (Applause.)

Ladies and gentlemen, it was not to have a cup of tea or, say, a glass of brandy that your President invited me to this country. I have companions with whom I could do that back home if I felt like it, without having to fly thousands of kilometers. The President, too, could do it at his home, and without me. It is clear to me, of course, that the U.S. President will not accept the communist point of view with regard to the development of human society, and I think the President, too, doesn't expect to convert me to capitalism. (Animation.)

Why has President Eisenhower invited me to the United States? It was wisdom that evidently prompted him to do so in order to find contact with the Soviet Union and reach an understanding to live in peace. We know that you don't like Communists. But we are neighbors. The Pacific separates us, but it also connects our countries. The question today is whether there is to be peace between our countries or whether there is to be war. I want to tell you frankly that I am deeply concerned about the persistence, the deliberate misrepresentation of the ideas expressed by me on the part of some of your spokesmen, who seek to maintain the state of cold war.

Make your choice: Shall we advance together to peace, or shall we continue the cold war and the arms race? I have not come to plead with you. We are no less strong than you. I have already made many speeches in the United States but have not once resorted to the word "arms," to say nothing of "missiles." And if I have spoken about it today, you must understand that I had no choice.

Perhaps some people would like to create the impression that we have come here as poor relations and beg you for peace as for alms. But don't fall into error. All peoples want peace. If armaments yield profits to your monopolies, if it is suggested that we should compete in arms production and not in peaceful pursuits, then it is a terrible course to steer! Think where that will get us, and make your choice. The point is this: Either our meeting with President Eisenhower will result in the relaxation of tension, in the termination of the cold war, or we will part without achieving the results desired.

This visit by the Chairman of the Council of Ministers of the Soviet Union is the first visit made to the United States by a head of our state in the history of our countries. Nevertheless, we lived. If you do not accept our idea of working for peace, for the promotion of friendly relations between our countries, perhaps we had better go home and then let everyone know who really wants peace and friendship and who obstructs them.

You may well say that you will carry on as you have done so far. But it should be clear to anyone that it is better to live in peace and friendship than to live with rockets trained on each other, that it is better to live in a pure atmosphere in which you can sleep peacefully, secure in the knowledge that you will have peace today and tomorrow, that it will be permanent and durable. *(Applause.)*

When I hear such talk I wonder sometimes whether some people have hit on the idea of inviting Khrushchev to the United States to give him a "rubbing-down," to show him the strength and might of the United States of America, so that his knees would bend a bit, so to speak. If that is what those gentlemen expect, they are sorely mistaken. It won't take us long to fly home from here. We took about 12 hours to fly here, and I suppose we can make the homeward trip in about 10 hours. What do you think, Comrade Tupolev?

A. A. TUPOLEV*: Yes, Nikita Sergeyevich, we can.

KHRUSHCHEV: Meet the son of Academician Tupolev, our famous aircraft designer.

I think we will be more sensible and find a common language. We should all strive for peace. And now I want to answer Mr. Lodge about his proposal to exchange books. Today, on our flight here, and while exchanging opinions, he suggested exchanging books on the history of our states.

I can say in this connection, let us not hide our identities. You represent the capitalist world and we, the socialist world. That being so, not all of our literature suits you, just as not all of your literature suits us. Let us not beat about the bush.

We are for exchanging cultural values, provided these exchanges serve to improve our relations, not to worsen them. When dealing

---

*Eminent Soviet airplane designer.

Khrushchev is seen here at the San Luis Obispo station on the way from Los Angeles to San Francisco.

with a partner, we should adhere to the right principle. If you palm off some bad goods on him today, he will stop buying them from you. The rule we stick to is this: You offer us your "merchandise," we choose and buy what we need. We offer you something in turn, and you buy what you like. If you don't like it, you don't have to buy it. *(Laughter, applause.)*

In the Ukraine we have a popular saying (there are probably some Ukrainians here, too): "Your eyes saw what you were buying, so now eat it even if they pop out." *(Laughter.)*

However, I agree to Mr. Lodge's proposal. But if in writing your history you advertise your ideology between the lines, you must bear in mind that Russians, Ukrainians, Byelorussians, Uzbeks—in short, all the peoples of the Soviet Union—are now educated, they know what is what and will not read any such books of yours. Our people will only buy what suits them, and we will sell you what suits you. We want to be good partners in exchanging cultural merchandise. *(Applause.)*

This is not an objection to Mr. Lodge. I repeat that I agree to his proposal. I am only saying on what terms such a deal can be concluded, so that you will not say later that Khrushchev heard you and agreed, and then refused to accept your merchandise. If the merchandise is good, we will take it; and if it isn't, we won't. *(Animation, applause.)*

Thank you for your attention. I wish you every success and happiness. *(Stormy applause.)*

IN SAN FRANCISCO

N. S. Khrushchev and his party arrived in San Francisco on the evening of September 20. A welcoming address was delivered at the railway station by Mayor Christopher. Replying to the greetings, N. S. Khrushchev said:

MR. MAYOR, LADIES AND GENTLEMEN:

I am very glad to have arrived in your remarkable city of San Francisco which is so famous. On approaching your city I saw places resembling the southern parts of our country.

I thank you, Mr. Mayor, for the good and kind wishes and for the promise of hospitality to me and my party in San Francisco.

As regards the questions which the Mayor mentioned, concerning our ideological views and your attitude toward them, I must say that I never evaded political arguments, to be exact, talks. If you wish, I am prepared to participate in controversy. I, of course, will defend my positions and show the good aspects of our system. You will have the opportunity of showing your good aspects. Please defend your positions in the discussion and I will defend mine. Talks and discussions on political subjects, if wisely approached, cannot spoil our relations or aggravate them; on the contrary, they could facilitate our *rapprochement* if every one will be tolerant toward the other side.

If we are to avoid talks and discussions on political subjects when we meet with you, then it would be like a meeting of two dumb people who only mumble instead of talking. This is not natural for normal people.

I consider that we should adhere to one rule, that these talks and discussions should not deepen our differences on the basic question, that of the necessity of having good—already not mentioning friendly—relations between us so as to ensure peace between our countries and between the peoples of all countries.

I express my thanks for the welcome to you, Mr. Mayor, to all the inhabitants of San Francisco who properly understand my visit and who correctly consider that I have come here in order to convey to you greetings from our people, wishes of friendship and cooperation between our countries. (*Applause.*)

MEETING WITH U.S. TRADE-UNION LEADERS

N. S. Khrushchev, Chairman of the Council of Ministers of the USSR, met with a group of U.S. trade-union leaders in San Francisco on September 20. The meeting took place on the initiative of some leaders of the American Federation of Labor-Congress of Industrial Organizations (AFL-CIO).

The Americans present at the meeting were James B. Carey, Vice-President of the AFL-CIO (President of the International Union of Electrical, Radio and Machine Workers); Walter P. Reuther, Vice-President of the AFL-CIO (President of the United Automobile, Aircraft and Agricultural Implement Workers); O. A. Knight (President of the International Union of Oil, Chemical and Atomic Workers); Karl F. Feller (President of the United Brewery Workers); Emil Rieve (Chairman of the Executive Council of the Textile Workers Union); Joseph Curran (President of the National Maritime Union); Paul L. Phillips (President of the United Papermakers and Paperworkers); George L. P. Weaver, (Union of Electrical Workers) and Victor G. Reuther (United Automobile, Aircraft and Agricultural Implement Workers).

Some questions about the international situation and Soviet-American relations were brought up during the discussion, which lasted over three hours and occasionally became sharp.

The U.S. press carried numerous contradictory reports of the meeting.

The source of information on what happened at the meeting was a news conference which the U.S. union leaders called late in the evening, immediately after parting with N. S. Khrushchev. It appears from the press reports that Walter Reuther, Vice-President of the AFL-CIO, made extraordinary statements at the news conference, about the remarks of the head of the Soviet Government, attributing to him things which he had not said or done. The news conference, according to the *San Francisco Examiner*, ended in chaos. According to the same newspaper, two of the union leaders present at the meeting—Rieve, President of the Textile Workers Union, and Curran, President of the National Maritime Union, told reporters that a considerable part of Reuther's statements about what had happened was a lot of nonsense.

On September 22 the *New York Times* published what it considered to be a complete transcript of the discussion. That transcript shows, however, that those who made it reported the discussion arbitrarily. They were apparently afraid to convey to the reader the actual statements made by the head of the Soviet Government.

To set the record straight, the Press Group of the Chairman of the Council of Ministers of the USSR published the following account of the discussion in question, the main points of which have been withheld from the public or distorted in the tendentious accounts given by some U.S. newspapers:

At the very beginning of the discussion, James Carey and Walter Reuther said that they and their colleagues were greatly interested in a frank exchange of views on major international problems of a pressing character. Carey stressed that they were interested in the new Soviet proposals for general and complete disarmament submitted by N. S. Khrushchev to the United Nations. He said that the American workers were concerned about the fact that enormous

Khrushchev greets citizens of San Luis Obispo on the way from Los Angeles to San F

sums are being spent on armaments. Reuther, for his part, said that the most urgent problem was that of how to preserve peace. Carey and others asked N. S. Khrushchev to tell them about the new Soviet disarmament proposals. But, in effect, they did not wait to hear the reply and went on to ask other questions—in particular, about economic aid to underdeveloped countries.

Answering these questions, N. S. Khrushchev pointed out that the proposals for general and complete disarmament submitted by the Soviet Government to the UN, which envisage the allocation of a certain percentage of the funds saved on arms reduction, could be instrumental in aiding underdeveloped countries.

"But we aren't waiting till an agreement is reached on disarmament," N. S. Khrushchev said. "We are giving the underdeveloped countries substantial economic aid right now. On the one hand, we

help them through the UN with funds, medical supplies and food. On the other hand, we help them on a bilateral basis. In India we are helping the government to build a steel mill, chemical and machine-building plants, and pharmaceutical factories. We grant the Indian Government credits; provide it with blueprints for industrial plants; send our specialists to help the Indians; and train engineers, technicians and skilled workers for plants under construction. We also render large-scale assistance to the Arab countries and countries in Africa. It is well known that the Soviet Union is extending friendly assistance to Cambodia, Burma, Ceylon, Yemen, Ethiopia and other countries."

Reuther interrupted N. S. Khrushchev and tried to discredit the Soviet Union's policy of assistance to economically underdeveloped countries. He went so far as to accuse the Soviet Union of using aid to underdeveloped countries for selfish purposes, for purposes of the cold war.

In repulsing that attack, N. S. Khrushchev said: "You are shooting your shafts in the wrong direction. The Soviet Union has never exploited anyone, nor is it exploiting anyone now. It helps underdeveloped countries as a friend, without any political strings attached. For example, we shipped thousands of tons of grain to Yemen. Yet its system is not socialist. It is a kingdom. Do you call that aid for selfish purposes? Just what selfish aims do we achieve thereby? We don't make any profit on that. We act as friends. But look at what the imperialists are doing. The U.S. monopolies are exploiting the riches of the underdeveloped countries and making big profits. Britain, France and other capitalist countries are doing likewise. Why cannot those countries expand their help to the underdeveloped countries out of the profits they derive in that way? The Soviet Government has put forward and submitted to the UN a proposal to that effect. The Soviet Union trades with all countries on a basis of mutual advantage."

Unable to counter N. S. Khrushchev's arguments in any way, Reuther suddenly shouted: "You are exploiting the people of East Germany!" This statement drew smiles even from Reuther's colleagues.

N. S. Khrushchev said:

"Where did you see that dream? Calm yourself, you have the shivers. Who empowered you to speak on behalf of the German people? Why do you keep trying to speak for other peoples? You are pampered by the fact that many countries depend on the United

States and are compelled to seek your aid. But the socialist countries stand firmly on their own feet. We don't take off our hats to you. The Soviet ruble has never bowed, is not bowing now and will never bow to the dollar."

The disarmament problem came up next. Reuther and some other trade-union leaders repeated the assertions of the commercial press to the effect that the Soviet plan for general and complete disarmament had been put forward merely for propaganda purposes and that the USSR spent as much on armaments as the USA, that is, 40 billion dollars a year.

"First of all," N. S. Khrushchev replied, "calculated in your currency, we spend 25 billion on defense and not 40 billion. In the second place, your statement that the Soviet proposals are propaganda makes me, a former miner, feel sorry for you. They say you were born in a working-class environment, but you talk like a spokesman for the capitalists. I can understand it when Hearst prints things like that. But when an American trade-union leader repeats them, I think bitterly of how thoroughly the monopolists have corrupted you!"

However, Reuther continued to repeat the allegations of reactionary propaganda, which distort the Soviet proposals. Among other things, he asserted that the Soviet disarmament plan did not envisage the establishment of control.

"Why is it," N. S. Khrushchev said, "that you know Dulles' arguments so well and are so ignorant of the Soviet stand? We are for all-embracing control, but how should it be organized? The United States proposes setting up control first and talking of disarmament afterward. At a time when the U.S. has encircled us with its military bases, control without disarmament can only mean one thing—military reconnaissance. What we propose, however, is to organize control by stages, accordingly as disarmament is carried out."

"But we propose organizing an equal measure of control for the USA and the Soviet Union," Reuther said.

"No, you don't, because those aren't equal terms," N. S. Khrushchev replied. "U.S. military bases surround our frontiers, while we have no bases on the American continent. How would you feel if there were Soviet military bases in Mexico and Canada?"

"Who is keeping you from having them?" said Victor Reuther, brother of the Vice-President of the AFL-CIO. "Set them up."

(This observation, provocative in effect, brought indignant protests from the entire assembly.)

"How can you, a spokesman for the working class, bring yourself to talk like that!" N. S. Khrushchev said to Victor Reuther.

Walter Reuther made a clumsy attempt to change the subject, saying that it was late and that the Prime Minister was "tired."

N. S. Khrushchev said that it was impossible to discuss things by jumping from one question to another like fleas. "Is it an earnest discussion you want or is it something else?" he asked. "You side-stepped one question, then another, and are now jumping to a third. Disarmament is the question of questions. We want you to get us right, so I must set out our stand in detail."

Nevertheless, Walter Reuther hastened to give the floor to Rieve for fresh questions. The latter raised several questions—about the role of state ownership in the capitalist and socialist countries, about democracy and dictatorship, control of the press and radio, exchange of information, and so on. He, too, repeated the attacks which hostile propaganda usually makes on the Soviet Union and the other socialist countries.

It was obvious from the manner in which Rieve put his questions that he had an exceedingly vague, and in many cases false, notion of Soviet realities.

Walter Reuther, who watched his colleague put questions according to the notes that lay in front of him, prompted Rieve to be sure to inquire about the one-party system. But Rieve ignored that.

N. S. Khrushchev said that the questions raised by Rieve were elementary and that in the Soviet Union they were studied in political study groups of the elementary type.

Then Walter Reuther, in an obvious effort to give the discussion a sharper turn, put an additional question. "Does the system of state ownership necessitate dictatorship which rules out democracy?" he asked.

While, in answering Rieve, N. S. Khrushchev described the difference between state ownership in the socialist countries, where the means of production belong to the entire people, and state ownership in the capitalist countries, where nationalization of the means of production leaves them in the hands of the bourgeoisie, the ruling class, Mr. Reuther suddenly said that "the highest degree of socialism has been achieved in Israel," where, so he said, 60 per cent of industry belongs to the trade unions.

Asked who in that case was in power in Israel, Mr. Reuther failed to give a direct reply.

N. S. Khrushchev explained that the fundamental issue in characterizing a particular social system is that of state power, of whom it belongs to—whether the working class, working people in general, or the exploiting classes. If state power is held by the people, the means of production are socialist, public property. Not so when nationalization of the means of production is carried out under conditions where power belongs to the capitalists. N. S. Khrushchev said that the Communists are proponents of the dictatorship of the working class and that the tasks of socialist construction can only be effectively carried out if state power passes into the hands of the working people. Working-class dictatorship, far from ruling out democracy, provides every condition for the development of genuine democracy. It is in itself the highest form of democracy.

Walter Reuther said again that the Prime Minister was probably "tired" and that they must hurry and ask other questions. This brought the following sarcastic comment from N. S. Khrushchev: "Will you have strength enough to vie with me? I'm in good form. I will not tire of fighting for the working-class cause as long as I live. Let us have a business-like talk if you want it. Our time isn't limited."

Joseph Curran, President of the National Maritime Union, said he wanted to ask what he called a question from everyday life. "I was in the Soviet Union in the thirties," he said, "when we delivered equipment purchased by you. We are pleased with the technical progress you have made. I should like to know whether the collective bargaining system will develop as technology makes progress in your industry, and whether the workers will have the right to strike. How do trade unions defend the interests of the working people?"

"I see what you mean," N. S. Khrushchev said. "I'm glad that you have the class instinct in dealing with questions of trade-union activity. But it seems that you have no idea at all of conditions in a socialist state, of the position of the working class there or of the role of the trade unions. You measure everything with the yardstick you are accustomed to in the United States."

Seeing that Curran took an interest in the explanation which the head of the Soviet Government was giving, Victor Reuther began talking about the "personality cult."

Curran cut him short. "Why do you butt in!" he said.

N. S. Khrushchev went on, speaking to Curran:

"I like your question because it is so forthright, and I will give you a forthright answer. We had strikes in the first few years after the October Revolution. I myself used to go to the striking workers to talk to them. Nowadays our workers do not strike. Why? You'll find the answer to that question if you recall certain facts. In what capitalist country would the government draw up plans to raise working-class living standards without the workers exerting pressure on it? It is more than one can imagine that in the capitalist countries wages would be raised while the working day was reduced, without the workers striking to achieve it. But in the Soviet Union this matter is being handled as a priority task. The government, the workers and the trade unions are cooperating closely in the matter of increasing wages further while reducing working hours. All we need is to lay the economic groundwork for it. Speaking tentatively, I think that if our proposal for general and complete disarmament were accepted, we could begin the transition to a six-hour working day and higher wages much earlier than 1964, the year envisaged in the seven-year plan. Soviet workers are always abreast of their country's economic development and know well whether or not there are, at any given moment, practical possibilities for a further rise in wages."

Curran thanked N. S. Khrushchev for his answer.

Walter Reuther made a fresh attempt to sharpen the discussion by alleging that the Soviet trade unions were "an extension of the government," and wanted to know why the Soviet trade unions did not come out against the Party. Some of the unionists asked for the floor but Reuther would not listen, and tried to speak for all of them.

"You are like a nightingale," N. S. Khrushchev said, smiling. "It closes its eyes when it sings, and sees nothing and hears nobody but itself." The audience burst out laughing and Mr. Reuther flushed. Nevertheless, he kept harping on his point, posing as a defender of Soviet workers.

"Why do you stick your nose into other people's plans?" N. S. Khrushchev asked. "The Soviet workers settle their problems by themselves, and get along without outside interference. There will be no real talk as long as you keep trying to lecture others."

"There is such a thing as international working-class solidarity," Reuther declared pompously.

"You dare talk about international solidarity after you've split the World Federation of Trade Unions and opposed your trade unions to those of most countries of the world," N. S. Khrushchev replied.

Reuther made no answer. He hastened to pass to another question as he did each time that he had nothing to say, and gave the floor to Knight.

Knight asked two questions. He casually raised the question of so-called free elections in Germany. His utterances on the so-called "Hungarian question" were in the same vein.

"Do you know anything about the German Democratic Republic?" N. S. Khrushchev asked him. "Have you ever been there? I have been there more than once and I can tell you that the German Democratic Republic is built on a most democratic foundation. All matters there are decided by a democratically elected government. Private ownership of the means of production has been abolished there and state power belongs to the working people. The working class of the German Democratic Republic is headed by the Socialist Unity Party of Germany, a party devoted to the interests of the working class. There are also other democratic parties there. As regards elections in Germany, that is an internal affair of the Germans themselves, as I have said repeatedly. Let them do as they decide between themselves. No one has a right to interfere in their internal affairs."

N. S. Khrushchev then firmly repelled attempts to pull the so-called Hungarian question out of the bag again.

During the discussion of this question Mr. Reuther unwittingly betrayed shocking ignorance. He began to "defend" Comrade Janos Kadar as if Kadar were a bourgeois nationalist. It was not until his colleagues burst out laughing, intimating that he meant Imre Nagy, that Reuther began to correct himself awkwardly.

Commenting on Reuther's attitude in "defending" the Hungarian people, N. S. Khrushchev said:

"The Hungarian People's Republic has its own Constitution, its legislation and its lawful government, elected by democratic procedure. It is developing freely, and has made considerable progress in socialist construction. What happened in Hungary in 1956? There was a revolt of anti-popular elements there, who were dissatisfied with the working people's rule. The Hungarian counterrevolution, instigated by international reactionary forces, sought to overthrow the socialist system. In doing so, the conspirators used arms received from the West. They acted on instructions also coming from the West. Having seized power in Budapest for a few days, the counterrevolutionaries began to commit outrages, to shoot and otherwise exterminate honest people. At that crucial moment, the Hungarian Revolutionary Government headed by Janos Kadar asked for our aid. We complied with that request, and we are proud of it. If we had not come to the aid of the people's government headed by Janos Kadar, the fascists might have seized power in Hungary. By render-

133

ing the Hungarian people fraternal assistance in their struggle against the fascist rebels, we did our international duty."

Phillips proposed passing to a fresh subject, and echoed the claims repeatedly made by capitalist spokesmen in interviews with N. S. Khrushchev in the United States regarding unhampered circulation of reactionary literature and anti-Soviet information in the USSR.

"What is your favorite dish?" N. S. Khrushchev asked Phillips.

"Roast beef," Phillips replied.

"And I prefer borshch," N. S. Khrushchev said. "You don't eat it, but I'm very fond of it. You are for capitalism and I am for socialism. Why am I not answering your question in greater detail? For the simple reason that I have been asked that question many times here and have answered it each time. It seems that you don't like my reply and wish to hear something different. But there's nothing to be done about it—you and we have different notions of freedom. When we were in Hollywood they danced the cancan for us. The girls who dance it have to pull up their skirts and show their backsides. They are good honest actresses but have to perform that dance. They are compelled to adapt themselves to the tastes of depraved people. People in your country will go to see it, but Soviet people would scorn such a spectacle. It is pornographic. It is the culture of surfeited and depraved people. Showing that sort of films is called freedom in this country. Such 'freedom' doesn't suit us. You seem to like the 'freedom' of looking at backsides. But we prefer the freedom to think, to exercise our mental faculties, the freedom of creative progress."

"Do you want such films to be banned?" Phillips asked.

"I think there should be such a law," N. S. Khrushchev replied, "a moral law."

"I'm free to see or not to see such films," Carey said.

"But your children see things like that!"

"I have no children."

"But other people have. Good children, who live on earth," N. S. Khrushchev remarked. "And you and we should protect them from bad influences spread under the guise of 'free cultural exchange.'"

Some of the unionists then contended that the Soviet Union was reluctant for some reason to expand Soviet-American cultural relations. N. S. Khrushchev refuted that false assertion. He stressed that in reality it was the American side which was stalling, and

Citizens of San Francisco welcoming Khrushchev.

suggested that G. A. Zhukov, Chairman of the State Committee for Cultural Relations, who was present, be asked to inform them on the matter. But the U.S. trade-union leaders avoided that.

"We'll read about it in the papers," one of them said.

Speaking of exchanges of information, N. S. Khrushchev pointed out that Soviet people are for exchanging truthful information, such as would make for a durable peace and closer relations between peoples. P. A. Satyukov, Editor-in-Chief of *Pravda,* who was present at the discussion, pointed out that *Pravda* had published in full the speeches made at the Washington conference on unemployment called by U.S. trade unions, without changing a single word in them, while the American newspapers for some reason had not carried them, describing them as "Red propaganda."

"You and we have different views regarding exchanges of information and a number of other matters," N. S. Khrushchev said. "But that doesn't mean we cannot find a common language on problems that are of interest to the peoples of our countries. We say to you: 'Rise higher, try to take a broader view of events. Don't look at things from the tower you've built for yourselves. Come to our country, see how Soviet workers live and work, how our trade unions function, how they defend the workers' interests. You and we ap-

135

proach things differently; we are advancing to communism along the path we have chosen, while you want to bolster capitalism.' In other words, our attitudes are different. Let us recognize this indisputable fact. But couldn't we try and find common ground for businesslike cooperation? We think we could. The whole working class needs such cooperation in the struggle for its fundamental interests, for peace.

"We did not come to this meeting to aggravate relations—they are bad enough as it is," N. S. Khrushchev remarked. "If we fling accusations at each other, it won't do the working class any good. Let's be reasonable, let's not bring up questions which separate us. Let's pool our efforts in the struggle for world peace."

But Feller asked another question in the cold war spirit. Reading from a sheet, he repeated the false propaganda that the workers are oppressed in the socialist countries and have to escape abroad.

A. I. Adzhubei, Editor-in-Chief of *Izvestia,* who was also present, pointed out that Feller was repeating word for word what was printed in that day's *New York Times.*

"Think of what you are doing," N. S. Khrushchev said, "You would repeat articles published in the bourgeois press, and I should answer you. Start reading the proletarian press and then you will see what's what sooner."

N. S. Khrushchev observed that Weaver, a Negro present at the discussion, had made several attempts to ask a question but that Reuther persisted in ignoring him for some reason.

"This isn't a democratic way of holding a discussion," N. S. Khrushchev said. "Let the black man speak. It's a shame, really. You still have places in this country which Negroes aren't allowed to enter."

Weaver said that the U.S. trade unions were fighting against racial discrimination and that they accorded him the honor of representing the U.S. labor movement at some international conferences. Two weeks ago, he said, he had attended a conference of the World Federation of United Nations Associations in Geneva.

At the conference, Weaver noted with satisfaction, the U.S. and Soviet delegations had cooperated closely. They had drafted a joint resolution aimed at ending the cold war, and it had been carried. Weaver pointed out, however, that the U.S. delegation and the delegations of the socialist countries had differed on many points and had had sharp clashes over them.

He asked N. S. Khrushchev how a start should be made and how common ground could be found for cooperation. "It's important for our people to have answers to the questions asked here tonight," Weaver said.

"I know that your trade unions are doing a good deal for the Negroes to become equal citizens of the USA," N. S. Khrushchev replied. "As regards the questions on which there is no agreement between your trade unions and those of the socialist countries, you know that you and we differ in our approach to many social phenomena, and appraise them differently.

"In our opinion, trade unions should have more frequent contacts. Everything cannot be settled overnight, of course. But should cooperation between trade unions begin to develop and strengthen on specific points, if only minor ones to begin with, the two countries will in the end come to join efforts. You cannot gain an understanding of the attitude of our trade unions overnight, just as our trade unionists cannot gain overnight an understanding of all that you have. That is why both you and we should take a good look at each other, examine each other's activities and get to know them better. We may have disputes and disagreements. But if you and we want to promote peace and improve the living conditions of workers, of working people, why aggravate relations? After all, that would benefit none but our common enemies.

"Do you want our socialist system changed? I hope not. We, for our part, don't want to interfere in your internal affairs and will not do it—won't try to bring about a change in the system you have. We have said in the past and say now: 'Let us be more tolerant toward each other. Though we differ with you on many questions, we have a common cause for the sake of which we should join our efforts. It is the struggle for peace. The peoples want peace, and are fighting for it.'

"As for specific questions of the trade-union movement, I must admit that I've never worked in that field and am no expert, but we have experienced trade unionists. Why don't you contact them? They will not try to make Communists out of you and I think that you, too, will not make supporters of capitalism out of them. But an exchange of views between you and them would, no doubt, be useful."

James Carey, Vice-President of the AFL-CIO, who spoke at the close of the discussion, thanked N. S. Khrushchev for the meeting.

"Thank you," he said, "for giving us so much of your time. Good-bye and good luck. Let's work together for peace, for the good of man."

The meeting ended in a friendly atmosphere. In parting, the

union leaders thanked the head of the Soviet Government again and again for the meeting.

In view of the foregoing, it was really surprising that a news conference was held right after the meeting, at which Mr. Reuther did not hesitate—in the opinion of the Soviet press group—grossly to distort the substance of the discussion and attack the man whom he and his colleagues had just received as a guest of honor. Mr. Reuther went so far as to allege that N. S. Khrushchev had in the course of the discussion "pounded the table and shouted, 'I am the dictator of the working class.'"

This sort of statement is plainly intended for people who have no idea whatever of the Soviet Union or its leaders. It is not mere chance that many bourgeois correspondents asked N. S. Khrushchev to comment on the utterly incredible statement which Mr. Reuther had made about the meeting.

"I don't know whether Mr. Reuther actually said that or whether it was attributed to him by unscrupulous journalists," N. S. Khrushchev replied. "Did he really say that?"

Journalists who had attended the news conference confirmed that Mr. Reuther had made the statement in question. Then N. S. Khrushchev said:

"If Mr. Reuther made such a statement, he acted dishonestly. It's a lie. I cannot respect a man who resorts to such methods. In our interview, we spoke of the dictatorship of the working class and not any personal dictatorship. Marxism-Leninism maintains that when power passes into the hands of the working class, it has to establish a dictatorship of its own to suppress the resistance of the overthrown exploiting classes. The forms of working-class dictatorship may vary in different countries. If the deposed class puts up no resistance to the new that is born in the course of the historical development of society, as a result of revolution, the working class has no need to use forcible means of suppression. But if the exploiters try to turn back the wheel of history, to prevent the people from taking power, if they try to strangle the revolution, then the working class, working people in general, must, in the name of their vital interests, use means of suppression to maintain their social gains and to defend the vital interests of the working masses, of the entire people."

N. S. Khrushchev stressed that as it advances to communism the Soviet Union is carrying out more and more extensive measures leading to the withering away of the state. "We have already carried out a number of far-reaching measures in that field," he said. "We are reducing our armed forces and militia, and cutting the number of state security workers. An increasing number of functions involved in the maintenance of law and order and in state administration are being transferred to public organizations."

What is the outcome of the interview between the U.S. union leaders and the head of the Soviet Government?

The very fact that the interview took place suggests that the political situation in the USA is taking a turn for the better. However strong anti-Soviet sentiment may be with some U.S. trade-union leaders, the growing urge of the American people for better U.S.-Soviet relations and for a durable peace is gaining the upper hand.

It will be recalled that so far the U.S. trade-union leadership has persisted in avoiding all contacts with the Soviet Union. Many speeches made by Meany, President of the AFL-CIO, hardly differed in substance from speeches made by reactionary-minded leaders of U.S. imperialism. Speaking at a trade-union congress in San Francisco as recently as September 21, 1959, Meany violently attacked the Soviet Union and the Soviet Government in the cold war spirit. This attitude of Meany's and his associates' is at variance with the sentiments of ordinary Americans, who want a durable peace and friendly relations between the USA and the Soviet Union.

This must have been the reason why the group of AFL-CIO leaders found it necessary to invite N. S. Khrushchev, head of the Soviet Government, to an interview to discuss some important problems of international life and Soviet-American relations.

It is reasonable to believe that that interview may serve as a good start and will help pave the way for the necessary contacts between American and Soviet trade unions.

Those contacts are indispensable and could be most fruitful in the struggle for the common cause of promoting universal peace.

As regards those who persist, trying to stay on the cold war bandwagon, they are merely exposing their true colors before the eyes of the working people of the world.

The vital interests of the working class call for unity in the struggle for peace. "Though we differ with you on many questions," N. S. Khrushchev said in his conversation with the U.S. trade unionists, "we have a common cause for the sake of which we should join our efforts. It is the struggle for peace."

It is deplorable that reactionary U.S. trade-union leaders are trying to aggravate matters at a time when there are signs of better relations between the Soviet Union and the United States, and of a more wholesome international climate.

No matter how hard reactionary-minded U.S. trade-union leaders try to conceal the appeal to unity voiced by the head of the Soviet Government or to distort his statements, the truth will triumph. One indication of this is the fact that Americans received the head of the Soviet Government with great warmth everywhere, all along the route of his U.S. tour. That warm welcome is a genuine expression of the American people's urge for peace and friendship with the Soviet people.

SPEECH BY N. S. KHRUSHCHEV AT A MEETING WITH LONGSHOREMEN OF THE PACIFIC COAST

N. S. Khrushchev called at the Longshoremen's Union of the Pacific Coast on September 21. At the request of the workers he addressed the people assembled with a brief message of greetings.

Allow me to address you the way we Soviet workers are accustomed to addressing each other—comrades! (*Stormy applause. Cries of greetings.*) I express sincere gratitude to Harry Bridges, the chairman of your union, for the kind invitation. During my stay in the United States I have met with ordinary Americans and with your public men. I received the impression that Americans want peace. We greet such a desire as we ourselves want a stable peace! (*Stormy applause. Cries in Russian and in English: "Mir!", "Peace!"*) I thank you dear friends for the warm reception. (*Stormy applause.*) I convey greetings to you from Soviet workers, and on returning home shall convey to them your greetings. (*Stormy applause.*) I would like to wish you what workers desire. And what do workers desire! (*Cries: "Peace!"*) That is true—peace. It is necessary that there be peace. Besides this, I hope that you always have work and good wages. (*Stormy applause.*) Good-bye friends! (*Stormy applause. Cries of "Peace!" "Friendship!" "Good-bye, Khrushchev!"*)

N. S. KHRUSHCHEV'S SPEECH AT THE IBM CORPORATION PLANT IN SAN JOSE

On September 21, N. S. Khrushchev and his party visited the IBM Corp. plant in San Jose, Calif.

Thomas Watson, president of the corporation, warmly welcomed the head of the Soviet Government. N. S. Khrushchev made a reply speech:

Mr. President of the Corporation, I wish to thank you from the bottom of my heart for the reception you have accorded my party and myself. I like very much the method of self-service used here in your cafeteria. We are using the same method, but not widely enough. Your example is worthy of imitation at our own factories.

I must point out an agreeable thing—when I meet businessmen, we find a common language in our conversations. Being men of action, we are quick to understand each other and get down to business-like talk. I like that.

But when I meet and talk with certain trade-union or other political leaders, things don't always take the desired turn. In your remarks, Mr. President, you spoke well of your system. And that is understandable, because everyone defends his own system. We keep our own opinion.

I remember a story for children, in which the following circumstance is aptly brought out: the snipe asks the quail to come and see him. They have the following conversation. 'Well, what's it like living in a field?' asks the snipe. 'It's dry there, with no water.' 'But I live in a marsh. It's good to live in a marsh!'

'You rot in your marsh,' answered the quail. 'You know nothing of dry land. But look how nice it is where I live, with the sun shining and flowers all around.'

The snipe and the quail didn't see eye to eye, and each thought he was right.

That's what sometimes happens to people. Each thinks his own system the best. Let us not argue this point. You believe your way of life to be better, and we think our way of life is better. Time will show who lives in a marsh and who soars in the sky. At any rate, our communist Lunik is now on the moon, looking down at the earth, wondering how soon its American brother will follow it. *(Laughter, applause.)*

We are having a peaceful, friendly chat with you. The President here has set the right tone like a good conductor. We mustn't aggravate relations, mustn't raise questions that can only be settled by reality itself in due course. Let us not argue those questions, because the deeper we get involved in argument, the more the strings will tighten, while we must loosen the strings, not tighten them, so as to come closer to each other, to be friends and do everything to assure world peace. *(Applause.)*

We want to be friends with the American people and the American Government—I stress, the Government, making no distinction between people and government, because that is the only condition on which we can achieve the results we are striving for, that is to say, friendly relations between our countries, and peaceful coexistence. Some people ask me what is peaceful coexistence. I have already explained that repeatedly and am willing to do so patiently again and again. If there's anyone who doesn't understand, let him reflect some more. If he still doesn't understand, he evidently isn't mature yet. Then let him develop some more, and reality will bring it home to him, perhaps he will knock bumps on his head before he realizes how essential is peaceful coexistence. To put it in a nutshell, peaceful coexistence means that states with opposite systems should live in peace, without wars. *(Applause.)*

Thank you for your attention. Thank you. *(Applause.)*

SPEECH BY N. S. KHRUSHCHEV
AT A RECEPTION IN SAN FRANCISCO

On the evening of September 21, the municipal authorities, business circles and public of San Francisco gave a reception in honor of N. S. Khrushchev.

The guest speakers were Chairman of the North California Council for International Affairs Rockwell, Mayor Christopher, Governor Brown, the President's special representative Henry Cabot Lodge and Chairman of the Commonwealth Club Johnson.

The floor was then given to N. S. Khrushchev.

MAYOR CHRISTOPHER, GOVERNOR BROWN, CHAIRMAN ROCKWELL, MR. JOHNSON, LADIES AND GENTLEMEN:

I am very grateful to you for this invitation to address such an esteemed gathering.

We came to San Francisco from Los Angeles. We traveled along the lovely coast, admired the beauties of the California landscape and saw your bountiful land. All along the route the California sun shone just as benevolently as the sun in the Crimea, where I spent my vacation before coming to the USA.

But it is not sunlight alone that warms our hearts so far from home. We are being met and received cordially by the Californians. We would like the friendship between our peoples to be as inextinguishable and bright as your southern sun. *(Prolonged applause.)*

It is a pleasure to see a rich and beautiful land. And it is an even greater pleasure to see how ably you utilize the riches of California. When the first European, the Portuguese traveler Juan Rodriguez Cabrillo, set foot in California in 1542 it was an unexplored territory with virgin forests of giant sequoias, many of which were already almost a thousand years old, and with incalculable wealth—oil and gold—lying untouched in the ground.

But are gold and oil the only riches of California? You have everything: trout and salmon, cotton—the priceless "white gold"— oranges, grapes and redwood, minerals and huge reserves of "blue coal."

Yours is a fertile land, ladies and gentlemen, and your city of San Francisco is magnificent. Its coast is lapped by the waves of the Pacific, whose waters also wash the shores of the Soviet Far East.

I did not have the opportunity of coming to your city by sea, but I know that the entrance there is through the Golden Gate. I would like to express the confidence that the day is not distant when this Golden Gate will open hospitably for Soviet ships bringing goods you need to your country, and American merchant ships will pass through this gate bound for ports in the Soviet Union. *(Applause.)*

At one time Russian people, too, reached California across the Pacific. You know, of course, that some of the towns and communities here still have Russian names.

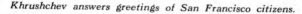

Khrushchev answers greetings of San Francisco citizens.

The American West traded with our country for many years. And it is just lately that Soviet-American trade has been brought to practically a standstill.

I have already said on several occasions that we have come to the United States with an open heart and honest intentions. We want only one thing: to live in peace and friendship with you and with other nations. I think that the esteemed Californians gathered here share these feelings and aspirations. *(Applause.)*

Americans who have visited the Soviet Union bring home different opinions about our country and about its life. But all of them will confirm that the words "peace" and "friendship" are heard at every step in the Soviet Union. These words are laid out in white stone along railways, they are written in flowers in gardens, squares and parks, and traced on the walls of houses. They are in the heart of every Soviet citizen. The reason for this is that through peaceful labor the Soviet people endeavor to protect themselves and the whole world from the horrors of war. We know very well what war is and although we are strong we do not want mankind ever again to go through the calamities and destruction of war. *(Applause.)*

It goes without saying that the best way to avert war, to eradicate it at its roots, is to destroy the means of waging war.

At the United Nations a few days ago the Soviet Government submitted a proposal on general and complete disarmament with the establishment of unlimited inspection. A little earlier, at the end of August, the Soviet Government passed a decision not to resume nuclear tests if such tests are not resumed by the Western Powers.

The Soviet Union will persist in its efforts to achieve a complete cessation of nuclear weapons tests, considering this to be an important step toward ending the nuclear arms race and removing the menace to the lives and health of millions of people.

Everybody is well aware that the settlement of these problems is not all that is essential for the preservation of peace. Survivals of the Second World War likewise harbor the danger of a new war, and therefore this problem, too, has to be settled.

In proposing a peace treaty with Germany, with due regard to the fact that there are two German states, we are not seeking any unilateral benefits or advantages for ourselves. What advantages can there be when the question is to extinguish the still smoldering embers of a past conflagration?

The Soviet Union has on many occasions pointed out that its

144

aim is to normalize the situation in Germany, which would also eliminate the abnormal situation in Berlin.

I shall not go into detail. We have already had and will still have frank talks on many questions with the President of the USA, Mr. Dwight D. Eisenhower. It is to be hoped that as a result of our talks both sides will draw considerably nearer to a settlement of pressing international issues, and that, in the final analysis, will strengthen world peace and security.

To arrive at a correct solution of urgent problems as quickly as possible, all prejudice and ill-will must be swept aside. It is just in this way that Soviet people approach the questions dividing us. We want to understand you and your motives better. But that calls for reciprocity. You must also understand us well and understand our motives. The Soviet Union is not seeking any benefits for itself. All we want is that war should not threaten people anywhere on earth. *(Prolonged applause.)*

Properly speaking, I have finished the address I prepared for such a representative and esteemed gathering. But if you have no objection I should like to add a thing or two. I feel I must share with you the impressions I have gained today. *(Applause.)*

It was a great pleasure to take a drive through the city, to see your bay from a ship, not for the purpose of spying out anything but of admiring your lovely coast and splendid bay with the most sincere feeling of friendship. *(Animation, applause.)*

I thank the officials of the Longshoremen's Union and the owners or contractors (I do not know how you call them), who organize shipments, for inviting me to visit them. The friendly talk at the Council of this trade union gave me pleasure. I shall long remember this wonderful day. I acquired one thing in San Francisco: A longshoreman gave me his cap, and in token of my appreciation I gave him my Soviet hat. *(Laughter, applause.)* For me it will be a pleasant souvenir of San Francisco. *(Applause.)*

When we drove with Mr. Lodge along the fine roads you have built, it gave me great pleasure to see the people meeting us. They came out into the streets, perhaps by chance or possibly with the express purpose of seeing what the foreigner who had come to them, and who was a confirmed Communist and the Prime Minister of the great Soviet Union, was like. We saw smiles and expressions of kind, friendly feelings. *(Applause.)*

It was a great pleasure to visit the computer plant, where we were accorded a very warm welcome. Allow me to express special thanks here to Mr. Watson, President of the International Business Machines Corp., who showed us great courtesy, talked warmly with us and spoke very well and with great understanding of the need to improve relations between our countries. He is a very likeable man, and for us he is all the more likeable for having been in the Soviet Union and seen the life and work of our factories. *(Animation, applause.)*

The plant we toured produces computer machines. That is evidently very interesting, but I am not a specialist in this field and for that reason in the given case my evaluation means nothing. In the Soviet Union we too produce computer machines, and I do not know who makes them better, or whose machines are better, yours or ours. That too remains to be seen. *(Animation.)* We have seen your computing machines, but you have not seen ours. Perhaps ours are better. The production of computing machines is kept secret for the time being, but I do not think much time will elapse before these secrets are made available to everybody who might benefit by them. *(Animation, applause.)*

I repeat that I can be shown factories of this kind, because I will not take advantage of any secrets. *(Laughter, applause.)*

Speaking of secrets, I remember when the preparations for the launching of our first rocket were completed, the scientists invited members of the government to inspect it. We walked round the rocket, peered here and there, examined it on all sides *(animation)*, but we do not know how it works, or, as people say, "what gravy it's eaten with." I think "secrets" like these can be shown to many people: They, too, will look, and feel, but won't understand a thing. *(Animation, applause.)*

I repeat, we are very grateful to the engineers, employees and workers of this factory, who were so kind to us during our visit to their factory. I am particularly satisfied with the cooks, who prepared a splendid meal. I enjoyed the dishes into which the cooks had put their culinary art, their skill. In this question of how meals are prepared, I think everybody, the specialist and the non-specialist alike, is more or less at home. *(Laughter, applause.)*

I very much regret that I had no opportunity today of visiting the Research Institute at Stanford, whose director or, to use your term, president, is the esteemed scientist Mr. Finley Carter. Our scientist, Professor Yemelyanov, went there today. That is good, of course, but I wanted to go, too. However, you cannot, as Kozma Prutkov said, embrace the unembraceable. You do not know and, in fact, nobody knows him, because he never existed physically, but the utterances, which in my country are known as the aphorisms of Kozma Prutkov, are really good. *(Animation.)*

I should like to add a few words to what I have already said about your lovely city of San Francisco. When the Second World War ended and our soldiers came home, the ones who had fought for the liberation of Bulgaria brought back a good song about that country. You know that the Soviet people are especially warmly disposed toward the Bulgarian people. The Russians and Bulgarians are brother nations. Their languages are very much alike. When the Bulgarians were ruled by the Turks, the Russians always had a brotherly feeling for them. Russians shed a lot of blood to help the Bulgarians free themselves from the Turkish yoke. We also helped the Greeks to liberate themselves, Mr. Christopher. *(Laughter, applause.)* (Mr. Christopher, Mayor of San Francisco, is of Greek origin.—*Ed.*)

Now then, this song contains the following lines: "Beautiful is the land of Bulgaria, but Russia is the best of all. . . ." I would somewhat re-word this song and say: "Beautiful are the cities of the United States that I have visited, but San Francisco is the best of all." *(Stormy applause, cries of approval.)*

Ladies and gentlemen, allow me now to express my most sincere gratitude to all of today's speakers. I shall not name them or single anyone out—all of them are worthy people and they spoke well. I do not know who among you is the chief organizer, but he has shown his skill in arranging this meeting. I tender you my heartfelt gratitude for everything. *(Applause.)*

The people of San Francisco have bewitched us. I felt I was among friendly people, who have the same thoughts as the peoples of the Soviet Union! To prove this I can tell you of something that happened when we drove about the city. Our car stopped accidentally in front of a house and I asked an ordinary woman, who happened to be near us, what she would like, what her wishes were. She replied, "My only wish is that there should be peace on earth, that there should be no war." I think she expressed the thoughts and wishes of all people—adults, men and women, and children, because peace is in the heart and on the lips of each one of them both in the Soviet Union and here in the United States of America. All the nations of the world want peace. *(Stormy applause.)*

The main thing we must now seek is not the questions on which we disagree. These have stuck so deeply in the throats of everyone that we cannot extract them, hard as we try. We must seek out what we have in common, so as to build up our relations on that, to achieve better mutual understanding, and to draw closer to each other in questions where we can find common ground.

Do you imagine you can convince me that the capitalist system is better than the socialist? Neither do I want to think that I can convince you that the communist system is better. Evidently, we shall each maintain our opinions, but that must not prevent us from living in friendship, from being good neighbors and showing concern about improving relations between our countries. *(Prolonged applause.)*

I would like to assure you, ladies and gentlemen, that I have no intention at all of calling you into the communist realm. I am simply telling you—perhaps you will yet recall my words when you get a better knowledge of Soviet people, their thoughts and aspirations. You may not agree just now, but the time will come when you will admit that Communists have the noblest of thoughts and aspirations. We strive to build a communist society based on the loftiest of ideals. Communism is not yet our present, but our future. But we are already building it. We are building a society where man is the friend of man, where no enmity exists, where no blood is shed, where all people are equal. These great human ideals should also be understandable to religious people, to people who are not Communists. From the Scriptures they ought to remember the exhortation to love their neighbor, and so on.

Do not judge Soviet people, Communists, only by the period of the Civil War. The Civil War was imposed on our people and they were forced to repulse their enemies. Your American ancestors also fought a bitter Civil War when the North fought the South, and killed one another in that war. The best people of your country fought for the democratic ideas held aloft by Lincoln, and they won.

At present we are waging our fight for communism with the best of human motives. We are not waging it, arms in hand, but with the word, by peaceful means, with our labor. Let those who do not wish to accept our convictions retain their own. We understand people who respect their own system. *(Applause.)*

Mr. Mayor Christopher, my friends and I greatly appreciate the kind feelings you have expressed. But I hesitate to speak in your praise. Your election campaign will soon start, and I would not like people to think that I am meddling in your internal affairs. Your

148

opponent might ask why Khrushchev spoke about you and said nothing about him. (*Laughter, applause.*)

We had a conversation with Mr. Christopher. I told him that I had not decided yet for whom I would vote were I given an opportunity to do so. I will give it further thought and perhaps tell him at the end of the dinner, depending on how good the dinner is. (*Animation.*) I must say that you are winning in that respect: The food has been deliciously prepared and served in abundance, so that by all outward signs I ought to vote for you; but, I repeat, I'll give that further thought. (*Laughter, applause.*)

From this distinguished rostrum I should like to thank the manager of the store which we were so kindly shown. It is an excellent store. America is a rich country, but we have no wish to impose upon your wealth. At the moment we are producing less than you, but we will put our backs to it and produce more. This will not harm you in any way, but will contribute to the prosperity of our country, of our people. (*Applause.*)

I consider it my duty here in San Francisco to say a few words about your neighbor, the city of Los Angeles and its people. (*Animation.*) I want to say some good things about these people.

We were pleased with the meetings we had with the population of Los Angeles. But something unforeseen happened there. I was told that when we were driving through the city, the car of the Chief of Police drove in front of us. Some individual who must have had either too much or too little sense, threw a tomato, perhaps even a good tomato, and it hit that car. (*Animation.*) The Chief of Police then displayed his authority and deprived us of the pleasure of seeing the fabulous world of Disneyland, which was put down in our itinerary. (*Laughter, applause.*)

I am grateful to the Chief of Police for his concern about my welfare, but I would say that he showed too much zeal. He should have acted more calmly. I am sure that if we had gone to Disneyland nothing but good would have come of it. But, after all, you do come across superstitious people! There was a case like this even with so great a man as Pushkin, the Russian poet. It is said that one day in winter a black cat ran across the road when he drove out in a sleigh, and because of that he turned back. But that was long ago. In our day we should not be deterred by a "black cat"; we should have carried on with the pre-arranged program. I think everything would have been all right. (*Applause.*)

149

Now I should like to say a few words in defense—and if not in defense, then in favor—of the Mayor of Los Angeles. *(Animation.)* When we arrived in Los Angeles, the Mayor and his family received us very cordially. He has a very charming wife and wonderful daughters. But at the dinner he made a speech which was not altogether happy. You do get unhappy speeches. Many of you have probably spoken on many occasions. Tell me frankly, ladies and gentlemen, are you always pleased with the speeches you make? As for me, there have been instances when I have not been pleased with my speeches. The same thing also happened to the Mayor of Los Angeles. So let us find it in our hearts to make allowances for him, for, after all, as religious people say, "We must forgive our neighbor his trespasses," especially if he perceives them. *(Animation.)* I think we should follow this good custom and consider the unpleasant incident which happened there as having simply been an accident—it did not come from the heart, nor from the mind. Let us consider the question closed. *(Applause.)* There is peace and friendship between us and the American people and, in particular, the Americans of Los Angeles and San Francisco. But as today I am speaking in San Francisco, I show just a little more preference for your city than for Los Angeles. *(Laughter, applause.)*

We had an amiable talk with the Mayor of Los Angeles before his speech, and during that talk I invited him to visit Moscow with his wife and daughters. I want to say from this rostrum that this invitation still holds good. We shall hospitably receive the Mayor of Los Angeles and his family in Moscow and drop no hint about his unhappy speech.

I would have also been pleased to invite you to Moscow, Mr. Christopher, but I do not know whether or not my invitation will be to your advantage in the coming elections. That is a very complicated question for me. I therefore extend this invitation to all of you here, to all the people of the lovely, verdant and sunny city of San Francisco—you are always welcome, come to the Soviet Union, come to our Moscow, we shall be happy to receive you. *(Prolonged applause.)*

We have a proverb that says, "He who has not been to Russia has not seen the world." See our country and perhaps you too will like it. *(Stormy applause.)*

Allow me to express the hope that our stay in the United States of America, our meetings with representatives of the business world and the American public will be of benefit, will help to bring our countries closer together, and, consequently, to arrive faster at mutually acceptable decisions in the interests of consolidating peace and friendship among nations. I thank you, ladies and gentlemen. *(Stormy applause, all rise, cries of approval.)*

> At the end of the reception, the Mayor of San Francisco, Mr. Christopher, presented N. S. Khrushchev with a gift—a chairman's gavel made of redwood. Expressing his thanks for the gift, N. S. Khrushchev said:

In my country we do not use chairmen's gavels at meetings or official conferences. I therefore do not know where I could use it.

I would like the first knock of this gavel to seal an understanding between the President of the USA, Mr. Eisenhower, and myself on the conclusion of an agreement—a treaty of peace, nonaggression and cooperation, and best of all—of friendship between our countries. That would be of great benefit to the peoples of our countries and to the cause of peace throughout the world. *(Stormy, prolonged applause.)*

It would also be good if an agreement were reached on the question of disarmament, so as to put an end to the arms race once and for all, so that people would not be threatened with war, so that they could live among themselves in peace and friendship.

I would be the happiest of men if that were achieved, ladies and gentlemen. *(Stormy, prolonged applause.)*

SPEECH BY N. S. KHRUSHCHEV ON ARRIVING IN DES MOINES

On September 22 N. S. Khrushchev and his party arrived in Des Moines, capital of Iowa.

He was met at the airfield by the Governor of Iowa Herschel Loveless, Mayor Iles and representatives of the Chamber of Commerce.

Replying to the greetings N. S. Khrushchev said:

MR. GOVERNOR, MR. MAYOR, LADIES AND GENTLEMEN:

I am very pleased to arrive in your state. We know quite a lot about your state of Iowa and we shall gladly acquaint ourselves with the life of the people in your state. We know that you occupy first place in the United States in the production of corn. We shall compete with you, and we think that this competition will be beneficial both for us and for you.

Thank you for the kind words, for the words of welcome. I think that our meetings and talks will bring us closer together and will create the necessary conditions for strengthening peace and friendship between peoples.

Many inhabitants of the city gathered at the entrance of the Fort Des Moines Hotel where N. S. Khrushchev was staying. Correspondents of local papers and the TV station asked the head of the Soviet Government to say a few words to the inhabitants of the state of Iowa.

N. S. Khrushchev expressed his satisfaction on arriving on the state's territory which is famed throughout the world for its achievements in growing corn and developing animal husbandry.

The people in the United States also strive for peace as our people do. I am very pleased to note this. It is precisely the striving of both our peoples for peace that induced me to accept President Eisenhower's invitation and to visit the United States.

Today I saw an interesting poster in English in Des Moines. It carried the following inscription: "We don't agree with you on many questions, but we welcome you." This is a sensible slogan. We also don't agree with you on many matters, but we also greet you. You can live the way you like best and we shall live the way we like best, but let us be friends in order to ensure peace between our peoples.

SPEECH BY N. S. KHRUSHCHEV AT THE RECEPTION
IN THE DES MOINES CHAMBER OF COMMERCE

The Des Moines Chamber of Commerce held a reception in honor of N. S. Khrushchev the evening of September 22. Speeches were made by Governor Loveless of Iowa, and by Henry Cabot Lodge, Jr., the President's special representative. N. S. Khrushchev made a speech in reply.

MR. GOVERNOR, MR. MAYOR, MR. PRESIDENT OF THE CHAMBER, LADIES AND GENTLEMEN, FRIENDS:

Allow me to thank you for your invitation to visit your state and its capital, the fine city of Des Moines, and for the warm reception extended to me and my companions. I am also grateful to the President of your Chamber of Commerce and his colleagues for giving me the opportunity to address you.

I avail myself of the occasion to convey to you, and through you to the people of the State of Iowa, the heartfelt greetings of the Soviet people and best wishes for success in life and in your work.

We are happy to visit the State of Iowa whose fame as a leading farming area has spread far beyond the United States.

In the Soviet Union we are well aware that your state occupies an important place in the world output of corn and that you have some fine achievements in livestock breeding. You will probably be interested to know that one of the largest farming districts of our country, Krasnodar Territory, wants to compete with Iowa in the output of farm produce. People in many Cossack villages in the Kuban area have a good knowledge of what your farms have achieved in the production of corn, meat, milk and other farm produce.

I have never been in your country before, but I have had many talks with representatives of the American people and with our people who had visited America. I remember, in particular, my talks with Mr. Garst, a farmer from your state, who has visited the Soviet Union several times. I remember my talks with Senator Ellender who also spoke about your agriculture. I never miss an opportunity of seeing films that depict different aspects of life in your country.

The agriculture of the United States, and of your state in particular, is of great interest to us, above all because it is highly mechanized. Some of your farms have achieved a high labor productivity by mechanizing field work and the feeding of all kinds of farm animals and poultry. The output per worker is today much higher on your farms than in our kolkhozes (collective farms). I must say, however, that some of your economists are mistaken when they mechanically compare the output figures of your farms and those of our kolkhozes

Iowa University students in Ames welcome the head of the Soviet government.

in terms of output per worker. In so doing they fail to consider the fact that farming in the Soviet Union and in the United States is based on absolutely opposite principles.

While your farms are private capitalist enterprises belonging to individual owners, the kolkhozes in the Soviet Union are socialized cooperative farms belonging to peasant collectives.

Everything that is economically unprofitable on your farms is deprived of the right to live and ceases to exist. Weaker farms that have no adequate income and working capital cannot cope with the situation. They are unable to effect such a high degree of mechanization as the large farms, fall behind and are ruined, and their places are taken by the stronger farms. The law of competition, inherent in capitalism, operates in your country.

In our country, on the other hand, farming is developing on other, that is, socialist principles. The kolkhozes are large cooperative farms established through the voluntary association of peasant farms. For this reason, the number of people working on a given farm is not the minimum necessary to till the soil, cultivate the crops and raise farm animals and poultry. Rather, it represents the number of able-bodied workers in the given cooperative. We cannot allow a state of affairs in which some members of the cooperative work, while others are deprived of the right to work. We realize that there

154

are shortcomings in the organization of labor and the employment of manpower in our kolkhozes, and are doing away with these shortcomings.

Of course, the lag of our farms in the field of mechanization and labor productivity, as compared with yours, is temporary. The socialist system of agriculture makes it possible to eliminate the lag in a brief space of time and to attain higher labor productivity than on your farms. The socialist system offers boundless scope for production development because it knows neither crises nor competition. In our country there is not and cannot be the danger that some farm or another will be ruined. We have a sufficiently high level of scientific farming, and skilled personnel, and a machine-building industry capable of providing farms with the necessary machinery. We are endeavoring to effect the comprehensive mechanization of all farming processes by using modern machinery and making more rational use of manpower to ensure a high output per farm worker. We have some fine specialists in mechanization who have achieved greater labor productivity in the cultivation of corn, cotton, sugar beet and other crops than that recorded by your best farms.

At the present time we are accelerating the development of the chemical industry. This will enable us to produce more mineral fertilizer, weed killers and insecticides, the extensive use of which will considerably raise the yield of farm crops and increase output per farm worker. This is one of our big potentialities. We also have some other big potentialities for the further growth of farm output. We have a large number of tractors and other farm machines.

Today, we are making very good progress in agriculture. In a short time—in just five years—we increased the output of grain from 82 million tons in 1953 to 141 million tons in 1958, the amount of grain purchased by the state rising from 31 million to 57 million tons. In the course of only three years we brought 90 million acres of virgin soil under the plow in the eastern regions of our country, and that is four times the crop area of the State of Iowa. Now we have considerably more fodder for our cattle. In those same five years the amount of silage stored increased from 32 million to 148 million tons in 1958, this amount including 108 million tons of corn silage, of which next to nothing was produced formerly.

In the last five years the cattle herds in our country have increased by 15 million head, pigs by more than 15 million and sheep by 30 million head. This enabled us to increase state purchases of meat for consumption by the non-farming population. In eight months of 1959 we have purchased three times more meat than in the same period of 1953, 2.3 times more milk, 2.2 times more eggs and twice as much wool.

Our agriculture has great potentialities and limitless opportunities to further extend the cultivated area, increase the yield of grain crops and develop livestock breeding.

American farmers, colleagues of yours, who have visited the Soviet Union, say that there are many points of interest in our country in the development of science, in biological selection, in the cultivation of industrial crops and in livestock breeding. I am sure that your farmers and specialists could make good use of many of the Soviet achievements in both practical farming and the agricultural sciences. And you, too, have much that is valuable and instructive. Soviet specialists who have visited the USA speak of your great achievements in corn cultivation and in poultry raising. You obtain the greatest increase in poultry weight per unit of feed—one kilogram increase to about two and a half kilograms of feed. We must learn from your experience. We pay due tribute to the knowledge, industry

Photo shows N. S. Khrushchev and his wife Nina Petrovna (center) talking with Iowa University students in Ames.

and experience of American farmers, scientists, and farm specialists. Your achievements are worthy of praise and your experience is worthy of study and imitation.

There is much of value that we can learn from each other. I think there is no need to speak of the great importance of studying experience gained in the field of agriculture and of sharing that experience. I know there are people who oppose such contacts and who believe that contacts, an improvement in the economic relations of our countries, would serve the more rapid economic development of the Soviet Union and the more successful fulfillment of its plans. Some of your country's periodicals carry articles in which an attempt is made to show that our seven-year plan constitutes the "danger of a Soviet economic offensive." But what, may I ask, is the danger of our endeavor, say, to increase the volume of farm output, and to whom is it dangerous? What harm is there in our desire to compete with you, say, in the output of corn, meat and milk? I don't suppose anybody will assert that a greater consumption of milk, butter and meat will make Soviet people more "aggressive"!

It is true that our people have adopted the motto: "Overtake and outstrip the United States in output per capita of population." But can this be regarded as a "danger" to Americans? We, for example, are by no means inclined to regard the farmers of Iowa as aggressive people simply because today they produce considerably more corn and meat than the Kuban kolkhozes. We challenge you to a competition in the output of meat, milk, butter, consumer goods, machines, steel, coal and oil, so that people might live better. This is far more beneficial competition than competition in stockpiling hydrogen bombs and all sorts of weapons. May there be more corn and meat, and no hydrogen bombs at all!

Farming is the oldest, the most vital and most peaceful branch of human industry. We want grain to grow in the fields and we want orchards to blossom, we want the earth to be turned up by peaceful plows and not by rockets and tank tracks.

You probably know the breath-taking prospects of peaceful development envisaged in our seven-year plan. You are business people and realize full well that whoever turns all his attention to developing peace economy, who employs his means and resources to that end, is not interested in war and war preparations. It is better to trade in agricultural and industrial produce than to continue the arms race and discrimination in world trade.

The Soviet people are applying all their efforts to peaceful

Khrushchev speaking to reporters in Des Moines.

construction. Our seven-year plan envisages an almost twofold over-all increase in industrial and agricultural output, while in many important branches the increase will be several times greater. In the field of agriculture we plan an annual output of 164 million to 180 million tons of grain, 76 million to 84 million tons of sugar beet; not less than 16 million tons of meat, and 100 million to 105 million tons of milk. The Soviet people are confident that we shall not only reach these targets, but even exceed them. In 1958, already, the Soviet Union surpassed the United States in over-all output of milk, especially of butter, and hopes to overtake and to outstrip the United States in the output of these items per capita within the next few years. Our country produces more wheat, sugar beet and wool than the USA. But I do not think this does any harm to the United States or to the farmers of Iowa.

In the past few years many Americans have visited the Soviet Union. Leading statesmen and men prominent in public life, Senators and Congressmen, businessmen, industrialists and farmers have been to our country. All of them enjoyed the hospitality of the Soviet people and were able to see for themselves that the Soviet people are a peace-loving people and that they are friendly toward the American people.

The purpose of our visit to the United States at the invitation of President Eisenhower is to help improve relations between the Soviet Union and the United States, and to strengthen peace.

As we know from history, there never have been in the past, and there are not at present, any territorial disputes between the

Soviet Union and the United States standing in the way of good, friendly relations. It is also known that among the Americans there are many people who want good relations with our country.

The peoples of the Soviet Union sincerely desire to strengthen and develop friendly relations with the American people. You know that in the past there have been many fine examples of friendly cooperation between our countries. In the Second World War the Soviet Union and the United States fought together, hand in hand, against the common enemy who threatened all mankind. And this speeded up victory and brought the peace whose benefits the nations enjoy.

The Soviet people want the experience of friendly collaboration between the peoples of our countries to be strengthened and expanded under present-day conditions in the interest of consolidating peace.

We are in favor of improving Soviet-American relations because we believe it to be in the interest of both nations. The establishment of friendly relations between the USA and the USSR would be an important step toward strengthening world peace and good relations among all peoples. The businessmen of your country can play an important part in improving Soviet-American relations. All mankind today hopes fervently that the Soviet Union and the United States will make a big contribution to the solution of the basic problems of our day, to the consolidation of peace.

If we succeed in improving relations between our countries, if we succeed in arranging mutually beneficial trade and in further extending our cultural, sports and other contacts, we shall thereby make a big contribution to the cause of relieving international tension, the cause of peaceful coexistence and the strengthening of world peace. And this will, in turn, have a beneficial influence on the lives of our peoples and of all mankind.

During our stay in the United States of America we have had many interesting meetings and conversations with representatives of various sections of the American people. These meetings and conversations show that the American people do not want war, that they desire peace. We have heard many warm words addressed to the Soviet people and many friendly good wishes. We are grateful for these expressions of good feeling and thank you for them, and for our part assure you that the Soviet people are awaiting President Eisenhower's visit to our country and will extend him a fitting welcome.

To conclude my speech I should once again like to emphasize

Photo shows N. S. Khrushchev shaking hands with a worker on Garst's farm.

Khrushchev with children at the Garst farm.

the unwavering determination of the Soviet people to uphold the cause of peace, to improve and develop friendly relations and cooperation between our countries, among the peoples of all countries. This is the purpose of the proposals for general and complete disarmament presented by the Soviet Government in the United Nations. This, too, is the purpose of the Soviet proposal to conclude a peace treaty with Germany. It is our opinion that these problems are not insoluble, provided, of course, there is a desire to adjust them. Where there's a will, there's a way. These problems can be solved because all the peoples have one object in view—the most noble and vitally important object—that of safeguarding peace.

For the sake of achieving this lofty aim all countries must make an effort and display the maximum desire. The cooperation of all the countries of the world, and, first and foremost, of our two countries, is essential to bring about a thaw and to melt the ice of the cold war once and for all. It's an ill wind that blows nobody any good. May the winds of peace and friendship blow over the fields, and may clouds appear in the sky only when a good shower is necessary for a good harvest.

May the two words, peace and friendship, be inscribed on the banners of each of our nations and may they guide the conscience and actions of our governments.

I wish you success in the further development of your excellent State of Iowa, and health and happiness for you all.

Thank you.

(N. S. Khrushchev's speech was frequently interrupted by applause.)

> N. S. Khrushchev, Chairman of the Council of Ministers of the USSR, spent all of September 23 in Iowa, one of the United States' major agricultural centers.
>
> On the morning of September 23, N. S. Khrushchev and his party drove from Des Moines to Coon Rapids to inspect the farms of Roswell Garst, who is well-known in the Soviet Union, and of other farmers.
>
> Giving his impressions of Garst's farm, N. S. Khrushchev said:

Before arriving here I had a picture of Mr. Garst's good farm from accounts and films. I have known Mr. Garst for several years. However, it is always better to see than to hear. I am glad that what I heard about this farm has been confirmed. I am happy over your achievements and I ask you also to rejoice over our achievements.

I must express my profound respect for the inhabitants of the state of Iowa, both urban dwellers and farmers, whom I met. I would

At the Garst farm in Iowa.

Garst and Khrushchev inspecting corn.

Khrushchev talking with Americans on the Garst farm in Iowa.

especially like to mention the editor of the local *Des Moines Register* who several years ago showed foresight and through his paper advanced the proposal of organizing an exchange of agricultural delegations between the United States of America and the Soviet Union.

> After inspecting the farms of Garst and Thomas, N. S. Khrushchev visited Iowa State College in Ames. Bidding the students and the teaching staff farewell, N. S. Khrushchev said:

Thank you for your cordial welcome. I was very glad to meet you, and to have even made a cursory acquaintance with your college. I knew something about it before, from what our comrades who visited it told us. We have a high opinion of the scientific research and teaching conducted in your college. I wish you the best of success.

Let us exchange experience. This will be useful for our countries.

Please convey my best wishes to all the students, and may they succeed in their studies so as to be of good service to their people and country. Please convey my best wishes to the scientists, the teachers, the laboratory personnel and all those who are advancing science and training specialists.

> N. S. Khrushchev and his party left by plane for Pittsburgh (Pennsylvania) on the evening of September 23. Before leaving Des Moines, N. S. Khrushchev addressed those seeing him off with a short speech.

N. S. KHRUSHCHEV SPEECH
BEFORE TAKING OFF FROM DES MOINES

MR. GOVERNOR, MR. MAYOR, LADIES AND GENTLEMEN:

I wish to express my gratitude to the Governor of Iowa, the Mayor of the city and to all the inhabitants of the city and the state I met. I am boundlessly pleased with the hospitality shown me, a representative of the Soviet state and of the Soviet people. On leaving I take with me and will convey to the Soviet people the friendly wishes which I received from the inhabitants of the state of Iowa.

I once again thank you and wish you happiness and prosperity. Good-bye.

N. S. Khrushchev and his party arrived in Pittsburgh at about mid-night. At the airfield the head of the Soviet Government was met by representatives of the local authorities and the public.

Mr. Thomas Gallagher, the city's Mayor, presented N. S. Khrushchev with a symbolic key to Pittsburgh.

SPEECH BY N. S. KHRUSHCHEV
ON ARRIVING IN PITTSBURGH

MR. MAYOR, LADIES AND GENTLEMEN:

I am very glad to be in your city. I accepted the invitation extended by the President of the United States to visit your country with great satisfaction. I have already sufficiently traveled around, and I have seen a great deal, heard a lot and have had many meetings in your country. It is very gratifying that the people of America have cordially welcomed me and have showed concern that relations between our countries be improved, that friendly relations and peace between all peoples be ensured.

Mr. Mayor, I highly value your confidence expressed in the fact that you presented me with a symbolic key of your city. I thank you and assure you that I want to be your friend and will never abuse your trust, and with this key I will only open those doors which you will allow me to open; I shall not make a single step without your permission.

I thank you for the good welcome and the kind words. I wish your city and your people happiness and prosperity.

SPEECH BY N. S. KHRUSHCHEV AT A LUNCHEON IN PITTSBURGH

The Governor of Pennsylvania, David Lawrence, the Mayor of Pittsburgh, Thomas Gallagher, and the President of the University of Pittsburgh, Edward Litchfield, gave a luncheon in honor of N. S. Khrushchev, Chairman of the Council of Ministers of the USSR.

Answering the greetings of his hosts, N. S. Khrushchev said:

MR. GOVERNOR, MR. MAYOR, MR. CHANCELLOR OF THE UNIVERSITY, LADIES AND GENTLEMEN, FRIENDS:

It is a pleasure to meet you. Perhaps it is because your city, a city of big industry, brings back vivid memories of the distant past, of my childhood and youth, of my work in the Donets Basin. Perhaps it is because, in general, I like to meet businessmen, but most likely I am happy to meet you for both these reasons.

There is a good tradition to begin a speech by expressing thanks to the audience for their patience. I will not break good traditions. Allow me to thank you heartily for your warm welcome and to wish you success in your affairs and in life. Meeting different people in your city, I got the feeling that contact of some sort had already been established between us.

We Russians and all Soviet people have long admired American efficiency, enterprise and the ability to value time. Of course, these are only a few of the qualities of the Americans.

We Soviet people also have our specific traits—revolutionary scope, courage and initiative. And so, if the efforts of both peoples were united on some common ground—in the struggle for peace and human progress, for example, the results would be good. *(Applause.)*

Ladies and gentlemen, I believe you will allow me not to continue my speech in Russian since the majority of you do not know the Russian language. I would like to ask my young friend, the interpreter, to read the text of the speech in English. That will be shorter. I am doing this especially because the Chancellor has said that we have to choose between a long and a short speech. So I choose the shortest. *(Laughter, applause.)*

Let us translate all of it into the language of business.

Your country has attained a high level of industrial development. The rapid development of industry in the United States of America astounded the whole world and aroused admiration and

Turnout to welcome the head of the Soviet government on the road to Pittsburgh.

even envy in other countries. Formerly, you did not have a worthy contestant in rates of development and in strength. Now you have one—the Soviet Union.

Under revolutionary conditions, on a new social basis, we utilized everything valuable that you had created, and we proved that your achievements could not only be equaled but also surpassed.

Today we are already catching up with your country in some things. To put it figuratively, we are now having an exchange of whistle calls. You hear our whistle getting louder and closer. Each year it will be heard better and better. And the day is not far distant when we shall draw level with you at the same station, salute you and move on. Then it will be we, and not you any longer, who are in front. And it won't be we who are following you, but you who will be following us.

Don't judge me too severely for my firm conviction that events will develop in just that way. We are prepared to compete with you in so lofty a cause as the satisfaction of the material and cultural requirements of the peoples.

You probably know that the Soviet Union is already the world's second industrial power. Incidentally, at one time your country was also second, but then it became the first. And you considered this to be perfectly natural. Why is it then that some of your compatriots think it impossible and even impermissible for us to set ourselves the goal of moving up from second place to first? We are going to compete with your country in all seriousness. The seven-year plan for the development of the Soviet economy has aroused considerable interest throughout the world. I don't wish to tire you and will quote only a few figures.

In 1958 we produced about 55 million tons of steel and in 1965 we intend to produce 86 to 91 million tons.

Last year our output of pig iron was about 40 million tons and we plan to produce 65 to 70 million tons.

Our output of rolled goods was about 43 million tons and we plan to produce 65 to 70 million tons in 1965.

I can tell you that, judging by the first of the seven years and by estimates for 1960, we shall have a greater rise in industrial output than we previously planned. We are, therefore, exceeding the targets, as we expected, and the seven-year plan will be fulfilled ahead of schedule.

As you see, we intend to take big strides forward and we are capable of doing it.

In a shop of the Mesta Machine-Building Plant in Pittsburgh.

Our country has accumulated valuable experience in developing industry, science and engineering. For example, we are making a better use of the effective volume of blast furnaces than you are in your country. Our steel workers get more steel per square meter of open-hearth furnace. In our country extensive use is made of oxygen blast in metallurgy. We are now successfully employing natural gas in metallurgy.

But how can I enumerate everything? And I've only touched on the subject of metallurgy.

Speaking figuratively, in the language of engineers, we can imagine the two giant industrial powers, the USSR and the USA, as moving along parallel lines. You on your own, and we on our own. There may be some people who would be satisfied with such a development of events. Even that sort of parallel and isolated development would, of course, be preferable to disputes and conflicts.

But it is also possible to imagine different relations between our countries. Sometimes, at a certain point, these lines, let us say, draw close to each other. In other words, contacts are established and economic, cultural, scientific and technical exchanges are arranged. We favor just this development and are prepared to disclose our technical achievements to you, making no secret of them. And you will do likewise with respect to our country. In your country, it is true, such things are not done. Everybody keeps his technical secrets to himself and does not even want his neighbor to know them, let alone disclose them to a foreign country.

And so what can we do?

We propose to approach the matter simply, on the basis of mutual benefit.

Although our peoples live differently, maintain a different way of life and have different customs, we have to live under the same sky. Although the climate in your country is much warmer and milder than in ours, the political chill comes from you and not from us. It is true, we are Northerners and not afraid of the cold, but still we would like warmer, more favorable winds, and not cold winds, to blow in the world.

Neither your people nor ours want war. Then let us live like good neighbors or, as we say in Russia, "To live with the people is to live in peace." Let us base our relations on the principle of peaceful coexistence. It gives nobody a one-sided advantage, nobody suffers losses from it, nobody makes any sacrifices, but everybody gains from it. And, most important of all, the cause of peace gains from it.

A good start has been made—visits are being exchanged on both sides at the highest level. My visit to the USA and the U.S. President's forthcoming visit to the Soviet Union will, we are sure, help us to know and understand each other better, and will help find a way to cooperation. If both our sides have the will for this, a way will be found.

The slogan "Overtake and surpass the United States" has become very popular in our country today. Some of your compatriots were frightened by this slogan. They saw in it a danger to America. But in what way is it a "danger" to you Americans? Our economic interests do not clash anywhere. Is not our country, engaged in such extensive peaceful construction, interested in a dependable and durable peace, in the development of comprehensive economic, technical and commercial relations with other countries? Certainly it is.

Could not the highly-developed industrial countries give substantial and constantly increasing aid to the economically underdeveloped countries?

I want to assure you that the purpose of our seven-year plan is a peaceful one. Our plan is calculated to improve the people's life. Unfortunately, we live in times when not all the steel produced is used for peaceful purposes. How happy the peoples of our countries and the peoples of the whole world would be if all the steel smelted in America, and here in Pittsburgh in particular, and all the steel in the Soviet Union and other countries, were used exclusively for peaceful purposes! (Applause.)

I think you will agree with me when I say that even if we had two lives they should be dedicated to this one great and worthy cause—the consolidation of peace between the peoples. (Applause.)

There is a distinguished sculptor in our country, Yevgeny Vuchetich. He has made a moving statue, called "Let's Beat Swords into Plowshares." It is a fine piece of work that deservedly attracts everyone's attention. It represents the figure of a blacksmith hammering a plowshare out of a sword. If any of you visited our exhibition in New York, you must have seen that gifted work of art. The sculptor has succeeded in embodying in bronze what millions upon millions of people are thinking and dreaming of today.

Is it not time, ladies and gentlemen, to use open-hearth furnaces to melt down the stockpiles of weapons, is it not time to beat tanks into tractors and guns into threshers, and to direct the entire might of the atom to peaceful purposes only?

As far as the Soviet Union is concerned, as I have already said at the United Nations, we are ready to do it this very day.

You and we are living in a rather complicated world situation, although at times there are bright patches in the overcast sky. Are these present days not one of them? It is not for nothing that the state of world affairs in recent years has been given the name of "cold war." Under conditions of tension the cold war can easily turn into a hot one, into a very hot one indeed, a nuclear war, that will not only scorch but will burn to ashes.

The surest way of avoiding such unenviable prospects is to destroy the means of waging war, that is, "to beat swords into plowshares." We propose that cold war be outlawed everywhere and for all time.

There are, of course, people who are interested in the very opposite. They are afraid that if there are no war orders, peaceful production will not bring in profits. They fear that if the output of weapons ceases and there is a change over to peaceful production, industry and the entire economy will be kept in a perpetually fever-

169

ish state. But this mood springs from sheer lack of foresight. Such people live by the principle of not looking farther than their noses. Indeed, if the weapons being manufactured today are ever used, the flames of war will consume not only the profits amassed on armaments production, but also very many of their owners.

I would like you to understand me correctly. I do not want to reproach anybody. I am merely trying to lay stress on the idea that wealth is of use only so long as it is not turned into ashes and cinders.

It is no secret that a special responsibility for the maintenance of peace rests with our two countries. Just imagine what world relations would look like if the USA, the largest and most powerful country of the capitalist world, and the USSR, the largest and most powerful country of the socialist world, were to establish good relations or, still better, collaboration, which we should like to grow into friendship.

I agree with Mr. Eisenhower, who once wrote that "no other division among the nations could be considered a menace to world unity and peace, provided mutual confidence and trust could be developed between America and the Soviet Union."

Those words were written shortly after the Second World War,

Khrushchev talking with executives of the Mesta Machine-Building Plant in Pittsburgh.

in which he had played so outstanding a part. Today Mr. Eisenhower is President of the United States of America. Why not realize those good ideas? We, on our part, are prepared to do everything to ensure mutual trust between America and the Soviet Union, and in this way help guarantee peace on earth for all peoples.

There are no serious obstacles to our two countries living in peace and friendship. There are, of course, ideological differences between our countries, but they are not an obstacle, for these differences existed during the Second World War but did not prevent our being good friends. Nor should they today prevent us from joining forces in the struggle for durable peace on earth. We are glad that here, too, in the USA, people who think realistically are inclined to adopt the same idea. The more people of that kind there are, the better it will be.

We must get to understand each other properly. We do not beg for peace. We only believe that peace, not war, is the natural state of mankind.

In connection with my trip to the USA, there appeared in some countries various conjectures about the purposes of the exchange of visits between representatives of our countries. Some even thought that Khrushchev was "going to divide up the world with Eisenhower."

I must state that such gossip is groundless and nonsensical. People who think along these lines take a gangster's view of all events. They have their own way of thinking: "If you're strong, grab everything you can." We, however, are people with entirely different principles. Our strength serves only the welfare of our people and of other peoples. We use our strength to ensure peace and universal security. It serves no other purpose.

The exchange of visits and our conversations on problems of the world situation and Soviet-American relations are useful not only to our countries but also to all other countries. The settlement by the Soviet Union and the United States of America of even a few disputed problems is bound to have a beneficial effect on the entire world situation and on the relations between our countries and all other countries, large and small.

Now I should like to share the impressions I gained today during my visit to the Mesta Machine Company's plant in West Homestead where we met the management, the office staff and workers. These were excellent meetings. On the way to the plant and back we were to some extent able to make contact with the inhabitants of Pittsburgh, even if at some distance. It was a pleasure to respond to the friendly greetings of the many thousands of people lining the streets.

Allow me to express my sincere thanks to the Vice-President of the Machine Company, Mr. Frank Mesta, who received us so kindly at the plant. Through him I would like to thank all the workers, engineers, technicians and other employees, who were very friendly to us during our visit to the plant.

We have gained a very fine impression of Pittsburgh and its people. But our visit here is coming to an end, and Mr. Lodge, if I may say so, must be glad: At last that "burdensome" job that has fallen to his lot—the job of accompanying me on my trip across America—is coming to an end. (Animation.)

LODGE: It has been a pleasure for me.

KHRUSHCHEV: Thank you. In a few days you will probably say: "Well, my dear guest, I have great pleasure at last in saying good-bye to you." (Laughter.)

(Lodge smiles and waves his hand in protest.)

KHRUSHCHEV: And what's wrong with that? Don't you want to give me a good send-off? (Laughter.) Or do you want to give me a bad send-off? (Laughter.)

LODGE: You have been a good guest. I regret that your trip to the USA is coming to an end.

KHRUSHCHEV: Thank you. I can tell you that when you come to us in the Soviet Union you will see that we are not only good guests but good hosts as well. (Animation, applause.)

We are very pleased with the attitude of the people of your fine city toward us Soviet people, with their warmth and cordiality, and chiefly with their appreciation of the significance of my visit to the USA, with their understanding of the necessity of improving relations between our states.

Allow me to express my sincere thanks to Bishop John Wright who, as Mr. Lodge informed me, appealed to his congregation to meet me and my party in a manner befitting good hosts in order to create conditions for an improvement in the relations between our countries.

I also render my sincere thanks to the Bishop who read a prayer before the beginning of our lunch here today. In his prayer, as translated to me, he prayed that our relations might improve, that there might be peace among people, between our countries and among all nations.

I can tell you, ladies and gentlemen, that all people in our country, atheists and religious people alike, the priesthood of all religions (and in our country there are many peoples and many different religions)—that they all have one thought, irrespective of their religious convictions or the color of their skin, that all Soviet people want peace and are doing their best to ensure peace between the nations, peace throughout the world. Our priests, mullahs and rabbis, like your bishops and clergy, pray to God that there may be peace on earth and friendship among the peoples. *(Applause.)*

I should like to assure you—it is easy for me to speak to you because many of those present have visited the Soviet Union and have some idea of our state and of our people and their hospitality—that we love our country and our state just as you love your country. Our people love their families, their children, just as you do yours. As we traveled through your towns and communities we saw many fine youngsters. Come and visit us, our successes in that field are no less *(animation)* than in the development of industry. Our people are just as fond of their children, their wives and their parents, and are solicitous of their well-being. *(Applause.)*

Your country is rich and you have achieved a high standard of living. When you were exhorted to pray for the liberation of the "slaves of communism," I said by way of a joke to Vice-President Nixon when we met in Moscow:

"Take a look at how the 'slaves of communism' live, talk to them and ask them whether they have anything to complain of."

And now that I am your guest I should like to repeat that joke—don't judge me too seriously—I have come here to see how the slaves of capitalism live. And I must say that you do not live badly. And neither do we; we live well and we are going to live still better. We shall stand up for ourselves and for our country, and are sure that we are going to catch up with you and outstrip you. We do not want to increase our wealth and catch up with you by using methods of piracy such as were used in the past—pirates never created anything, they only plundered what other peoples had created. We want to overtake and outstrip you by applying our own physical and spiritual efforts in order to create more material values than you create. I repeat, we are confident that we shall catch up with you and outstrip you. And we warn you, like honest contestants, pull up your socks or you may find yourselves behind us. We say that our riches will never be used to the detriment of any nation. In the interests of peace we must march in step with you, in step with all nations. *(Stormy applause.)*

Speaking with workers at the Mesta Machine-Building Plant in Pittsburgh.

You, ladies and gentlemen, like your capitalist system. We are very fond of the socialist system which our people have built up. You say that your system is better. Well, stick to your opinion until you are convinced of the opposite. We tell you sincerely that the socialist system is better. It provides better conditions for the development of the productive forces and, consequently, can do more for the progress of economy and culture. So far you do not admit this, although the advantages of socialism have been very well demonstrated by the example of the Soviet Union and other countries. Different views on the social system must not prevent us from cooperating. You like capitalism so have it your own way—live under capitalism, continue riding your old horse. We are mounted on a new, fresh, socialist steed, and it will be easier for us to overtake and outstrip you. But this is a question of the economic competition between the two systems. If we take the path of peaceful competition, it will be to the advantage of all nations, because there will be no

174

wars between states and human blood will not be spilled. *(Applause.)*

Allow me to thank all those who have spoken here, the Governor, Mr. Lawrence, Mr. Lodge and Mr. Litchfield, the Chancellor of the University, who is in the chair. I can subscribe to all the speeches made here today, yet there is something I should like to clarify and one point I should like to raise about the Governor's speech which, in general, I liked. All the speeches were well conceived and the speech of the Governor, especially the closing part of it, was very aptly, I might say even very cleverly, constructed. I envy you, Mr. Governor, as one speaker envies another. *(Laughter, applause.)*

At the end of your speech, Mr. Governor, you said that your people are united in their support of the government's policy, that the Republican and Democratic Parties of the USA display complete unity in defense and support of your system and your state, that they support the President and his foreign policy.

Such a statement could have two meanings. I want to say how, in my opinion, that speech may be interpreted. One meaning could be: "Listen here, Khrushchev! *(Laughter.)* We have two parties, but we are one."

God knows what difference there is between your parties. I wonder if you know; I'm sure I don't. *(Laughter, applause.)* To put it more precisely, I don't see any difference between them. But the Governor's speech might also contain a hint of this sort: "Tomorrow, Khrushchev, you're going to talk with our President. We tell our President: 'Be steadfast! Stand firm! We are behind you.'"

To this I can reply: "Ask your Ambassador, Mr. Thompson, and Mrs. Thompson." Mr. Thompson has represented your country in Moscow for several years, and if I'm not telling the truth, let him correct me. Our Soviet people are united, they are rallied solidly around their Communist Party, they support their own Party, which they believe to be the best party in the world. Our one Communist Party is better than your two parties. *(Animation.)* That's my opinion. What do you expect me to say? That your parties are better? If I thought so, I'd join one of them. *(Laughter.)*

Our people support their Soviet Government. Before I left for the USA many people said to me what you say to your President: "Comrade Khrushchev, go to America, try to achieve peace and friendship with the American people and the American Government, but stand firm." *(Animation.)*

If we adopt this over-simplified approach and take up adamant positions—I, mine, and the U.S. President, his—there won't be any businesslike talks tomorrow. There would be no negotiations to find reasonable solutions, but sheer stubborness that, to put it figuratively, would be like the stubbornness of two bulls—which has the stronger legs, which has the harder forehead, which has the longer horns and which can first gore the other.

But is that what the peoples of the Soviet Union and the United States, the peoples of all countries, expect of us? You have strong legs, but ours don't bend either. So let's compete in solving disputed questions by reason and not by force. That is what all the peoples expect of us. *(Applause.)*

It is a pleasure for me to negotiate with a head of state who enjoys the support, respect and love of his people. *(Applause.)* I represent our Soviet people. I am grateful for the confidence and respect the Soviet people have for their Government and for me as the head of the Soviet Government, representing the Soviet Union, the great Soviet people, in your country.

In these circumstances it will be easier for us to seek mutually acceptable solutions, that is, solutions acceptable to both our peoples. If a people are not united and do not support the head of their state, then that head of state cannot make sensible decisions. He would always be looking first one way and then the other, first at the Democrats, say, and then at the Republicans, and then at nobody knows whom; for he is never quite sure whether they will support his position or not.

So I should like to interpret your statement, Mr. Governor, as a real mandate of the Americans' confidence in and love for their President, as a wish that he, in his negotiations and conversations with me should find reasonable arguments, that by our joint efforts, we should find mutually accepted solutions that would really guarantee mutual understanding and friendly relations between our states and a sound peace between us and among all countries.

I came to the USA with the confidence of my people and of my government. And that is what will guide me during my meetings and talks with your esteemed President, Mr. Dwight D. Eisenhower.

If our two countries establish relations of trust instead of mistrust, and pool their efforts in the struggle to consolidate peace for themselves and for everybody, the peoples of the whole world will support us.

Thank you. *(Prolonged applause. All rise.)*

N. S. Khrushchev and his party left by plane from Pittsburgh to Washington at 4:38 P.M., local time.

IN WASHINGTON

On September 24, N. S. Khrushchev and his party returned to Washington.

Following are N. S. Khrushchev's speeches and talks in the U.S. capital September 24-27.

MEETING WITH A GROUP OF REPRESENTATIVES OF THE U.S. BUSINESS AND COMMERCIAL WORLD

In Washington on September 24, Mr. Eric Ridder, publisher of *The Journal of Commerce,* gave a dinner for N. S. Khrushchev, which was attended by representatives of the U.S. business and commercial world. The Press Group with the Chairman of the Council of Ministers of the USSR published the text of the talk held during the dinner.

In his opening remarks Mr. Ridder greeted N. S. Khrushchev and thanked him for consenting to meet a small circle of businessmen in order to exchange views on some important questions, including the question of Soviet-American trade. Mr. Ridder noted that in March, 1958, when he was received by N. S. Khrushchev in Moscow, he had asked him many questions and had been given comprehensive replies. Such an opportunity had now arisen for his colleagues. He was confident, he said, that N. S. Khrushchev would be asked many questions and that, in turn, he could ask American businessmen a series of questions.

QUESTION: Do you think, Mr. Chairman, that your trip to the USA will help to promote Soviet-American trade?

KHRUSHCHEV: Yes, I expect it will, but I should imagine that American businessmen could answer that question better than I.

RIDDER: I would ask my guests to give their points of view on this remark of Prime Minister Khrushchev.

PHILIP CORTNEY (*President of Republic Steel Corporation*): I don't see how Mr. Khrushchev's trip will help Soviet-American trade.

RIDDER: I hold a different view and believe that an improvement of political relations will help to promote business relations between our countries.

177

CHARLES WHITE (*President of Republic Steel Corporation*):
Trade with the USSR is nothing new to us. We used to sell sheet
steel to the Soviet Union. The Union Carbide and Carbon Corporation used to buy ore from Soviet organizations. We have been working with the Russians for 30 years. I want to say that today Russians
are producing many of the goods we are making in the USA and
that this fencing-off of markets has caused difficulties in trade. I have
a good knowledge of the situation in the USA and of our American
problems. We have frequent conflicts between management and labor.
Communists are mixed up in all these conflicts. They add fuel to
them and in that way make it difficult to adjust relations with the
USSR.

JACK STRAUS (*President of R. H. Macy and Company*): Another difficulty is that the American consumer does not want to buy
goods coming from behind the "Iron Curtain."

W. T. MOORE (*President of the Moore-McCormack Lines*): We
have been working with the Russians since 1928. We carried large
shipments of freight from the USSR to the USA and from the USA
to the USSR, and are doing so to some extent today. We know the
Russians well. Our business relations with them have always been
good. We believe that business relations will improve with the improvement of political relations, because trade always develops
together with friendship.

I cannot agree that Americans are refusing to buy goods coming
from the Soviet Union and the other socialist countries. For instance,
we transport ham from Poland to the U.S., and various goods from
Czechoslovakia. I do not know how they are being sold in the USA
(we are not associated with that), but I do know that their sales
are increasing all the time. For example, the import of Polish ham
to the U.S. has, I think, tripled lately. We also bring Soviet goods,
caviar among them, and I would like to see more of that in the
U.S. (*Laughter.*)

CORTNEY: In the interview with Eric Ridder, Mr. Khrushchev
said that Russia wanted to buy all the goods she needed and to sell
those she had. But an exchange of goods and payments is always
made by means of gold. Regrettably, the Soviet Union does not
publish data about its gold output and gold reserves. That worries
us, because all other countries supply this information. The lack of
such information with respect to the USSR undermines trust and
worries us.

KHRUSHCHEV: I have listened attentively to your questions, gentlemen, and have not interrupted you. But I cannot understand to what extent and why commercial circles in the U.S.A. are worried and anxious over the fact that we do not publish data about gold reserves. In general, I cannot understand what gold has to do with it. I must tell you that we do not value gold very highly. I could cite what V. I. Lenin said about gold, but I do not think it would be the suitable thing to say at dinner. *(Laughter.)*

LODGE *(the U.S. President's personal representative with N. S. Khrushchev):* I am a small capitalist and I have no gold at all.

KHRUSHCHEV: But I have. Here it is *(N. S. Khrushchev points to two gold Hero of Socialist Labor medals),* but it does not belong to me. When I die it will be turned over to the state.

REMARK: You mean your family won't be able to make use of this gold?

KHRUSHCHEV: It won't. But as regards gold and foreign trade, you can ask all the people with whom we have had dealings and they will tell you that we are always punctual in our payments and have never been in debt. Now, as regards the question asked earlier, —When you enter a shop to make a purchase, is it customary in

...rushchev at the experimental station of the Department of Agriculture in Beltsville (Maryland).

your country to ask when some item or other was made and who made it?

I myself bought a hat in one of your shops because I gave mine away to a longshoreman in San Francisco. Now then, when I bought this hat I did not ask who had made it and showed no interest in the shopkeeper's political views. I did not know that, when making purchases in your country, one is expected to ask who made the item concerned, who is the father of the shopkeeper, who is his wife and what their names are. That makes commerce very complicated. (Animation. Cries of "Quite right!")

REMARK: But under our laws it is important where the goods come from. For instance, there was a time when German goods were banned.

KHRUSHCHEV: My good tradesman, you are making a hash of everything—trade, economics and politics. You speak of things that have nothing to do at all with any of the laws of political economy. When you could not buy German goods, you were at war with Germany. But we are not, after all, at war with you! I am sure that if shops selling Soviet goods are opened, your people will buy those goods with pleasure. I know that you have no liking for the Russian Revolution, as you call the Great October Socialist Revolution, but you do like Russian caviar, for instance, and I have noticed that you are ready to consume it in fairly large quantities. (Laughter.)

STRAUS: But would you let Macy's open a store on a reciprocal basis?

KHRUSHCHEV: Now that is put in a businesslike way. We are willing to negotiate. But are you, gentlemen? (Animation.) You must, of course, understand that I am speaking of goods and not of shops. American businessmen can organize the sale of our goods themselves and extract a profit from it. The only trouble is that many of our goods cannot be imported into the USA at present because the duties on them are exorbitantly high.

MIKHAIL A. MENSHIKOV (Soviet Ambassador to the USA): The duty on some Soviet goods is three, four and more times higher than that on the same goods from other countries. The duty on vodka, for example, is four times higher.

KHRUSHCHEV: I want to make one thing clear. I did not come here to sell you goods that found no market. Besides, we don't have goods of that kind in our country. We produce a lot and sell quickly. Our warehouses are not crammed with stale goods. Goods make the path from industry to shop and consumer in double-quick time. If you don't want to trade with us, you don't have to. We'll wait until you yourself come knocking at our door. Let me repeat, we'll wait. The wind isn't blowing in our faces. Go ahead, sit by the shore and wait for fair weather. (*Animation.*) We are doing excellent business with China and other socialist countries. We are making good progress in our trade with India, Britain, France, West Germany and Italy. Our affairs are in good shape. Our economy is expanding at a rate which is two or three times faster than yours. We offer thanks to God, so to say, and go ahead with our good work. (*Animation, applause.*)

G. B. MILLER (*President of Allied Chemical and Dye Corporation*): I think that better relations between our countries and greater contacts between the peoples will enable us to improve economic relations as well.

KHRUSHCHEV: Quite right. I think so, too. That, is why I said that improved political relations will most certainly bring about an improvement in trade relations as well. The important thing is that you should understand that we have not come to stretch a long hand into your pocket. We keep our hands in our own pockets. (*Laughter.*) Even if you keep your pocket open, I'll pass by and not so much as glance at what you have in it. (*Laughter, applause.*)

The present bad trade relations between our countries are not an economic but a political factor. You did not recognize the Soviet Union for 16 years, but you traded with us. (*Animation.*) Now you recognize us, but do not trade. How much longer will this continue, 16 years or more, I cannot tell. That is your affair, reflect on it and decide for yourselves.

R. T. REED (*American Express Company*): Greater contact between the business people of our countries would go a long way toward increasing trade. There has lately been an increase in tourist travel between the USA and the USSR. It appears to be useful.

KHRUSHCHEV: I consider it a step in the right direction. We support such contacts and will do our utmost to broaden them.

REED: The Soviet side had agreed to let American firms open their offices in the USSR to promote tourism. But nothing has yet been done about it. I realize that that is only a detail, but I should like to bring to your notice that such a question exists.

KHRUSHCHEV: I shall bear your remark in mind.

REED: Would you say that trade between our countries would be more successful if we had a trade agreement?

KHRUSHCHEV: Why not? In general, why can we trade with others—Krupp, for example—and not with you?

CORTNEY: All the same, there are many difficulties in Western trade with the USSR. One of these is the monopoly on foreign trade.

KHRUSHCHEV: You are again mixing trade up with politics. The question of monopoly on foreign trade was resolved in our country 42 years ago and is not subject to revision. If it is difficult to trade with us, you don't have to. Do business with those with whom it is easy for you, but the system in our country will remain unchanged.

CORTNEY: But both you and we want to trade.

KHRUSHCHEV: Well, we did have considerable trade with many American firms. With Ford, for example. And it was profitable both for Ford and for us.

CORTNEY: Perhaps it was profitable for Ford but not for America? *(Animation.)*

KHRUSHCHEV: But the American business world is made up of Fords! *(Laughter.)*

RIDDER: Would you, Mr. Khrushchev, tell us of the impressions of your tour of the USA?

KHRUSHCHEV: I am pleased with my U.S. tour. The Americans are a peaceful people and, like all nations of the world, they do not want war. In saying so, I emphasize again that I do not divide the American people into business and political circles. Nor do I make any distinction between them and the government. Businessmen are, possibly, more inclined toward a peaceful development of events. But I do not want to dig into souls. That is a difficult thing to do. It is also possible that some businessmen, those who have large war orders, are not inclined toward a peaceful development of events. But that is only my assumption, I may be wrong.

You have many politicians who are afraid that the cold war might end. They have made too many speeches connected with the cold war. They have galloped into Congress on the cold war hobby-horse and want to stay in the same saddle. *(Laughter.)* But that is also an assumption and I cannot say exactly how many people of that kind you have.

I want to speak frankly, just as I shall report on the trip to my government. It seems to me that the American people want to come to an agreement and live in peace. But apparently it will take some time before we build up complete trust in our relations. *(Remark of "That's right!")*

Now a few words about trade. I have already said at the Economic Club that our economy suffers nothing from the fact that trade is not developing between the USA and the USSR. But if there were

182

Photo shows N. S. Khrushchev chatting with journalists after his visit to the Lincoln Memorial in Washington.

trade, it would be better both for you and for us. *(Animation. Voices: "That is reasonable.")* Everybody knows that trade utilizes the benefits of the international division of labor, the benefits of specialization in industry. We would not be developing the manufacture of many kinds of machines in our country, but would be buying them from you. But since there is no trade we are compelled to develop our own manufacture of such machines, and are doing so successfully. Today, for example, I was told at your Mesta Machines Company plant that the most powerful press made in the USA has a capacity of 50,000 tons, but we have made a 70,000-ton press.

If we do not have something, we will make it ourselves. Some of our machines are better than yours and we are selling them to you. For example, you have bought a license for a turbodrill for the oil industry. But we would also buy machines from you. We would be willing, for example, to buy chemical equipment, because you have moved ahead in that. We could make it ourselves, but that would

183

take some time. For that reason, we are ready to buy that equipment from you and to pay for it in the way established by international practice. We would purchase equipment for the oil-refining industry.

In the past we have had dealings with Du Pont. We are ready to deal with the company today as well, if there are no State Department bans on this. But if you won't sell us equipment for the oil-refining industry, we shall make it ourselves and fulfill our plans—fulfill them ahead of schedule.

I must tell you that we buy chemical equipment in other countries and it is better than yours. Last year we bought two chemical plants from Krupp. The Americans have also bought a similar plant from the Germans. We bought an automobile tire factory in Britain. The equipment for it has already arrived in the Dnepropetrovsk Economic Area and it is already being installed. We were told that in this field the British have outstripped you Americans.

N. A. TIKHONOV (*Chairman, Dnepropetrovsk Area Economic Council*): The USA does not have such improved technology for the production of tires.

KHRUSHCHEV: After signing a trade agreement with Britain we concluded many deals with British firms. Italy is prominent in the manufacture of equipment for the production of artificial fiber. We are buying this equipment there and also in France. In short, all your allies are selling us what we want, and we are buying it. America is the only country that does not trade with us. Very well, we have a saying that if you sulk and don't eat your *kasha* you'll gain nothing by it. (*Animation.*) Please, don't eat our Russian *kasha*. That is your business. Perhaps our *kasha* is bad for your stomachs. (*Laughter.*) If that is so, we will not be offended. If it is profitable—sell, if it isn't—don't sell; if it is profitable—buy, if it isn't—don't buy. Such are the laws of trade. (*Applause.*)

I see that Americans fear communism as much as the rabbit fears the boa constrictor, and are losing their common sense. Very well, we'll wait until you recover your senses completely and begin to trade. (*Laughter.*)

QUESTION: Why, in spite of all this, do you adopt a lot of what there is in the capitalist countries?

KHRUSHCHEV: Because we are not fools! (*Laughter, applause.*) Why should we turn our backs on useful experience? You have set many examples in organizing production. Ford, for instance, started line production. We have adopted that method and are developing it for the better.

QUESTION: We are interested in trading with you. But why are Soviet organizations buying only sample machines?

KHRUSHCHEV: I'll tell you frankly. If John Deere wants to sell us tractors and agricultural machines, that is not realistic, because we are making our own agricultural machines. We are buying and can buy, say, ten or a hundred tractors and other agricultural machines. That is done to compare them with our machines, to see which are better. But why are you displeased with that? How many tractors or combines do you sell to a farmer? Would Garst buy a thousand tractors from you? I should think that not a single farmer would buy even as many as ten machines. He'll buy one or two, but we'll buy 10 or 100. The argument about samples is unrealistic. I'll tell you frankly that in the sense of purchases we are not interested in tractors, combines, aircraft or rockets. (Laughter.) We are interested in chemical equipment, in equipment for engineering works and oil refineries. (Animation.) We can sell you tractors ourselves, gentlemen. If you like we can even sell you one tractor. (Animation.)

RIDDER: Mr. Khrushchev, you have raised the question of credits. What is your attitude now?

KHRUSHCHEV: We are not asking for credits. But if American manufacturers want to get big orders from us, they will get them, provided they give us credits. I have in mind credits from firms, such as the English have given us. As regards government credits, these are evidently impossible with the present state of relations between countries. If credits are forthcoming from firms, we shall pay a reasonable interest. But I stress, a reasonable interest. We shall not agree to a high interest.

MILLER: What is a reasonable interest?

KHRUSHCHEV: Not more than you get from others—the interest that operates in the world market. We are not in a position where we have to ask for credits to help us out. You are businessmen and can see for yourselves how fast we are advancing. Overfulfillment of our economic plan by one per cent amounts to 11 billion rubles. This year we are over-fulfilling the plan by five per cent. This means that at the end of the year we shall have an additional 50 billion rubles. At the close of the seven-year plan period, one per cent will amount to 19 billion rubles. I say this to illustrate the fact that we have drawn up a realistic plan. I have even received a letter from an American economist who declared that Soviet economists had calculated the seven-year steel target incorrectly. Our target is 91 million tons, while according to his calculations we shall be producing 104-105 million tons.

F. PACE: I make movie cameras. I have been told that your cameras are bad. If we taught you to make cameras, would we get paid for it? As you know, we make cameras better than most people, including the Germans.

KHRUSHCHEV: If we got a license from you, the Soviet Union would pay for it in accordance with international practice. But I cannot agree that you make better cameras than others, including the Germans. Our cameras are also good.

WHITE: For normal economic relations to develop between us there must be trust, but there is no trust because the American Communists try to create all sorts of conflicts between management and labor.

KHRUSHCHEV: I can be of no help to you there, my dear sir. You know so little about our system that it is difficult for me to tell you why. Is it that you want me to tell your Communists not to do what they are doing?

WHITE: Yes.

KHRUSHCHEV: If we told your Communists that, their reply would be: "Keep your nose out of other people's affairs."

We would tell the American Communists the same thing if they interfered in our affairs.

RIDDER: Mr. Chairman, you have seen the American people and you have recognized that they are a peace-loving people. Did you have the same view before, and do you believe that the American Government is just as peacefully inclined?

KHRUSHCHEV: My tour of the United States has not changed my convictions. I have always regarded the Americans as a peaceful people. As regards an appraisal of the actions of the American Government, that depends on concrete conditions. We must not judge by words but by deeds. We have submitted the question of disarmament. But if you only say that you are for peace and at the same time have military bases around the USSR, then we'll also be forced to have rocket bases against you. We have submitted a proposal for a peace treaty with Germany. If you sign it, that means you want peace; if you don't, that means you are steering a course towards worsening relations. We want to live in peace and to trade with you. Trade is litmus paper—it shows the state of relations between states. It shows whether they want to live in peace or not. You do not want to trade with us. But why? That makes us think and puts us on our guard. Apparently you are planning some evil. You cannot expect me to tell my people that you are for peace, but do not even want to trade in such a trifling item as herring. If I did that, the Soviet people would tell me that I am a simpleton and that evidently they need another Prime Minister. But I shall not tell the Soviet people that.

If you do not want to trade with us, you don't have to, but end discrimination. So long as there is discrimination we shall have a thorn in our hearts. But if we find a common language on questions of disarmament, and if we have a peace treaty with the two German states, that would mean that you want to live in peace. If not—that means you want war. Everything consists of concrete deeds. If you, gentlemen, think that our economy will buckle under the arms race you are imposing on us, you are making a big mistake. In our plans for peaceful economic development we have also made provisions for the manufacture of the armaments necessary to defend the interests of the Soviet Union. We want peace, but we are ready to defend ourselves against any aggression.

That is what I wanted to tell you, gentlemen, in reply to your questions. Thank you.

Eric Ridder, who presided, in turn thanked N. S. Khrushchev for the frank and useful talk. Ridder's guests warmly took leave of N. S. Khrushchev and wished him success in his struggle for improving the relations between the United States of America and the Soviet Union and among all countries of the world.

SPEECH BY N. S. KHRUSHCHEV AT LUNCHEON GIVEN BY U.S. SECRETARY OF STATE CHRISTIAN HERTER

On September 25 the Secretary of State of the United States Christian A. Herter gave a luncheon in honor of N. S. Khrushchev, Chairman of the Council of Ministers of the USSR.

Mr. Herter proposed a toast to the Chairman of the Council of Ministers of the USSR and to the people of the Soviet Union. N. S. Khrushchev returned the toast:

MR. SECRETARY OF STATE, GENTLEMEN, FRIENDS:

I was very glad to hear Mr. Herter's friendly words. I fully agree with all he said. On my own behalf and on behalf of my comrades, I must with all sincerity say that we are very pleased with the President's invitation to visit your country, are very pleased with our stay here and with the meetings which we had in your country.

I must say that nothing unforeseen happened, in our opinion, during this trip. You think that when we object to what we do not agree with, we thus express our dissatisfaction. No, we simply express our disagreement with the point of view of others, and this is quite normal.

I understand your train of thought; you have a poor knowledge of our system. We have no less and perhaps even more differences and disputes over practical questions than you have. But your system operates in such a way that differences are presented in a more dramatic and sensational light.

When differences arise in considering various questions, we discuss matters in a calm atmosphere. Indeed, people who do not agree with one or another draft which is under review proceed, in the final analysis, from the same considerations which guide the authors of the draft. That is why we have arguments but no sensations arise.

Of course, we sometimes also have differences on essential problems which end rather dramatically. I shall not cite any concrete

Secretary of State Christian A. Herter shakes hands with his luncheon guest, Soviet Premier Khrushchev, as the latter arrives at Anderson House in Washington. In center is Khrushchev's interpreter, Oleg Troyanovsky.

examples—all present here know what I have in mind. However, all this should not prevent us from improving relations between our countries. An agreement which would correspond to the interests of both countries can and should be found, if there is a desire to do so.

At present I would like to say, and I am pleased to do this in such good company, Mr. Herter, that the meetings with the American people have confirmed that we acted correctly in having accepted the President's invitation, and that they have filled us with a hope that this trip to the United States will yield useful results.

We, on our part, shall do everything so that the talks with the President, which we start today, may produce beneficial results. We shall do everything on our part so that, following these talks, the relations between our countries may become better than previously.

On returning home, I shall report to our people on the results of the talks, and I am certain that our people will understand us and approve the strivings which guided us in the talks here, that a gradual improvement of relations between the USSR and the USA will lead to friendship between our countries in the interests of strengthening the cause of peace.

Allow me to propose a toast to the health of President Dwight Eisenhower of the USA, to the American people, to our host, Mr. Herter, who received us so kindly, to all present. *(Applause.)*

JOINT SOVIET-AMERICAN COMMUNIQUE

The Chairman of the Council of Ministers of the USSR, N. S. Khrushchev, and President Eisenhower have had a frank exchange of opinions at Camp David. In some of these conversations, Minister of Foreign Affairs of the USSR, A. A. Gromyko and United States Secretary of State Christian Herter, as well as other officials from both countries, participated.

The Chairman of the Council of Ministers of the USSR and the President have agreed that these discussions have been useful in clarifying each other's position on a number of subjects. The talks were not undertaken to negotiate issues. It is hoped, however, that the exchange of views will contribute to a better understanding of the motives and position of each, and thus to the achievement of a just and lasting peace.

The Chairman of the Council of Ministers of the USSR and the President of the United States agreed that the question of general disarmament is the most important one facing the world today. Both governments will make every effort to achieve a constructive solution to this problem.

In the course of the conversations, an exchange of views took place on the question of Germany, including the question of a peace treaty with Germany, in which the positions of both sides were expounded.

With respect to the Berlin question, an understanding was reached, subject to the approval of the other parties directly concerned, that negotiations would be reopened with a view to achieving a solution which would be in accordance with the interests of all concerned and in the interests of the maintenance of peace.

In addition to these matters, useful conversations were held on a number of questions affecting the relations between the Union of Soviet Socialist Republics and the United States. These subjects included the question of trade between the two countries. With respect to an increase in exchanges of persons and ideas, substantial progress was made in discussions between officials and it is expected that certain agreements will be reached in the near future.

The Chairman of the Council of Ministers of the USSR and the President of the United States agreed that all outstanding international questions should be settled not by the application of force but by peaceful means through negotiation.

Finally it was agreed that an exact date for the return visit of the President to the Soviet Union next spring would be arranged through diplomatic channels.

Washington, September 27, 1959

PRESS CONFERENCE IN WASHINGTON September 27

STATEMENT BY N. S. KHRUSHCHEV

My esteemed fellow-traveling journalists. You will excuse me for this somewhat unusual form of address. Many of you have been traveling with me through the United States and therefore I look upon you as my travel companions, my sputniks.

To begin with, allow me to make public the text of the joint Soviet-American communique.

(At N. S. Khrushchev's request, the interpreter, O. A. Troyanovsky, read the text of the communique in English.)

KHRUSHCHEV: Now I would like to thank you for the work you have done and for your rather complete coverage of my trip. You have had to work pretty hard.

I know that each of you wrote in a different way about my visit to the USA and about my talks with President Dwight Eisenhower. I have read some of your stories and I can see that they were written in a well-meaning spirit, with a knowledge of what was what. But that was not always the case. Some find it difficult to give up cold-war methods. It is gratifying, however, that most of the journalists with whom I have had contact tried as best they could to be objective in covering our visit to the United States.

Now, a couple of words about my impressions. I have a great many impressions. Today I shall speak to you as a man enriched by all that he has seen and heard in your great country. I had meetings with the President, with well-known statesmen and civic leaders in your country, with businessmen and ordinary Americans. Our talks were frank and straightforward, and that is good. All this helped us to understand each other better. Of course, twelve days is a short period to hope to see everything. But for us it has been a lot of time in which to learn many things and to discuss many things with Americans. As you know, in addition to Washington, we visited New York and Los Angeles, San Francisco, Des Moines and Pittsburgh.

You are naturally most interested in my impressions of the meetings we had with the President of the USA, Mr. Eisenhower. We had pleasant talks. On all the subjects that we touched upon, we had a great deal in common both as regards our evaluation of the situation and the need to improve relations between our countries.

Everybody realizes that it is not so easy to throw off all the litter that has piled up in the many years of cold war. We cannot count on a sudden change in the situation. The process of improving relations between our countries will require much effort and patience and, above all, the desire of both sides to achieve that end.

The Soviet Union, whose government and people I represent, is guided by the interests of consolidating peace and friendship between nations. We have made and will continue to make every effort to end the cold war and improve relations between our countries.

I have no doubt whatsoever that the President is sincere in his desire to improve relations between our countries. It seems to me that the President of the USA is in a more difficult position than I am. In the United States the forces obstructing an improvement of relations between our countries and a relaxation of international tension are, evidently, still influential. And that must be taken into consideration. But I believe that, in the long run, common sense will

191

indicate the right course in settling international problems—a course leading to the consolidation of peace throughout the world.

My meetings with representatives of the business world of your country showed that there is a mutual interest in reviving the relations and ties which would be beneficial to both countries. At the same time, this would afford an opportunity to consider in a calm atmosphere the ways and means of replacing military production by civilian production.

I would like to say a great deal about my meetings with workers and farmers, students and intellectuals of your country. I like your people. Just like the Soviet people, they want one thing—peace and prevention of another war. They want to know more about the Soviet Union and the Soviet people in order to utilize the grand potentialities of our countries for the good of the people and an improvement of the international situation.

I have been asked everywhere whether I like your way of life. Naturally, I like our way of life better. But I do not want to disappoint you and will frankly say that regardless of the difference in the way of life of our countries, we can work together well and usefully in the international arena. After all, we did have good relations in the years of our joint war effort against the common enemy. And there are no insurmountable obstacles to reviving and developing that cooperation also in the struggle for peace.

Our meeting with the President, Mr. Eisenhower, will be followed by his visit to the Soviet Union. Our people will receive him just as cordially and hospitably as your people received me and the other representatives of the Soviet Union accompanying me.

I am now prepared to answer your questions.

QUESTION: You have called for a vast expansion of consumer goods trade between the United States and the Soviet Union during your earlier press conference at the National Press Club. Do you think now your visit to America will result in increased peaceful trade?

KHRUSHCHEV: In replying to this question, I would, first and foremost, like to stress, so that the gentlemen of the Western press would understand clearly, that the Soviet Union is not a colony. Our country is one of the biggest industrial powers. Its industry, economic potential and level of scientific and technical development enable us to produce all kinds of goods, both the articles needed to promote a rapid growth of industry and agriculture, and consumer goods. So if some people in the United States of America think of selling us sausages or shoes, those, of course, are not the kind of goods for expanding trade between our countries. Let them look for buyers of such goods elsewhere. We want to buy what interests us and sell what interests you, and this includes consumer goods and goods for the development of industry—machine equipment, for example.

QUESTION: Do you not think that there will be more progress now in the development of Soviet-American ties in the cultural field?

KHRUSHCHEV: We shall not be behind in that respect. We favor a broad exchange of delegations, an exchange of spiritual values, and are ready to do all in our power to develop Soviet-American relations in the cultural field on a reasonable, mutually acceptable basis. We would like the United States of America likewise to be ready to do that.

QUESTION: Do you feel that there was any planned attempt to hinder your reception in America and, if so, who do you think planned it?

KHRUSHCHEV: I agree with you, Mr. Schorr, with what you had in mind, when you were planning this question. (Laughter.) But it would be discourteous for a guest to point a finger at the people, who, so to say, forced themselves to accept, or by force of a certain necessity accepted, my visit. I, naturally, do not imply high-placed persons, but speak of certain people who play quite an important role in the general state machine of the United States of America. True, not everybody favored my visit. But the persons who counted on preventing a good reception for me in the USA have failed.

QUESTION: Mr. Chairman, the joint communique says both sides expounded their views on Berlin. Has the position of the Soviet Union changed as a result of your talks with President Eisenhower?

KHRUSHCHEV: That is a very complicated question and a simple answer will not do. Besides, I do not know how the author of the question understands this problem, how he understands our position on Berlin. But since our position on the Berlin question has been expounded fairly comprehensively, the President and I exchanged views on this question as well and we found much in common in our understanding of it. I think that is quite sufficient for a press conference. (Animation.)

QUESTION: What will you tell the Russian people about the United States when you return?

KHRUSHCHEV: Have patience until tomorrow. My plane arrives in Moscow at 3 P.M., Moscow time, and at 4 P.M. I shall address the people of Moscow. If you want to listen in (I don't know if my speech will be broadcast in your country), you will learn by radio what I shall tell the Muscovites. If you don't, my speech will be published in the press on the next day and you can read it in the newspapers. *(Laughter.)*

QUESTION: Which questions do you consider the most mature for discussion at a meeting of the heads of government of the Great Powers?

KHRUSHCHEV: All questions which tend to worsen international relations and hinder normal relations with the United States and other Western countries should be discussed at a conference of heads of government. They must be resolved and the obstacles hindering normal relations between countries must be removed so as to create a warmer atmosphere in international relations, so that relations between countries could develop in more favorable circumstances, so that they could improve steadily and become friendly.

QUESTION: At the National Press Club you said that capitalism, being more progressive than feudalism, replaced it, and that socialism will replace capitalism for the same reason. What, in your opinion, will in turn follow communism? *(Laughter.)*

KHRUSHCHEV: Having built socialism, we in the Soviet Union have started to build communism and are in the first stage of the building of communism. To one degree or another, the other socialist countries are completing the construction of socialism. We have still, if one can say so, not tried what the communist system gives people and society. Yet here among you is a man who demands that he be given a new pie. *(Laughter.)* Why should I look for a new pie when I consider the communist pie the best. We shall eat it with pleasure and will share it with anyone who wants it. *(Animation.)*

QUESTION: Mr. Chairman, do you think that a summit meeting is now assured? When and where would you propose to hold it?

KHRUSHCHEV: Only a director of some institution could use such a tone with his employees and say that everything is now ready as far as he is concerned and all that remains is to sign an order and everything will proceed as he wants it.

A summit meeting requires the consent of all the heads of government concerned. I therefore cannot say that everything is ready for such a meeting. Agreement has yet to be reached on this. I believe that the conditions necessary for calling a meeting of heads of government have already ripened. Personally, I am ready for the meeting to be held anywhere. It will have to be held where the majority of the heads of government find it most convenient. So far as we are concerned, this is not a special question and it is not worthwhile making a principle of it. Geneva, for instance, is a good place for a meeting of heads of government.

QUESTION: Has the hope for permanent world peace increased as the result of your talks with President Eisenhower?

KHRUSHCHEV: I have never relinquished the hope for peace and have always believed that if people make an effort to ensure peace, peace will be preserved. After meeting with Mr. Eisenhower, the President of the United States, my hopes are now stronger than ever before, because during my talks with him I felt that he, too, is showing a concern to ensure peace just as we are doing.

QUESTION: Do you still believe that the only way to solve the German problem is to sign peace treaties with both East and West Germany?

KHRUSHCHEV: Day follows night, and after war, peace must come. That is why a peace treaty must be signed. With whom? With the two existing German states, because there is no united Germany. There is no other way; at least, I can see no other. If you have some other solution, tell me about it. I think you will not find another solution either.

QUESTION: Before your arrival and during your stay in the United States, some people here said that you ought to be taught a lesson with a demonstration of American power, with a display of the American way of life, so as to convince you of the advantages of capitalism. How do you feel, Nikita Sergeyevich, after these heavy lectures?

KHRUSHCHEV: To teach a lesson is not a suitable phrase with regard to representatives of the great Soviet Union. Whoever thought that way was not a sensible person. As regards my convictions and which system I think is better, this is not the suitable place in which to hold a discussion on that score. We are not forcing our system on anyone and, personally, having been in the United States, I am convinced more than ever that the holiest of holies, the best that man can create is socialist society, the communist system, where man is indeed a friend and brother to man. How do I feel after my trip? To put it in a nutshell: God grant that you may feel as well as I do! (Animation, applause.)

QUESTION: Would the Soviet Union allow foreign observers on its soil at the precise moment that proposed disarmament begins, allow them to travel at will during the process of disarmament, and allow them to remain there until all disarmament is completed?

KHRUSHCHEV: If you carefully read our disarmament proposals, which I expounded in my speech at the UN General Assembly, you will find, I think, that our position on this question is explained there quite exhaustively. If you like, I can repeat it. Our idea is that when disarmament starts there should be a corresponding stage of inspection at each stage of disarmament, that is to say, the representatives of the other countries should be present and there should be inspection in the regions subject to inspection by agreement. And that will take place throughout the process of disarmament, until it is completed. After there is complete disarmament, then inspectors must, of course, remain in the countries concerned to see that the disarmament agreement is religiously observed by each state.

If our proposals are accepted and there is general disarmament, the question of secrecy will fall away. People will then be able to go wherever and whenever they please, with the exception, perhaps, of places where the permission of the housewife must first be asked. *(Laughter.)*

QUESTION: What reasons did President Eisenhower give you for postponing his visit to Russia until spring?

KHRUSHCHEV: I shall let you in on a secret, although I have not asked the President's permission to do so. But he promised to listen in and he will know what I shall say. For that reason I shall take the liberty of telling you how it happened.

Yesterday the President kindly invited me to his farm and introduced me to his wonderful grandchildren. I had, so to speak, direct contact with them—a kind of "conference." I asked them if they thought they could accompany their grandfather and, if so, when would they like to go with him to the Soviet Union.

At that "conference," jointly with the President's grandchildren, we unanimously decided that they definitely must come to Moscow. The question of the most suitable time for such a trip arose, and I must admit that I suggested that the best time for the President, and especially for his grandchildren, is in summer or spring, when everything is in bloom and fragrant, when no cold autumn or winter winds blow. Then, in a most amiable manner, we had an exchange of views on this question with the President and came to just such a conclusion. Therefore, do not look for fleas where no fleas exist, and try to understand how these questions are resolved in a human way. *(Laughter.)*

Well, I have told you how that happened. If the President considers that I, as a partner, have overstepped my authority and revealed some special secrets about our talks, I ask him to forgive me.

I think that my grandchildren, too, will approve of our decision. So, if we are to speak of our grandchildren, then they are agreed that the visit of the President of the USA to the Soviet Union should take place in spring or summer, and the grandfathers also agree with this. *(Laughter, applause.)*

QUESTION: What do you now think of the United States, of the American people, and of the possibility of peaceful coexistence and cooperation between the USSR and the USA?

KHRUSHCHEV: Experience tells all nations that countries with different social systems must coexist, live in peace, be friends and develop normal relations. That has always been my position, and my conviction that it is a correct one is now firmer than ever before.

QUESTION: If disarmament is effected, how many men would you thus release for your civilian economy? *(Animation.)*

KHRUSHCHEV: This, I think, is not only journalistic but also overflowing female curiosity. *(Laughter.)* I will tell you frankly that if we get disarmament, and that is something we want, then all the soldiers, generals, officers, admirals and airmen who are now doing military service will go home.

QUESTION: When President Eisenhower asked you for assurances that Western rights in West Berlin would continue to be respected, what was your answer?

KHRUSHCHEV: The President and I have exchanged views on many questions and I think it is not necessary to make everything public. We have already made a lot public. We shall meet again and talk and after that again tell you what we consider necessary. How inquisitive you are! Have patience and we shall tell you. When the time comes, we shall tell you everything.

QUESTION: Those of us who went to the USSR with Vice-President Nixon were surprised at the number of young people in church. If there is an increasing interest in religion, what will be your attitude toward churches?

KHRUSHCHEV: First, by asking that question you confirm our repeated statements that we have complete freedom of religion. Secondly, people also go to church simply out of curiosity. Generally speaking, curiosity is characteristic of young people. For example, I told the President how, one day, immediately after the war, Marshal Tolbukhin, with whom I had spent a lot of time at the front near Stalingrad, paid me a visit. I had invited him for dinner. My children

197

were still small then. When Marshal Tolbukhin arrived, they all gathered and gazed at him from around a corner, out of curiosity, and then said among themselves: "There, at last we have seen a living marshal."

Similarly, children and young people who hear elderly people speak of religion, of the saints and of God, want to go and see for themselves what goes on in church. It is interesting to them. But if each young man and girl were to go to church out of curiosity just once, the doors of churches would never close. They would be creaking all the time with people going in and out.

Or take the case of me, a Communist, coming to your country now. How many people came out into the streets to see a living Soviet Communist! Suppose a prominent capitalist comes to the Soviet Union. How many people would want to take a look at him, to pull him by the tail, so to speak, if he has such an appendage to his person! (Laughter.) A very large number of people would gather, and there would be nothing surprising in that.

Ladies and gentlemen, there are still many more questions and I would have answered them all with pleasure, but the clock keeps its own count. I shall soon have to speak on television. Therefore, in conclusion, allow me to thank you most sincerely for your attention and to wish you success. I would ask you to spare no effort in ensuring good relations between our countries, so that there is friendship and peace between our countries, so that there is peace throughout the world. (Applause.)

Good-bye. Thank you. (Prolonged applause.)

N. S. KHRUSHCHEV'S BROADCAST OVER U.S. TELEVISION

September 27, 1959

Good evening, American friends.

I am glad of this opportunity of talking to you before leaving for my country. We liked your beautiful cities and fine roads, but most of all your amiable, kind-hearted people. And let these words of mine not be taken as the guest's customary tribute of courtesy and respect to his host.

Those who have visited the Soviet Union will have told you about the very good feelings which the Soviet people have for you and about their wish to live in peace and friendship with you. And I will now take with me the certainty that you feel the same way about the Soviet people. I am going to tell them about it.

I have had very pleasant talks with President Dwight Eisenhower. In all matters touched upon in our conversations, we had much in common, both as regards our appraisal of the situation and the need for better relations between our countries.

You will realize that it is not so easy to overcome all that has piled up in the many years of cold war. Think of all the speeches that did not promote better relations but, on the contrary, aggravated them! That being so, we cannot expect an abrupt change in the situation. The process of improving relations between our countries will require great effort and patience, but above all else a mutual desire to create conditions that will facilitate a shift from the present state of tension to normal relations, and then to friendship in the interests of durable peace throughout the world.

The Soviet Union, whose government and people I represent, is guided by the desire to promote peace and friendship among nations. We have always done our utmost to end the cold war and improve relations between our countries, and we do so now.

I have not the slightest doubt that the President sincerely desires better relations between our countries. It seems to me that the position of the U.S. President is more difficult than mine. It would appear that the forces obstructing better relations between our countries and a relaxation of international tension are still influential in the United States of America. And that must be taken into account. I think, however, that common sense will in the end suggest the right course in the settlement of international problems. And that course, the only correct course, is the termination of the cold war and the promotion of universal peace.

But it takes more than two states to end international tension. This can only be done if all states desire it and work for it.

There can be no stability or peace in the world as long as the two mightiest powers are at odds.

Picture two neighbors. Each disapproves of the way the other lives and runs his household. So they fence themselves off from each other. And together with their families, they revile each other day and night. Is that a happy life to live? Anyone will say that it is not; sooner or later the two neighbors may come to blows.

Bad neighbors have a way out, at least—one of them could sell his house and move into another. But what about states? They cannot move elsewhere, can they? What is the solution then?

You have capitalism in your country, and we have socialism. Must we on this account push things to the point of a world-wide free-for-all? Or shall we establish normal relations and live in peace, each in his own way? Everybody in the Soviet Union wants all countries to live in peace, everybody wants peaceful coexistence.

Have you ever given any thought to the following? Why do you and we need all these armaments if we have no intention of going to war? I have been told that your country annually spends an average of more than 40 billion dollars on armaments. What about us? There's been no point in concealing the fact that we spend about 25 billion dollars a year for the same purpose. Couldn't a better use be found for the people's money?

To be sure, it is not easy for any country to accept disarmament unless it is certain that the others will do likewise. Every country has fears of being attacked.

You probably know that a week ago the Soviet Government submitted to the United Nations a proposal for general and complete disarmament and for the most rigid, comprehensive control. What have we in mind? We propose that all armed forces be completely abolished, that all weapons, including atomic, hydrogen and rocket weapons, be destroyed. The states should retain no more than strictly limited contingents of police armed with small arms. But if our partners should be unwilling to take measures as far-reaching as that, we are prepared, for a start, to reach agreement on partial steps toward disarmament.

We are gratified that many statesmen and political leaders are giving serious thought to these proposals of ours and on their part are taking steps to bring about the necessary agreement on disarmament. Unfortunately, some people still cling to the arguments of the cold-war period. We should like to hope that the governments of the USA and other countries will take a correct view of our peaceful proposals and will, for their part, take appropriate steps in the same direction.

We discussed this problem in detail during our conversations with your President. The President, like ourselves, is concerned about the fact that so far we have not succeeded in ending the armaments fever. I am going home in the hope that the U.S. Government will be able to overcome deep-rooted prejudices and that sooner or later, in common with all the other countries, we will find the correct approach to the solution of the disarmament problem.

We have also discussed other pressing matters, of which quite a number have piled up these days. I will, first of all, single out the problem of removing the aftermath of the Second World War. Many people ask why the Soviet Union is so concerned about the question of removing those vestiges. After all, it's a thing of the distant past, they argue. I will speak plainly: We are not afraid of German militarism. But we know its insidious ways and habits only too well. The absence of a peace treaty creates an atmosphere which stimulates revanchist sentiment. Don't misunderstand me. The survivals of war must not be allowed to stay if we are to have peace.

The Soviet Union has proposed that a line be drawn through the Second World War. This can and must be done by signing a treaty with Germany.

The argument is sometimes used against us that since the war was waged against Germany when she was a single state, a peace treaty can only be concluded after Germany is unified. But it is well known that, at present, two German states exist in reality, and each of them lives in its own way. Neither of the German states wants to give up its social system. And surely there can be no question of forcing one German state to surrender to the other. Let the Germans themselves reach agreement on how they should live, on how they should shape their mutual relations.

Would it not be best to conclude a peace treaty with both German states without further delay, and thereby put out the sparks buried in the ashes before they set off a new conflagration? Conclusion of a peace treaty would also put out the live spark in West Berlin, with the result that a normal situation would be created.

The question of a German peace treaty, like the disarmament question, is not an easy one. But precisely because these are difficult questions, they must be settled and not shelved.

During my stay in your country I have acquainted myself with the life of the American people as best I could in so short a time, and have seen and heard a good deal. I am most grateful for the warm reception and cordiality accorded to me, as head of the Soviet Government, and to my companions. We were strengthened in the conviction that the American people are striving for friendship with our people and that they love peace and their country. They have created great riches and achieved a high standard of living. Like you the Soviet people love their country and want peace. They want to live in friendship with your people, and with all the other peoples of the world.

The peoples of the Soviet Union have made great progress, thanks to the victory of socialism. And though we are not yet as rich as you, we are on the right path that leads to the achievement of the highest standard of living. Our people are striving for it, and it shall be achieved.

The question of social and political structure, that is, whether to live under socialism or capitalism, is the internal affair of each people, and noninterference by states in each other's domestic affairs should be strictly adhered to.

If all countries are guided by these principles, there will be no particular difficulties in assuring international peace. To live in peace, we must know each other better. Allow me to tell you, if only briefly, about our country, the life of our people and our plans for the future. I hope you will not misunderstand me when I say that the impressions which I have gained here, and indeed the things that I liked in your country, have not shaken my conviction that the political, economic and social mode of life in the Soviet Union is the most progressive and just.

The Soviet Union is a state of working people. We have no capitalists. Our factories and mills belong to the people and so does all the land with its riches. Peasants work on that land as members of collective farms. Each has an income that depends on the amount of work he puts in, not on capital invested.

Under socialism, the remuneration paid to a worker depends on the quantity and quality of the work he performs for the good of society. When we have expanded production still more and accumulated greater wealth, we will go over to distribution according to the communist principle, which means that each will work according to his ability and enjoy the good things of life according to his needs.

The Constitution of our state is, in fact, the most democratic. It guarantees universal, direct and equal suffrage by secret ballot. It guarantees the right to work, to education and to rest and leisure.

Before the Revolution in our country, he who had capital was considered wise. For the first time in history, our country has established the just principle: He who works well enjoys social distinction.

Take the composition of the Supreme Soviet of the USSR, which is the country's highest organ of state power. There are 1,378 deputies elected to the Supreme Soviet of the USSR, of whom 366 are women. Over 1,000 deputies are directly engaged in industrial or agricultural production—they are workers, engineers, collective farmers, agronomists. The other deputies are statesmen, public leaders, scientific or cultural workers, men of letters, art workers, teachers, doctors. As you see, there are no capitalists in our country and no capitalist representatives in the Supreme Soviet. Those who make up our government are the sons and daughters of working people.

I will tell you about myself. My grandfather was an illiterate peasant. He was the landlord's property and could be sold or even, as was often the case, traded for a dog. My father was a coal miner, and I, too, worked in a coal pit as a fitter. I fought in our Civil War. Then the Soviet state sent me to a workers' school and later to the Industrial Academy. Now the people have entrusted me with the high office of Chairman of the Council of Ministers.

Recently, both my First Deputies, Anastas Mikoyan and Frol Kozlov, visited your country. Who are they? Anastas Mikoyan is the son of a carpenter, and Frol Kozlov is the son of a blacksmith and was himself a worker and later an engineer. There is no such thing as inheriting capital or high posts in our country.

All members of Soviet society enjoy genuine freedom. The only thing we do not have is the freedom to exploit other people's labor, to privately own factories or banks.

We people of the older generation started life in a capitalist environment. But why do we consider the socialist way more just? For hundreds of years mankind had developed under conditions where a minority appropriated the riches created by the majority. And always people had sought a better social structure under which there would be no exploitation of man by man.

We are grateful to Marx, Engels and Lenin who blazed the trail to that society, and we have taken that trail. And the same path was taken after us by many peoples of Europe and Asia. Having taken power into their hands, the working people put an end to the urge for profiting at other people's expense. Human greed is a terrible thing. Has there ever been a millionaire who did not want to be a multimillionaire?

I want to be understood correctly. It is one thing when a person has a pair of shoes and wants to have two or three pairs more, when he has one suit and wants to have a few more, or when he has a house and wants to build himself a better one. That is a legitimate desire. Socialism does not limit people's tastes or requirements. But it is quite another thing when a person owns a factory and wants to have two, or when he owns one mill and wants to have ten. It should be perfectly clear that no one, even if he is helped by his entire family, and even if he were to live more than one life, can earn a million, and still less a billion dollars, by his own labor. He can do that only if he appropriates the labor of others. But surely that is contrary to man's conscience. You will remember that even the Bible says that when they who engaged in trade turned the temple into a house of usurers and money-changers, Christ took a whip and drove them out.

That is why religious people should not oppose the new socialist system if, in accordance with their moral code, they are guided by the principles of peace on earth and love of one's neighbor. For it is a system which establishes the most human and truly just relations in society.

To help you understand why we are so proud of our Soviet country, I must say a few words about our pre-Revolutionary past. The people had a very hard life in those days. Almost 80 per cent of the population was illiterate. Hunger and disease killed millions of people.

You will now find it easier to understand why Soviet people are so happy that their country has in a short time become the world's second greatest industrial power. We have increased industrial output 36-fold, eliminated illiteracy, and are now graduating almost three times as many engineers as the USA.

Our people would still be better off today if, out of 40 years, we had not spent almost two decades on wars imposed upon us, and on postwar economic rehabilitation.

Do you know that during the war the German fascist invaders burned down or otherwise destroyed 1,710 towns and townships and upward of 70,000 villages, leaving about 25 million people homeless? We lost many millions of people and suffered material damage amounting to nearly 500 billion dollars.

But for these fearful losses and destruction, we would probably have caught up with the United States by now both in volume of output and in living standards.

Today our people are busy fulfilling the seven-year plan. In the current seven-year period we will double industrial output. In this period, we will invest the equivalent of nearly 750 billion dollars in the national economy.

Today the United States is economically the most highly-developed power. Your country's economic indices are the peak of what has been attained in the capitalist world. But don't forget that, on the average, the Soviet Union's annual rate of industrial growth is three to five times as high as yours. That means that in the next ten to twelve years we will exceed the United States both in physical volume of industry and in per capita output. And in agriculture this task will be fulfilled much earlier.

Our country is carrying on large-scale housing construction. Here is an example: In the past eight years alone more housing was built in Moscow than throughout the 800 years of its pre-Revolutionary history. Next year the people of Moscow will have additional housing whose total floor space will exceed one quarter of all the housing available in our capital before the Revolution. In the current seven-year period we will build about 15 million apartments in towns and 7 million houses in the countryside. That is roughly equivalent to some 50 new towns as large as San Francisco. An important point is that our country has the world's lowest rent—a mere 4 or 5 per cent of the family budget.

We are seeing to it that there are more comfortable homes and that Soviet people get more and better consumer goods. And we are as good as our word. In the last six years Soviet agriculture has trebled meat sales to the urban population, and more than doubled those of milk.

It will not be long before we abolish—I repeat, abolish—all taxation of the population. I believe you fully appreciate the significance of this measure.

The Communist Party, the Soviet Government and the trade unions are working for the welfare of all Soviet people.

Soviet people need not fear anything like unemployment, for example. The term "unemployment" is long forgotten in our country. In the Soviet Union, it is not people who look for work, but work that looks for people.

All our children go to school. In the Soviet Union tuition is free not only in secondary schools, but also in higher schools. Students receive state allowances. We give a very great deal of attention to the education of children. Nursery school, kindergarten, boarding-school, and then a start in life—such is the clear road of our rising generation.

The merits of the Soviet educational system are widely known. It is the people educated in Soviet schools—scientists, engineers, technicians and workers—who amazed the world with the first man-made earth satellites. We are proud that the Russian words "sputnik" and "lunik" are now understood all over the world, without having to be translated.

Two million teachers and almost 400,000 doctors are serving the welfare of Soviet people.

We are taking care of the health of our people; the sick rate has sharply declined in our country and the death rate is the lowest in the world. Every factory or office worker is granted paid leave every year. The working people have the best sanatoriums, health resorts and vacation resorts at their disposal. Medical treatment is free for all in our country, and neither a minor operation nor the most complicated one entails any expense for the patient. Sometimes you don't understand certain aspects of our way of life. And Soviet people find it hard to understand how it can be that when you are in trouble because someone in your family is seriously ill and has to be operated on or sent to a hospital, you have to pay money for it. And what if you have no money? What happens then—must the sick man die?

When somebody is ill in our country and cannot work, he gets his pay just the same. And when old age comes along he does not feel abandoned, for he gets a state pension. Peasants are pensioned out of the funds of their collective farms.

You may ask: "Is everything really so good and smooth in your country?" I am afraid not, because we also have our difficulties, shortcomings and unsolved problems. I can assure you that we Soviet people are the most scathing and uncompromising critics of our own shortcomings.

Esteemed citizens of the United States of America, in a few hours our plane will leave American soil. I wish once again to thank the American people, President Eisenhower and the U.S. Government for the hospitality and good feelings shown us. I credit these good feelings and the attention shown to me, as head of the Soviet Government, to the people of my country.

During my stay in your country I have received thousands of letters and telegrams of greeting from American citizens. They express friendship for the Soviet people. Many of them invited my companions and myself to visit their homes and meet their families and their children. I should like to go to all the places I was invited to, but unfortunately that is out of the question. To do it, I should have to stay here a long time. And that, you will realize, is something I cannot do. Allow me to give my heartfelt thanks to all who extended their friendly invitation, to all who expressed friendly sentiments.

Allow me, in conclusion, to wish the American people prosperity and happiness, and also to express the hope that our visit to the United States, and President Dwight Eisenhower's forthcoming visit to the Soviet Union, will be regarded not only by the American and

Soviet peoples, but also by all the other peoples, as the beginning of joint efforts in the search for ways of bringing our countries closer together and promoting universal peace.

Good-bye and good luck, friends!

SPEECH BY N. S. KHRUSHCHEV
ON HIS DEPARTURE FROM THE USA

On the evening of September 27, N. S. Khrushchev, Chairman of the Council of Ministers of the USSR, on his departure from the USA, in reply to the speech of Richard M. Nixon, Vice-President of the USA, who was seeing him off, said:

DEAR MR. NIXON, LADIES AND GENTLEMEN:

Our visit to the United States of America at the kind invitation of Mr. Eisenhower, President of the United States, has ended. We visited various cities in your country from the Atlantic to the Pacific; we had many pleasant meetings and talks with Americans, with business people of America, political and public figures; we met workers, farmers and intellectuals.

As a result of the useful talks we had with President Eisenhower, we reached a mutual agreement that all outstanding international issues should be settled, not through use of force, but by peaceful means through negotiation.

When we come home we shall tell the Soviet people of our impressions, of the meetings and talks on American soil. The entire Soviet people are striving to live in peace; they want friendly relations to be established between our great states. We are convinced that the American people also desire peace.

There are quite a number of complicated outstanding questions in our relations; nevertheless, let us not return to the past, but look to the future and do all we can for that future. Let us join efforts to consolidate peace, to improve mutual understanding among all the nations of the world.

I thank you from the bottom of my heart for the kind hospitality—for your bread and salt. I would like to wish that we more and more frequently use in the relations between our countries, the short and good American word—"O.K."

Good-bye, friends!

TO PRESIDENT DWIGHT D. EISENHOWER
OF THE UNITED STATES OF AMERICA

Radiogram from the TU-114 plane

Crossing the frontier of the United States, I beg you, Mr. President, to accept, on behalf of the members of my family and the persons accompanying me, and also on my own behalf, cordial gratitude for the invitation to visit your great country and for the warm reception extended to us by you personally and by the American people. Our acquaintance with the life of the American people was extremely interesting and useful.

The exchange of opinions on most important international problems and on questions of Soviet-American relations has shown that the trend toward undertaking the efforts needed to end the cold war and to create a climate of confidence and mutual understanding between our countries is on the ascendancy. Our meetings will definitely help to ease international tension and to strengthen the cause of universal peace.

I thank you sincerely once more, Mr. President, and I thank the American people for their hospitality. We assure you that the Soviet people and the Soviet Government will, in turn, extend to you as hospitable a reception when you come to the Soviet Union.

I wish you, Mr. President, your wife, your son and your wonderful grandchildren, with whom it was so easy for me to agree on the time of your visit to the USSR, I wish all of your family happiness and well-being.

I wish happiness and prosperity to the entire American people.

N. Khrushchev,
Chairman of the Council of Ministers of
the Union of Soviet Socialist Republics.

September 27, 1959.

HIS EXCELLENCY NIKITA S. KHRUSHCHEV,
CHAIRMAN OF THE COUNCIL OF MINISTERS
OF THE UNION OF SOVIET SOCIALIST REPUBLICS

Reply Radiogram

Dear Mr. Chairman:

I am grateful for the cordial message you sent to me from your plane, as you left the United States, and glad that you found both pleasant and interesting the brief visit to our country by yourself, your family and members of your official party. For my part, I found the meetings with you most interesting, instructive and pleasant.

It is gratifying to know that you feel our discussions may constitute some small step in the promotion of mutual understanding and the reduction of the causes of those international tensions which have brought us great difficulty in the past. We share the hope that concrete and meaningful progress in the important field of disarmament can be made. Nothing could be more useful than progressive and mutually fair discussions in the promotion of the just and durable peace which I am sure the peoples of both our countries earnestly seek.

The members of my family join me in greetings to you and your family, and the assurance that we look forward to our later visit to your country.

With the prayerful hope that such meetings as this will prove of real benefit to the world, and with personal wishes for the health and well-being of yourself, your family and the people of the Soviet Union.

Sincerely,
DWIGHT D. EISENHOWER

MEETING OF THE PEOPLE OF MOSCOW
IN HONOR OF N. S. KHRUSHCHEV'S RETURN
TO THE SOVIET UNION

On September 28 a meeting of the people of Moscow was held in the Sports Palace of the Central V. I. Lenin Stadium in honor of the return of the head of the Soviet Government, N. S. Khrushchev, from his trip to the United States of America.

The tremendous hall is filled to capacity. Over the rostrum a crimson streamer bears the words, "Long live the peaceful policy of the Communist Party and the Soviet Government!"

In a single impulse all present rise from their seats and a storm of applause flares up when N. S. Khrushchev, A. B. Aristov, I. I. Brezhnev, K. Y. Voroshilov, N. G. Ignatov, A. I. Kirichenko, F. R. Kozlov, O. V. Kuusinen, A. I. Mikoyan, N. A. Mukhitdinov, E. A. Furtseva, P. N. Pospelov, D. S. Korotchenko, J. E. Kalnberzins, A. P. Kirilenko, A. N. Kosygin, K. T. Mazurov, V. P. Mzhavanadzo, M. G. Pervukhin, N. V. Podgorny, D. S. Polyansky, the members of N. S. Khrushchev's party in his tour of the USA and others appear on the rostrum. Also present on the rostrum is Mr. E. L. Freers, Charge d'Affaires ad interim of the USA in the USSR.

Present in the hall are the heads of diplomatic missions accredited in Moscow.

V. I. Ustinov, First Secretary of the Moscow City Committee of the CPSU, addressed the meeting with a short speech.

On behalf of the working people of Moscow he warmly and heartily congratulated N. S. Khrushchev on the successful completion of his historic visit to the United States of America.

"Muscovites, like all Soviet people, followed your trip with great attention and impatiently awaited every report about your meetings and talks on American soil," Comrade Ustinov said, addressing N. S. Khrushchev.

"Your trip has yet again graphically proved to the whole world that the Communist Party and the Soviet Government indefatigably and consistently work for lasting peace and friendship among nations. The forcible call: 'Let us carry out total disarmament!' which you made at the United Nations to all the states of the world, is unanimously upheld and approved by the working people of Moscow, by all Soviet people. This call meets with the most ardent response in the hearts of ordinary people in all lands! *(Applause.)*

"Your speeches and pronouncements addressed to the American people contained the great truth about the first country of socialism, about the inspired creative effort of Soviet people, the builders of communism, about our people's ardent aspiration for peace. And we Muscovites were particularly pleased that your simple and convincing words were understood by ordinary Americans and found a vivid response among them.

"The Soviet people are happy that your visit to the USA took place at a time of such outstanding achievements of our people as the successful launching of the Soviet space rocket to the moon and the completion of the atomic icebreaker, *Lenin.* The scientists, engineers, technicians and workers of Moscow are proud that these wonderful achievements contain a share of their modest labor.

"The working people of Moscow are working with great inspiration for the implementation of the seven-year plan, and with their selfless effort they are enhancing the might of our great country.

"Allow me, dear Nikita Sergeyevich, to express, on behalf of all present at this meeting and on behalf of all the working people of Moscow, our warm gratitude for your tireless activity in the name of peace and the happiness of the Soviet people and to assure the Leninist Central Committee of our own Communist Party that Muscovites will spare no effort or labor for the implementation of the stupendous tasks of building communism! *(Applause.)*

"Long live the great Soviet people, the builders of Communism! *(Applause.)*

"Long live the Communist Party of the Soviet Union, the standard-bearer of peace and friendship among nations!" *(Prolonged applause.)*

V. I. Ustinov declares the meeting open. The strains of the State Anthem of the Soviet Union resound in the great hall.

The floor is then given to Y. N. Nikolayev, a machine-tool adjuster of the Likhachev Motor Works.

SPEECH BY Y. N. NIKOLAYEV

DEAR NIKITA SERGEYEVICH:

Expressing the sincere desire and thoughts of the many-thousand collective of the Likhachev Motor Works and all the working people of the capital, I convey to you heartfelt gratitude for your indefatigable struggle for peace and happiness of the Soviet people. *(Prolonged applause.)*

The greatest feeling we are experiencing now, Nikita Sergeyevich, is the feeling of tremendous joy from the knowledge that you are again in our midst, on our native Soviet soil. *(Applause.)* If we may speak figuratively, we did not part with you! Our hearts were with you during your historical tour of the United States. We of the Motor Works, like the entire Soviet people, warmly applauded you when you put forward the bold and clear-cut plan for complete and general disarmament. You expressed the opinion of all the Soviet people when you spoke of our friendly feelings for the American people, and our fervent wish to live in peace with all nations.

We noted with great satisfaction the statement contained in the Soviet-American Communique to the effect that all outstanding international questions should be decided by peaceful means, by negotiations, and not by use of force.

We Soviet workers found it a matter after our own hearts when you, Nikita Sergeyevich, with the folk wisdom characteristic of you, gave in your speeches and talks a telling rebuff to those who hate communism and are the champions of the cold war. *(Applause.)* The workers avidly read your striking speeches and said to each other:

"Nikita Sergeyevich is crushing the ice of the cold war with the strength of an atomic icebreaker and striking the enemies of peace with the accuracy of the Soviet moon rocket!" *(Prolonged applause.)*

Frankly, we cannot understand those people across the ocean who praise the capitalist way of life and at the same time envy our great achievements. No fables about a capitalist paradise can muddle us Soviet people. We are proud of the socialist system. We are proud of our sputniks and the Soviet pennants planted on the moon.

We are proud of our majestic seven-year plan and are working with great enthusiasm to fulfill it ahead of time. The many thousands employed at the Likhachev Motor Works are making their contribution to this nationwide cause. By September 22 the workers of the plant had successfully fulfilled the plan for the first nine months of the year and gave our country 85 million rubles' worth of goods in excess of the plan. (Applause.) I also am not lagging behind my comrades: I am topping my work assignment by 80 per cent, and more. (Applause.)

Soon our plant will switch over to a seven-hour working day. We consider this to be a fresh and striking manifestation of the care the Party takes of the Soviet people. We assure the Central Committee of our Party and the Soviet Government, that in seven hours we shall produce as much as in an eight-hour day. (Applause.)

It is neither thirst for profit nor need that make us fulfill our plans. Work for the people, for ourselves, for our Soviet state, the great aim towards which we are marching—communism—this is what inspires us to great patriotic accomplishments. And I am convinced that the time will come when the workers of America too will know the joy of free labor in their own factories. (Applause.)

Long live peace and friendship among all nations!

Long live our own Communist Party, which is leading the Soviet people to the triumph of communism! (Prolonged applause.)

U. M. Trofimova, team-leader of the Put Novoy Zhizni Collective Farm, Kuntsevo District (Moscow Region), is the next speaker.

SPEECH BY U. M. TROFIMOVA

DEAR NIKITA SERGEYEVICH:

Permit me to congratulate you from the bottom of my heart on the successful end of your mission of friendship and peace to the United States, and to convey to you the ardent greetings of the collective farmers of Moscow suburban area. (Prolonged applause.)

The people at our collective farm, like all Soviet people, followed your tour of the United States with great emotion and deep interest.

We felt and realized that this was no easy tour. Besides honest and peace-loving people, there are other people in America who are opposed to a relaxation of tension in international relations.

You, Nikita Sergeyevich, spoke to the Americans on behalf of your people. You defended the cause of peace with great ability and fervor. Your voice is the mighty voice of all Soviet people.

Ordinary people understand who is for peace and who fears a thaw in relations among the Great Powers. Speaking in our own collective-farm language, everyone today realizes that the road to peace is the road to Moscow. We were pleased that the American people met you with warmth and expressed friendly feelings for the Soviet people.

Your visit, Nikita Sergeyevich, turned out to be a good lesson for the capitalists. It is high time for them to understand that the Soviet Union is no longer that ragged Russia where the only fare of the poverty-ridden *muzhik* was thin cabbage soup with hardly a crumb of bread to go with it. *(Applause.)* No, the USSR is a mighty state who should be addressed as an equal among equals and with whom it is necessary to live in peace and to maintain good-neighborly relations.

We heartily approve the proposals you submitted on the question of preserving peace and ending the cold war. Only our country could propose general and complete disarmament.

The clouds of the cold war are dispersing. Life and work have become more cheerful. And look what's being done! We have decided that the seven-year plan should be fulfilled in five years. *(Applause.)* Let the Americans see what the collective farmers are capable of. We assure you, Nikita Sergeyevich, that we shall hold our own in the competition with the farmers, that we shall catch up with America and surpass it in output of agricultural produce per capita! *(Prolonged applause.)*

Facts themselves point to this. You remember, of course, Nikita Sergeyevich, what our collective farm was like about five years ago. And now? Preparing to mark the next plenary meeting of the Central Committee of the Party in a fitting way, we shall produce at least 10 tons of meat and 100 tons of milk per hundred hectares of land. *(Applause.)* Our collective farm has introduced cash payment for labor as well as annual holidays. From the beginning of next year we will start issuing pensions to aged collective farmers. *(Applause.)* This is how our life is changing. This is most striking proof of your words that the Soviet system is bringing the working people greater benefits than the capitalist system. *(Applause.)* We firmly believe that the future belongs to communism. *(Applause.)*

We most heartily wish you, an outstanding champion of peace and friendship among nations, many years of life. *(Prolonged applause.)* Thank you for your great efforts for the good of the Soviet people and for the whole of working mankind. *(Applause.)*

Long live our own Communist Party and the Soviet Government! *(Prolonged applause.)*

The floor is given to Academician L. I. Sedov.

SPEECH BY L. I. SEDOV

OUR DEAR NIKITA SERGEYEVICH:

Soviet scientists, like all our people, are heartily congratulating you on your return home from the United States of America where you went on a peace visit. *(Applause.)*

With great attention and pride we heard your historic speeches in which you expressed the Soviet people's desire for peace. We admire the tireless energy, persistence and patience with which you selflessly fight for strengthening peace and friendship among the nations. *(Applause.)*

The old methods and conceptions for solving outstanding issues between states by the use of force are becoming outdated. War in our day is a catastrophe which spells doom to tens and hundreds of millions of people. It is absolutely clear that war should not be allowed; it can and must be banned from the life of society.

We are proud and happy to know that our Party, the Soviet Government, and our people are in the front ranks of the struggle for peace, and that the initiative and the main constructive proposals as well as practical steps, aimed at consolidation of peace, come from the Soviet Union. We are profoundly confident in the victory of plain and sensible ideas, in the possibility of peaceful coexistence of different social systems, in the cessation of the cold war, and in the establishment of an atmosphere of good-will and cooperation among nations.

The Soviet Union's historic proposals on general and complete disarmament which you, Nikita Sergeyevich, made in the United Nations, are in accord with the vital interests and aspirations of broad sections of the population in all countries of the world. There is no doubt that there are still very many obstacles on the path to the realization of these proposals. Yet the things which were only a dream yesterday are becoming a reality today.

It is generally known that not more than two years ago there were skeptics among scientists who did not believe that it was possible to launch successfully artificial earth satellites.

Our scientists, engineers, and workers have turned into reality man's age-old dreams and were the first to pave the way to space and interplanetary flights. We are proud to say that the first artificial earth satellite and the first rocket flight to the moon were made by the Soviet Union.

The socialist system provides unlimited opportunities for the advancement of science and engineering.

We are living in a great era and are witnesses of the fact that human society develops in a great measure under the influence of the wise policy of the Soviet Union. This gives us confidence in the fact that, in spite of all the difficulties, an end will be put to the cold war. The achievements of science and engineering will go to serve mankind's spiritual and material requirements.

Dear Nikita Sergeyevich, Soviet scientists realize the responsibility they bear before their people and history, and will spare no effort in solving the majestic problems of construction of communism, our country's bright and happy future. *(Applause.)*

Glory to our Communist Party and the Soviet Government! *(Prolonged applause.)*

Long live peace the world over! *(Prolonged applause.)*

L. M. Selivanova, student of the Moscow Bauman Higher Technical School, made a speech on behalf of the Soviet youth.

SPEECH BY L. M. SELIVANOVA

DEAR NIKITA SERGEYEVICH:

We feel particular joy greeting you today in our wonderful capital on your return from a long and difficult trip. *(Applause.)*

If you only knew how excited the Soviet youth was during your stay in America! How impatiently we waited for the news on the radio and television, stood in long queues for newspapers, and with what ardor we discussed every bit of news from overseas! There is nothing surprising in this, for peace—and that means our future— was at stake.

It is a joy to live, work and dream when you are confident in your future. What a great happiness men will feel when all tanks, guns and bombs remain only on the pages of history textbooks and civil dress will be the only uniform worn on earth. *(Prolonged applause.)*

Dear Nikita Sergeyevich, on behalf of our people, you have clearly stated this in America, and the Soviet youth and the youth of the globe is grateful to you for defending with such fortitude and so passionately its future from the threats of a new war. *(Applause.)*

It makes us laugh when we learn that there are still people on earth who assert that we are intending to wage war against somebody. There is, indeed, a militant spirit in the Soviet youth! We are storming and will continue to storm nature's most treasured secrets, the severe ice of the polar regions and the stellar voids of the universe. The fire in our hearts helps to light new blast furnaces, build new power stations, plants, towns in the Siberian taiga, so as to make man's life happier. Our new space rockets carry to the distant stars our daring dreams of the future. (*Prolonged applause.*)

Our youth has many friends in all countries and we would like to see among them ever-growing numbers of young Americans. The difference in our ideologies should not prevent us from living in peace, having sport-competitions and meeting each other at festivals and on tourist routes.

We are not imposing our ideas on anyone, but we are firmly convinced that our system is the most progressive and the most humane in the world, and that the future belongs to it, and not to capitalism. There is nothing that can shake this assurance in us!

The main thing which will not be obscured in us is our love for the land of the Soviets, Soviet freedom, Soviet flag and Soviet sun! (*Prolonged applause.*)

We have been reared in this spirit by the Communist Party which opened for us broad horizons and gave us wings for daring flights into the future. Learning today the fundamentals of science, we students, like all Soviet youth, make our contribution to the fulfillment of the great plans mapped out by the Party.

We assure you, Nikita Sergeyevich, our own Party, and all Soviet people, that we shall always and everywhere act as most loyal and tireless fighters for the great cause of communism, as did Communists, our fathers and older brothers. (*Prolonged applause.*)

Glory to our wise Communist Party! (*Applause.*)

May there be stronger friendship between Soviet youth and youth of all countries in the struggle for peace! (*Prolonged applause.*)

The next to take the floor was N. S. Khrushchev. The participants of the meeting, standing, greeted the head of the Soviet Government with stormy, prolonged applause.

SPEECH BY N. S. KHRUSHCHEV

DEAR COMRADES:

We have just stepped off the plane which made a nonstop flight from Washington to Moscow. (*Applause.*) We have come straight here to this meeting, dear Muscovites, in order to share our impressions with you and to tell you about the results of our stay in the United States of America, which we visited at the invitation of President Dwight D. Eisenhower.

In accepting that invitation, we were prompted by the consideration that the international situation and the relations between our states—our two Great Powers, the Soviet Union and the United States—have for a long time been strained. To preserve such a state of affairs would mean to preserve a situation in which there may be all kinds of surprises fraught with grave consequences for our peoples and for the peoples of the whole world. That is why the more farsighted statesmen in a number of countries have come to realize the need to make some effort to put an end to the cold war, to remove the tension in international relations, clear the atmosphere and create more or less normal relations between states. The peoples could then live and look to the future without fear. The Twentieth Century is one in which human intellect and talent have attained the greatest heights. In our day, the dreams mankind cherished for ages, dreams expressed in fairy-tales which seemed sheer fantasy, are being translated into reality by man's own hands. How, then, in this age of flourishing human genius that is fathoming nature's secrets and harnessing her mighty forces, can one reconcile oneself to the preservation of the primitive relations between men that existed when men were no more than beasts?

If such relations in the remote past may be explained by the fact that man was still at the initial stage of his development and little different from animals, then today, when man has reached such heights of scientific knowledge and is step by step subduing the forces of nature, compelling them to serve the needs of society— today there can be no justification for preserving the kind of relations that existed among primitive men.

Our time can and must become the time of the triumph of great ideals, the time of peace and progress. *(Prolonged applause.)*

The Soviet Government has long since perceived this. And that is why we have repeatedly proposed to the Great Powers to organize a meeting of the heads of government in order to exchange views on urgent international issues. When we made these proposals, we believed in the power of human reason. We believed that, with a rational approach, representatives of different political views, of states with different social systems, could in the interests of peace, find a common language in order to arrive at correct solutions to the problems agitating all humanity today. In our age of tremendous

218

technological progress, in circumstances where there exist states with different social systems, international problems can be successfully solved only on the basis of the principles of peaceful coexistence. There is no other way. Those who say that they do not understand what peaceful coexistence is, and are afraid of it, are wittingly or unwittingly helping to further the cold war which is bound to spread unless we intervene and stop it. It will reach a point of such intensity that a spark may at any moment set off a world conflagration. In that war much will perish. It will be too late to discuss what peaceful coexistence means when such terrible means of destruction as atomic and hydrogen bombs, and ballistic missiles, which practically cannot be intercepted and can carry nuclear weapons to any point on the globe, go into action. Not to reckon with this, means to close one's eyes and stop one's ears, to hide one's head in the sand as the ostrich does at the approach of danger. If we humans imitate the ostrich and hide our head in the sand, then, I ask you, what is the use of having a head if it is incapable of averting the danger to life? *(Prolonged applause.)*

No, we must show human reason, we must have faith in the human intellect, faith in the possibility of achieving agreement with statesmen of different countries and in combining efforts to mobilize people for the task of averting the threat of war. We must have the courage and determination to act in defiance of those who persist in continuing the cold war. We must stop it from spreading, melt the ice and normalize international relations.

From this lofty rostrum, before you Muscovites, before my whole people, my government and Party, I must say that President Eisenhower displayed wise statesmanship in appraising the present world situation, displayed courage and determination. *(Stormy applause.)* Notwithstanding the complex situation prevailing in the United States, the President, a man who enjoys the absolute confidence of his people, proposed an exchange of visits between the heads of government of our two countries. We give him due credit for this important initiative aimed at strengthening the cause of peace. *(Prolonged applause.)* In taking this step, he was confident that we would accept the hand he proffered us, inasmuch as we have repeatedly addressed both President Eisenhower and other heads of government to that effect. And the President was not mistaken. *(Applause.)*

Dear comrades, it gives me great satisfaction to report to you that we have fulfilled part of our arrangement with President Eisenhower concerning the exchange of visits. At the President's kind invitation we have visited the United States of America, where we have had some important meetings and talks.

I would like to share with you my impressions of that visit and to tell you briefly of its results. I believe it will be best to tell you exactly what happened. The more candid our account, the better it will be for strengthening relations between the peoples of our two countries. *(Applause.)* It would not be true if I were to say that our tour of some American cities, and our meetings and talks with many Americans have ironed out all the controversial issues. Only a politically blind man could expect that whatever he says will be done.

No, in order to settle such important questions, one visit, one trip is not enough. Much effort is required. It will take many more meetings before complete mutual understanding is achieved, before we reach the goal which our Party, our people and our Soviet Government have always pursued—to ensure peaceful coexistence between states with different social systems, and to safeguard the security of the peoples on the basis of noninterference in internal affairs.

I would like to tell you how we felt when we first set foot on American soil.

Frankly speaking, my own feelings were somewhat mixed. The reason for this was that as soon as the first reports of the coming exchange of visits appeared, many press organs and some United States spokesmen launched a propaganda campaign against my coming to the United States. The atmospheric conditions they created did not warm me, although the temperature in the United States is much higher than in Moscow. They wanted to meet me with a cold shower. I was particularly disappointed when, in the plane en route from Moscow to Washington, I read a speech by Vice-President Nixon timed to coincide with my arrival. He chose an audience which could hardly be suspected of being bellicose. He was addressing an association of dentists. *(Animation.)* However, Mr. Nixon's speech was far from medicinal in content. *(Laughter.)* He, so to speak, added a chill to the toothache. One would think he was afraid of the atmosphere really turning warmer, of the cold war really ending. I cannot understand why this was necessary.

However, when we arrived in Washington we were accorded a reception worthy of our great country, our great people. *(Prolonged, stormy applause.)* We must give due credit to President Eisenhower for having done everything appropriate for a meeting at such a level.

(Applause.) You probably read the newspaper reports about the reception in the U.S. capital and the President's speech on that occasion. I shall not repeat all that. It was a warm reception.

Shortly after our arrival in Washington, the President received us at the White House. The Vice-President, Mr. Nixon, and the Secretary of State, Mr. Herter, were present. I am a rather restless, straightforward sort of person, and although it may not have been altogether diplomatic of me, I asked at our very first meeting why the Vice-President had to make such a speech on the eve of my visit, not to mention the unfriendly statements and articles by people of lesser rank.

The President said he had not read Nixon's speech. I told him he need not bother to read it, since it was already past history. *(Applause.)*

This is a little detail that gives some idea of the preparations made to meet the visitor from overseas. *(Animation.)*

Here is another. You Muscovites, and not only you, but all Soviet people—Russians, Ukrainians, Byelorussians, Uzbeks, Georgians, Kazakhs, Armenians—all our peoples alike, always give a guest a proper welcome. No matter what country he may come from, whatever his political views, once he is our guest we put our bread and salt on the table and show him not only formal, but sincere respect. *(Applause.)* Here is what I witnessed on my first day there, in the United States: As we drove with the President through the streets lined with crowds, I noticed that here and there someone would raise his hand and wave, but the next moment the hand would drop abruptly as though it had touched a live wire. *(Laughter.)*

I could not understand it at first. And so I decided to look more closely at the faces of the people lining the route. I began to nod to them in greeting, and many of them nodded in response. Now what was the trouble?

Later I was told that ten minutes before we drove through with the President to the White House, an automobile had passed along the route carrying a poster inscribed to the effect that the guest should be met with dignity and politeness, but without applause or greetings. *(Animation.)*

Afterwards I asked Mr. Lodge, the President's personal representative accompanying me on my tour of the United States, whether this was true, and was told that a car with such a poster had indeed passed along the route, but whose car it was no one seemed to know. *(Laughter.)* It was said to have broken through the police guard.

When I was given this explanation by official spokesmen, I told them I could not imagine how the police, who were guarding me so well, could have failed to notice a car carrying a poster of that sort. *(Animation.)*

I am convinced that the President knew nothing of all this and that it was all done without the knowledge not only of the President but of the others who organized our reception. But, as the saying goes, you cannot take a word out of a song.

From the moment we set foot on American soil I was so well guarded that it was quite impossible for me to come into contact with rank-and-file Americans. Police protection developed into a sort of house arrest. *(Animation.)* I was driven around in a closed car, so that I could catch glimpses of the people who came to greet us only through the window. And the people greeted me, even though they could not always see me.

I am far from suggesting that all the friendly feelings expressed by the American people were addressed to me personally or even to our communist ideology. By their greetings, the Americans were telling us that they, like ourselves, stand for peace and friendship between our peoples. *(Stormy applause.)*

I shall not give you a detailed account of all our meetings with the Americans. You have no doubt read about them in the papers. We spent some time in Washington, then in New York, where I had the honor to submit on behalf of the Soviet Government from the rostrum of the United Nations a plan for general and complete disarmament. *(Stormy applause.)*

From New York we went to the West Coast of the United States, to Los Angeles and San Francisco, and from there to the state of Iowa, and to Pittsburgh, the big industrial center of Pennsylvania. And, finally, we returned to Washington. It was quite an extensive tour. We visited various parts of the United States, and met all sorts of people. We had many very good meetings and frank talks. But there were meetings of a different nature, too.

During the first half of our tour, we could not help noticing that one and the same story was repeated each time. Speakers claimed that I had once said that we would "bury the capitalists." At first I patiently explained what I had actually said, that we would "bury capitalism" in the sense that socialism would inevitably replace that moribund social system, just as in its time capitalism had replaced feudalism. But as time went on, I saw that the people who persisted in repeating this sort of question did not really need any explanations. They were pursuing a definite purpose, namely, to use the communist bogey to frighten people who have only the vaguest notion of what communism is.

At a reception in Los Angeles, at which the Mayor, who is no worse than other mayors though perhaps less diplomatic, again began to speak in this spirit, I felt compelled to speak my mind.

I said to them: Do you intend to make an unfriendly demonstration in every city and at every gathering? Very well, if that is how you are going to receive me, then, as the Russian proverb says, "From the stranger's gate, the road home is straight." *(Applause.)* If you are not yet ripe for talks, if you haven't yet realized the need of ending the cold war and fear its termination, if you want to go on with it, we can wait. The wind isn't blowing in our faces either. We have the patience to wait, and the wisdom. Our country is getting along fine. Our people have more than once shown wisdom, strength and determination, and such capacity to surmount difficulties that they can stand up for their country and for the cause of peace. *(Prolonged applause.)* They will be able to give a fitting answer if the aggressive forces should try to probe us with their bayonets. *(Applause.)*

I was obliged to start diplomatic negotiations on this score. I asked Comrade Gromyko, our Minister of Foreign Affairs, to go and tell Mr. Lodge, the President's representative accompanying me, that unless the matter was rectified I could not continue my tour and would be obliged to return to Washington, and thence to Moscow.

All this evidently had its effect. Mr. Lodge conveyed to me through Gromyko that he advised me to continue with the program and to go on to San Francisco and other cities, and that the local authorities would see to it that this would not happen again.

I must tell you that the talks through Comrade Gromyko took place at night, and when I woke up in the morning everything had indeed changed. When we left Los Angeles for San Francisco, the "handcuffs" figuratively speaking, were removed and I was able to get out of the train and talk to people. *(Applause.)* People shook my hand and I theirs, and they applauded and smiled, exactly as you Muscovites do when you meet a guest, because you are glad to see him and wish to do your best to make him feel that he is welcome. *(Applause.)*

When we arrived in San Francisco, the sun was shining, it was a beautiful day, like our own summer day. The climate of this wonderful city was quite different, the sun's rays warmed us, but warmer still to us was the cordial, unconstrained reception we were given. *(Applause.)*

We are very grateful to Mr. Christopher, the Mayor of San Francisco, to Mr. Brown, Governor of California, to the people of San Francisco, to all those who showed an understanding of our visit—a visit of peace and friendship between our nations, between the peoples of all countries. *(Applause.)*

We were given every opportunity to meet and talk to ordinary people. True, the physical possibilities were limited, but that was due to the brevity of our visit. To tell the truth, my suspicions concerning the ill intentions of the local authorities were dispelled. We at once established good contact with the inhabitants of that large and beautiful city.

I want to make special mention of my meeting with the longshoremen. Mr. Bridges, the leader of the Pacific Longshoremen's Union, invited me and my companions to come and talk to the workers. That was a most cordial meeting. Among the longshoremen, simple and sincere folk, I felt as if I were among our Soviet workers. *(Applause.)* The greetings I conveyed to them on behalf of Soviet workers were met with enthusiasm, and they asked me, in turn, to convey their hearty greetings. *(Stormy applause.)*

I also recall our visit to the computer plant in San Jose, near San Francisco. The manager of the plant, Mr. Watson, and the employees gave us a warm welcome, and acquainted us in detail with the complex production processes. The explanations were given in Russian—a mark of consideration which it is particularly pleasant to note. The plant itself, the layout, and the organization of production, made a good impression.

I observed that one of the men who was showing us around the plant spoke Russian with a Ukrainian accent and I asked him in Ukrainian:

"What is your name?"

"Marchenko," he replied.

"Glad to meet you," I said. "Are your parents living?"

"Yes," he answered.

"Give my regards to them."

He thanked me.

But our stay in hospitable San Francisco came to an end, and we had to continue our journey by plane to another American city, Des Moines, in the state of Iowa. Des Moines is one of the principal agricultural centers of the United States.

After a cordial reception by the Governor of the state, the Mayor of the city, and representatives of the business community and public leaders, we drove out to the corn fields so dear to my heart. *(Animation, applause.)* I must say that the Americans know how to grow corn. It is planted everywhere in squares and the fields are in good condition. True, there too, in the fields of the leading corn expert himself, my old acquaintance Garst, I found a few shortcomings. *(Laughter, applause.)* His corn was crowded in clusters, and I drew his attention to that fact—in a friendly way, of course.

We were shown great hospitality by our host, Mr. Garst, who arranged an interesting meeting for us with the farmers. We met Adlai Stevenson there—the prominent Democratic Party leader who had come from Chicago, and we had a most frank and friendly talk with him.

I recall this episode. When we visited the local college, one of the young people gave me a copy of the students' newspaper. It contained a long article in which, I was told, the students welcomed our arrival. The article, however, said that the students would meet us without enthusiasm or cheers. Yet those very students in whose name the article had been written—those lively, eager young people —showed exactly the same sort of enthusiasm as our own youth. They shouted, and applauded, and expressed their feelings most vociferously. I heard them shout: "Tovarishch Khrushchev!" "Nikita!" and other simple, friendly words. *(Animation, applause.)*

I must also tell you about the warm welcome we were given by the inhabitants of Pittsburgh—one of the biggest industrial centers of America, the city of steel-makers and machine-builders. They showed us great friendliness and respect. I even felt a trifle awkward as I drove from the airfield. We arrived in Pittsburgh at midnight. It was a dark night, yet all along the road people stood beside cars and I saw their smiles and heard their words of welcome.

In Pittsburgh we visited the Mesta Company's machine plant. We felt that the plant management had done their best to show us the plant and to enable us to acquaint ourselves with working conditions. We went through the plant and talked with the workers. I would like to mention one detail: When we first arrived we were greeted, but with restraint. However, the longer we were with the workers, the warmer the atmosphere grew. The workers enthusiastically expressed their respect for us representatives of the Soviet state and Soviet people.

I also remember the meeting I had with Pittsburgh businessmen and intellectuals at the local university. There was the usual dinner and speeches, but speeches which seemed to me to display a more realistic understanding of the need for amicable relations between our countries.

Hearing me speak now, some people may be thinking: Khrushchev is speaking only of the friendly meetings, he says nothing about the hostile demonstrations. No, I do not intend to hush up the fact that there were instances of hostility and unfriendliness towards us. Yes, there were such instances. I must tell you that just as the American newspapermen accompanied me throughout my tour of the United States, so did some fascist-minded refugees from different countries, who went with us from town to town, parading a few miserable posters. We also saw grim and morose American faces.

There was a great deal that was good, but one must not forget the bad either. The little worm, or rather the great big worm, is still alive and is liable to show its vitality in the future.

Why do I speak of this? Is it in order to cool relations between the Soviet Union and the United States? No. I mention this because it is necessary to know the truth, because you must see not only one side, the pleasant side, but also the other, the backstage side which should not be hidden. In America there are forces which are operating against us, which are against lessening tension and for preserving the cold war. To close one's eyes to this fact would be to display weakness in combating these evil forces, these evil spirits. No, they must be dragged out into the open, exposed and publicly flogged, they must be roasted like devils in a frying pan. *(Laughter, prolonged applause.)* Let those who wish to continue the cold war fume. No ordinary people anywhere in the world, no sensible human being will support them. *(Applause.)*

Our visit to Pittsburgh rounded out our tour of the United States.

In winding up my account of our tour I should like to express our sincere thanks to the mayors of the towns and the governors of the states we visited, to the representatives of the business world and to the intellectuals, to the personnel of the factories and universities, to workers and farmers, and to all the representatives of public organizations. I particularly want to express my appreciation of all that was done for us by the Mayor of New York, Mr. Wagner; the Mayor of San Francisco, Mr. Christopher; the Mayor of Pittsburgh, Mr. Gallagher; the Governor of Pennsylvania, Mr. David Lawrence; the Chancellor of the University of Pittsburgh, Mr. Litchfield; the President of Iowa State College of Agriculture and Mechanical Arts, James Hilton; the representatives of the business world Eric Johnston, Robert Dowling, Cyrus Eaton, Thomas Watson, Frank Mesta, Roswell Garst; and others. *(Applause.)*

The numerous gifts we received were a splendid token of respect for our country and for its great people. The Mayors of New York and Pittsburgh presented us with a medallion of New York and the key of Pittsburgh.

I said, by the way, that I was accepting the key as a symbol of trust, "And you can rest assured," I said, "I promise you, that this key will never be used without the hosts' permission." *(Prolonged applause.)*

International Harvester Company presented us with a film dealing with the mechanization of corn production; President Eisenhower gave a pedigree heifer from his private farm; Admiral Strauss, a steer and a heifer; and farmer Coolidge, a pedigree hog. Many other gifts were presented, for which we are grateful and appreciative. *(Applause.)*

I would like to say that the American press, radio and television gave extensive, and on the whole correct, objective coverage of our visit to the United States. There were, of course, some unfriendly attacks on the part of individual journalists, but it was not they who set the tone in the American press.

My comrades and I were accompanied on our tour of the United States by the President's personal representative, Mr. Lodge; Mr. Buchanan, Chief of the Protocol Division of the State Department; Mr. Thompson, U.S. Ambassador to the USSR; their wives; and other officials. I would like to thank them all, and especially Mr. Lodge. He did his best to create the necessary conditions for us on our tour and to acquaint us with the life of the great American people. *(Applause.)*

I remarked in jest to Mr. Lodge that if he, a representative of the capitalist world, and I, a representative of the working class and the Communist Party of the Soviet Union, were to be cast away on a desert island, we would probably find a common language and would be able to coexist peacefully. *(Animation, prolonged applause.)* Why could not states with different social systems coexist? Our countries are also on an island, as it were; after all, with modern means of communication which have brought continents closer together, our earth indeed seems like a small island, and we ought to realize that. And once the need for coexistence is realized, it is necessary to pursue a peaceful policy, to live in friendship and not to brandish weapons but to destroy them. *(Applause.)*

Comrades, on September 25 I met the President again in the White House and together we flew by helicopter to Camp David, his country residence. We spent September 25, 26 and 27 there. We held frank and friendly talks, set forth the positions of our governments on vital international issues and also on questions of improving Soviet-American relations. Mr. Herter, the U.S. Secretary of State, and Comrade Gromyko, the USSR Foreign Minister, as well as other comrades in my party took part in these meetings and talks and did useful work.

The principal result of our exchange of opinions is given in the joint communique which has been published today in the press. There can be no doubt that this document will be received with satisfaction by all who are interested in strengthening peace. *(Prolonged applause.)*

It should be borne in mind, however, that naturally the President and I could not at one sitting clear away all the accretions of the cold war that have piled up in the course of many years. It will take time to sweep away that rubbish and, not only to sweep it away, but to grind it to dust. Certain things that divide us are still too fresh. It is sometimes difficult for some leaders to discard old positions, old views, old definitions.

But I can tell you in all frankness, dear comrades, that as a result of my talks and discussions of concrete questions with the U.S. President, I have gained the impression that he sincerely wishes to see the end of the cold war, to create normal relations between our countries and to help improve relations among all countries. *(Stormy applause.)* Peace today is indivisible, it cannot be secured by the efforts of two or three countries alone. Hence it is necessary that all nations, all states participate in the fight for peace.

The President and I exchanged views on the question of disarmament. He stated that the Government of the United States was studying our proposal and that the United States, like ourselves, wants total, controlled disarmament.

It would seem that there are, at present, no reasons for delaying settlement of this question. But, on the other hand, disarmament is too serious a question for one to expect one's partners to settle it hastily, right off the bat. It must, of course, be studied with a view to finding a solution that would really create confidence and ensure disarmament and the peaceful coexistence of states.

So let us not be hasty in our judgement, let us be patient and give the statesmen time to study our proposals. But we will not be idle, we shall continue to urge the need for complete and general disarmament. *(Applause.)* We regard our proposals as a basis for agreement. We are prepared to discuss any amendments to our documents, to our proposals. We are prepared to discuss any other proposals that may be made if they are directed towards the same aims as those we pursue.

The President and I also exchanged views on the German question, on the question of concluding a peace treaty. We tried to show him, and I believe we succeeded, that our proposals for a peace treaty had been incorrectly interpreted in the West. Some people had sought to whip up undue passions by claiming that this was an ultimatum, and so on. Those who did so were clearly prompted by a desire to prolong the cold war. They went so far as to declare that our proposals for a peace treaty with Germany were little short of a declaration of war. To think that anyone could distort the peaceful stand of the Soviet Union in such a fashion!

We also exchanged views on holding a meeting of heads of government. We both outlined the positions of our governments and agreed that such a meeting is necessary and useful.

We exchanged opinions on the date of President Eisenhower's return visit to the Soviet Union. At first the President intended to come to the USSR in the latter part of October. However, he asked me what time of the year was best for touring our country. That made me think. We Muscovites like Moscow at all seasons of the year. But, like all people, we find spring, the season of joy when nature awakens to life, pleasantest. And so I said that it would perhaps be best if he came later in May or early in June. And it would be good if the President would bring along his wife, his son and daughter-in-law, and his grandchildren. We would also be glad to see the President's brother, who has been to our country with Mr. Nixon.

The President was kind enough to invite me to his farm. He showed me his corn—I couldn't very well visit the President without having a look at his corn, could I? *(Animation.)* He showed me his calves and his steers. Fine animals. True, I must say that the Eisenhower farm is rather small for the President of such a huge and wealthy state. It is not a rich farm and the soil is not very good. But the President said that he wants to work to improve the land and thereby leave behind a good memory of himself.

At the farm I met the President's grandchildren and had a conference with them. *(Laughter.)* I asked them if they would like to go to Russia. And all of them, from the youngest to the eldest, declared that they wanted to go to Russia, to Moscow. The eldest grandson is eleven, the youngest granddaughter is three or four. I won their support. I remarked jokingly to the President that it was easier to agree on a return visit with his grandchildren than with himself *(laughter, applause)*, because his grandchildren have a good environment, whereas he evidently has some obstacles to contend with which prevent him from realizing his wishes as and when he wants to. *(Applause.)*

I would like to tell you, dear comrades, that I have no doubt that the President is prepared to exert his efforts and his will to bring about agreement between our countries, to create friendly relations between our two peoples and to settle pressing problems in the interest of a durable peace. *(Applause.)*

At the same time, it is my impression that there are forces in America which are not operating in the same direction as the President. These forces stand for continuing the cold war and the arms race. Whether these forces are great or small, influential or uninfluential, whether the forces backing the President—and he has the support of the absolute majority of the American people—can win, are questions I would not be too hasty to answer.

Time is a good counsellor, or as the Russians say: "The morning is wiser than the evening." That is a wise dictum. Let us wait until morning, the more so since we have arrived by plane at the end of the day and it is now evening as I speak here. And perhaps more than one morning will pass before we will be able to tell for sure. But we shall not sit with our arms folded and wait for the dawn, wait to see which way the arrow of international relations will point.

We, for our part, will do everything we can to ensure that the barometer points not to "storms" or even to "change," but to "fair." *(Prolonged applause.)*

I am confident, comrades, that in the present circumstances, when the forces of peace have grown immeasurably, when the socialist camp numbers nearly one billion people and possesses enormous productive capacities, when the Soviet Union has such vast achievements in industry and agriculture, science, engineering and culture— we can do a great deal for peace.

In our actions we base ourselves on reason, on truth, on the support of the whole people. Moreover, we rely on our mighty potential. And those who wish to preserve the cold war with a view sooner or later to turning it into a hot war had best know that in our time only a madman can start war, who himself will perish in its flames. *(Applause.)*

The peoples must strait-jacket such madmen. We believe that statesmanship, that human reason will triumph. *(Applause.)* In the splendid words of Pushkin, "Let reason triumph! May darkness be banished!" *(Prolonged applause.)*

Dear comrade Muscovites! We are boundlessly happy to be home again, to see the dear faces of Soviet people. *(Applause.)*

Long live the great Soviet people who are successfully building communism under the leadership of the glorious Party of Lenin! *(Prolonged applause.)*

Long live Soviet-American friendship! *(Prolonged applause.)*

Long live friendship among all the peoples of the world! *(Stormy, prolonged applause. All rise.)*

A standing ovation greeted the end of the speech made by the head of the Soviet Government. Nikita Sergeyevich went over to E. L. Freers, Charge d'Affaires ad interim of the United States in the USSR and shook his hand. A burst of applause once more broke out in the hall.

The meeting was declared closed, and the majestic strains of the national anthem of the Soviet Union filled the hall. For a long time the audience remained in the hall, warmly applauding N. S. Khrushchev.